100 *Places Every Woman Should Go*

STEPHANIE ELIZONDO GRIEST

TRAVELERS' TALES
AN IMPRINT OF SOLAS HOUSE, INC.
PALO ALTO

Travelers' Tales and Solas House are trademarks of Solas House, Inc., 853 Alma Street, Palo Alto, California 94301. www.travelerstales.com

Art Direction: Stefan Gutermuth
Cover Photograph: © John Wilkes/Taxi/GettyOne
Author Photo: Alexander Devora
Interior Design and Page Layout: Howie Severson
Research/Editorial Assistant: Emilia Thiuri

Library of Congress Cataloging-in-Publication Data

Griest, Stephanie Elizondo, 1974-
100 places every woman should go / by Stephanie Elizondo Griest. -- 1st ed.
    p. cm.
Includes index.
ISBN 1-932361-47-2 (pbk.)
1. Travel. 2. Women travelers. I. Title. II. Title: One hundred places every woman should go.
G151.G76 2007
910.4082--dc22

2007043032

First Edition
Printed in the United States
10 9 8 7

For my niece and nephew,
Analina and Jordan,
May your journeys take you far and wide!

Table of Contents

SECTION II
PLACES OF ADVENTURE

SECTION III
PLACES OF PURIFICATION AND BEAUTIFICATION

SECTION IV
PLACES OF INDULGENCE

SECTION V
PLACES OF CELEBRATION AND WOMANLY AFFIRMATION

SECTION VI
PLACES OF STRUGGLE AND RENEWAL

SECTION VII
PLACES OF INSPIRATION AND ENLIGHTENMENT

Introduction
By Holly Morris

TIME DISAPPEARED WHEN I SPUN THE GLOBE AND DROPPED MY young finger on a hunk of foreign land—a pink continent, a green island, a *republic* or a *highland* or a *range*. The *italics,* the **bold,** the ragged coastlines, the vast teal-blue oceans: to me, it all added up to potential. In some nascent way, even then I understood that seeing the world would be among life's sweetest nectars.

And now, with a good bit of road dust under my nails, and a keener than ever sense of years flying by, traveling with a *reason* (rather than the way of the peripatetic) seems more important than ever. But *Where?* And *Why?*

It's a wide, wide, wide, daunting and thrilling world out there, and we could all use a bit of direction. Sure, there are stacks of guidebooks that offer ample information about bus fares, hotels, and arcane history—the kind of stuff that flies out of your mind the minute you find yourself dancing on a sturdy Greek table, or watching an offering glide down the holy Ganges, or gazing across Cambodia's killing fields.

We ladies could use a book that limns the world in a way that makes sense for us; a book that encourages us to lead with our inspirations and chase down their manifestations around the globe. *100 Places Every Woman Should Go* does just that. This is the brain trust of an intrepid traveler who lashed on her estro-lens, filled a few passports, and is now handing over all the juicy liner notes so others can engage the world in a similarly spirited, pro-woman way.

There are lots of good reasons to travel far, near, and widely. Sometimes we simply need to escape the numbing demands of the work-a-day grind; sometimes we've lost our way and need the life-altering clarity one can achieve from leaping outside the comfort zone; sometimes we hope to connect with our contemporaries around the globe who face challenges similar and different from our own: poverty, land mines, spiritual angst, potty training. Sometimes we simply need to remember that there's a two-steppin' cowgirl within each of us—and that she could use a top-notch massage now and then.

This practical paean serves as a fresh reminder that every trip can be a votive journey of sorts. Reading it sparked memories of my own long-delayed pilgrimages: that intriguing Virgin festival in a tiny nook of South America that I've been meaning to get to—for a decade; the magical Hindu temple in Kerala that has long beckoned; the sites of my own matrilineal roots.

100 Places Every Woman Should Go touches on all the best reasons to travel, and delivers a hot list of destinations that is sure to enliven the *Where* and *Why* of your next adventure. Onward!

—HOLLY MORRIS, BROOKLYN, USA

Holly Morris is executive producer/writer/host of the award-winning PBS series *Adventure Divas* and is the author of *Adventure Divas: Searching the Globe for Women Who Are Changing the World*, which was named a *New York Times* "Editors' Choice."

She has written for many publications including *Outside*, *The New York Times*, and numerous anthologies. She is also the former editorial director of the book publishing company Seal Press and developed the Adventura imprint, which features international travel and adventure writing by women.

Morris works as a television correspondent for the series *Globe Trekkers*, *Treks in a Wild World*, *Outdoor Investigations*, and has worked and traveled all over the world—from Lapland to Guyana, the Middle East to the Far East, the top of the Matterhorn to the depths of the South Pacific.

Preface

WANDERLUST PUMPS THROUGH MY VEINS: I'VE EXPLORED TWO dozen countries and all but four of the United States in the past decade, and ache for more. Every place is glorious in its own special way, but now and then, I stumble upon somewhere sacred. It usually takes a moment to recover, and when I do, I scan the room (or wilderness) for a pair of eyes to share it with. No matter where I am—downtown Manhattan or the Mongolian steppe—it is inevitably in the eyes of another woman that I find a similar spark or sense of wonderment. Afterward, I can only describe the place as one where "every woman should go."

When Travelers' Tales approached me with this project, memories of these places surged forth. I scribbled down half the list in half an hour, then started calling my girlfriends (and a few select boy friends). Nearly one hundred interviews later, this book was born. Within its covers, you'll discover places where women made history, where we battled for our rights to rule, to speak, to vote, to be free. You'll find places of inspiration and enlightenment, such as the 88 Sacred Temples of Japan, and places of purification and beautification, such as the mud bath volcanoes of Cartagena, Colombia. Looking for a little adventure? There's surfing in Costa Rica, mountain trekking in Pakistan, canyoneering in Utah, pearl diving in Bahrain. Or do you just want to indulge? Choose between white-sand beaches in Zanzibar, champagne tours in France, and chicken tamales drowned in black *mole* sauce in Oaxaca. For every site of struggle on this planet (Rwanda, Beirut, Cambodia, New Orleans) there is a site of celebration (rumba clubs, full moon *haflas*, flamenco festivals, Carnivale).

In short, this book documents places where being a woman is affirmed and confirmed; where you will be energized and impassioned.

Perhaps you are wondering: does this mean there will be no men? Not a chance: in some locales—Rio de Janeiro, Havana, Bali—they are a main attraction! But we all know how catcalls from street corners and wandering hands in crowded subways can tarnish an otherwise fabulous trip. So pains were taken to include places populated by men who are at least somewhat respectful to foreign women. Of course, not all women are similarly received on the open road. A Bulgarian friend of mine, who has dark Mediterranean features, strolled across southern Italy without incident, while a busty blonde American friend got harassed at every turn. Our perceived race, class, religion, and sexual orientation can have just as much—or more—impact abroad as at home.

Another initial goal was to choose only places where local women, indigenous people, and the environment are treated with kindness, but it was nearly impossible to find 100 of them: inequities are too omnipresent. Instead, I tried to highlight the work of local community activists so that if you, like me, feel guilty downing a glass of Chardonnay in Napa Valley while undocumented farm workers are hunched over in the sun, you know where to volunteer or send a check afterward.

These destinations can be visited with your girlfriends, your mother, your daughter, or your partner. But hopefully you'll someday travel to at least one alone, to take on Mother Road on your own terms and experience what she has to offer. Be fore-warned that she will push you to your physical, spiritual, and psychological limits—then nudge you a few steps further. But at the end of the journey, you'll be more self-reliant and self-assured, and ever more the woman.

May your travels take you far and wide! And if you discover yet another place every woman should go, please post it on our website at www.placesforwomen.com. It just might make it into our next edition.

—STEPHANIE ELIZONDO GRIEST
CORPUS CHRISTI, TEXAS

Ten Tips for Wandering Women

1. *Networking.* A month before your trip, send an email to everyone you know with your travel itinerary. You'll probably be amazed at how many people have old friends/ex-lovers/third-cousins-twice-removed along your route. Ask for their contact information and arrange to meet them for coffee (or *chai,* or *nargileh*) when you arrive to get the scoop on their home turf. Also check in with other travelers by posting a note on Lonely Planet's Thorn Tree Forum at www.thorntree.lonelyplanet.com. Any burning questions you have will likely be answered within 24 hours (if not minutes), and you can find travel partners as well.

2. *Packing.* Take only what you can carry half a mile at a dead run. This is the golden rule of foreign correspondents and should be adopted by travelers as well. Lay out everything you think you'll need, then pack half of it and double the money. A few things I never leave home without: earplugs, a versatile pocket knife, a strong piece of nylon rope, a flashlight (or better yet, a headlamp), a combination padlock, a rain poncho, blank paper, pens, a journal, condoms, and a mountain of tampons. Which leads us to Tip No. 3.

3. *Feminine Hygiene.* A friend once traveled the developing world for nearly two years with a single device—a menstrual cup— and swears it is the greatest contribution to womankind.

Simply insert it into your vagina and empty it a couple of times each day. No strings, no wings! Another friend eliminates her menses altogether by taking Depo-Provera, a shot of progesterone that can prevent ovulation for intervals of up to three months. Otherwise, pack o.b.s or other non-applicator tampons, which take half the space of regular tampons and are less likely to be tampered with by customs agents searching for drugs. Chances are you'll be able to buy tampons abroad, but if you're picky or have a heavy cycle (as in, only super-absorbency-plus will suffice), bring your own.

4. *Money Storage.* Some travelers sew little pockets on the insides of their clothes; others stash emergency bills and contact information in their bras or shoes. I advocate spreading the wealth. I usually keep a copy of my passport, a couple of travelers' checks, and some money in a hidden waist belt, then store the critical documents (passport, airline tickets, credit cards, bulk of money and travelers' checks) in a hidden thigh pouch. If theft is a serious problem in your destination, carry a decoy purse—that is, something to hand over in case of a robbery.

   Before you leave, give a trusted friend a folder containing your itinerary, contact information, and copies of your passport, visas, driver's license, travelers' checks, and credit cards. Save your passport number, 1-800 credit card replacement numbers, and pertinent contact information in a folder in your email account.

5. *Male Repellent.* Some women wear fake wedding bands and carry photos of hulky men they call husbands to ward off advances. I try to learn key phrases in the local language.

("I'm meeting my boyfriend here. He is a lieutenant in the U.S. Marine Corps," is a useful one.) Public guilt and humiliation are the best way to deal with men who molest you on crowded buses or subways. Loudly and firmly, say: "How would you like it if someone treated your wife/daughter/sister like that?" or simply: "Shame on you!" Chances are, your fellow passengers will come to your rescue. (If you turn around and slug him, they likely will not.)

6. *Safety.* As a general rule, pensions, homestays, bed and breakfasts, and hostels are more "women friendly" than hotels or motels. Use only a first initial when checking in and request a room that is not on the main floor. Take the elevator instead of the stairs, and never leave your key where someone can see your room number.

7. *What to Wear.* Conforming to local gender roles/social customs can be a challenge sometimes. While foreign women might be forgiven or excused for pushing the limits of local dress codes, it is simply disrespectful to wear tank tops and shorts in conservative or religious societies. Also beware that many cultures take fashion seriously: my mud-brown corduroys and hiking boots made me look and feel like an androgynous pauper in Eastern Europe, and my ripped jeans were crudely inappropriate. Flip through magazines and rent contemporary movies from your destination to help you pack accordingly.

8. *Staying Healthy.* Parasites just love to hitchhike. Keep them away by avoiding the following, especially in the developing world: salads and other raw vegetables, unpasteurized prod-

ucts like milk and yogurt, iced drinks, cold meat and cheese platters in Soviet-era hotels (where it's probably been sitting out for hours, if not days), and shellfish. When choosing a restaurant, check out the bathroom first. If the Board of Health would condemn it, the same probably goes for the kitchen. Give your body time to adjust to local spices before hitting the street stalls, and only patron the busiest ones when you do. If you wind up somewhere even remotely sketchy, go vegetarian—or at the very least, avoid chicken and fish, as it goes bad fast. If you do get sick, drink Sprite, ginger ale, or carbonated beverages (or electrolytes if you have severe dehydration) and monitor your stool. If it turns yellow, bloody, or has pus in it, get to a doctor fast.

9. *Tears Work.* While I hate to recommend that women rely on their perceived fragility or weakness to get by, there really is something about a lonesome foreign woman crying that magically opens the doors, wallets, and hearts of the people of this planet. It is how I got all of my stolen documents replaced one miserable day in Turkey in record time, without penalty or rush fees. It is how my friend Daphne evaded costly traffic violations across Africa and literally stopped a departing airplane in Angola. Use only as a last resort, but if you're going to do it, go all the way. If seeking to avoid an exorbitant fine, jail, or getting thrown off the Trans-Siberian train in the middle of the night for not having your papers in order, think: Oscar. Drop to your knees. Convulse. Make such a scene, passersby get involved. If the situation is truly critical, consider fainting (but *only* if you've gotten enough sympathetic people involved that your oppressor can't just toss your body off the train!).

Another strategy is pretending to get sick. I once read of an elderly expat in China who never left home without his doctor's business card. Whenever his cabbies hit 80 miles per hour, he would hand it over with an ominous "If I have a heart attack, drop me off here." The cabbies promptly screeched to a halt. Younger travelers may have a harder time pulling that off, but if your taxi really needs to slow down, shout: "I'm getting carsick!" and heave.

10. *Return the Good Sister Karma.* Spread the love. Be nice to female travelers you encounter at home, and help out your local sisters abroad. Support female artisans, vendors, tour guides, and taxi drivers wherever you wander. Your money will almost certainly go where it is needed most.

I

Powerful Women and Their Places in History

1 *Madonna Sightings Around the World*

MARY JUST MIGHT BE THE MOST VENERATED WOMAN TO HAVE graced the planet. Nearly all cultures worship her in some form or fashion: she has been named Mother of God, Earth Mother, and the Bodhisattva of Compassion. Great feasts are thrown in her honor in the Roman Catholic and Eastern Orthodox churches. Although she died some two thousand years ago, her spirit still makes public appearances now and then, and shrines commemorating these "miracles" abound. The following spots are considered especially sacred:

* In December of 1531, campesino Juan Diego Cuauhtlatoatzin was resting on a hilltop near Mexico City when he heard some fantastic singing, "like the songs of various precious birds." A woman dressed in clothes "like the sun" suddenly stood before him and asked his help in convincing the local bishop to build her a shrine. Juan Diego hurried off to the church, carrying the Castilian roses she gave him as proof of her presence. When the bishop expressed skepticism, he opened his cloak to show him the roses, and lo and behold—her olive-skinned image was emblazoned on its fabric. La Virgen de Guadalupe has since become the symbol not only of Mexico's faith, but of the very nation itself, and many indigenous and activist groups have adopted her image in their call for social

justice. The famous cloak can be viewed via a moving walkway at the Basilica de Santa Maria Guadalupe in Mexico City, near the La Villa-Basilica metro station. During the weeks of the Feast of the Virgen de Guadalupe (December 12) and Easter, millions of Mexicans make pilgrimages to the Basilica, some hobbling on their knees as an act of penance.

* In May of 1917, a woman "more brilliant than the sun" appeared before three children tending their family's sheep outside Fatima, Portugal. After revealing three secrets  (including a description of hell and instructions on how to save souls from it), she asked them to pray the rosary every day, and visited on the thirteenth of the next five months to ensure they did. Word quickly spread of this vision, and thousands flocked into the fields to catch a glimpse. By August, authorities deemed the children disruptive and threw them in jail, but they refused to divulge the secrets that the Virgin passed on—even under threat of being dunked into a cauldron of boiling oil. That October, the Virgin rewarded some seventy thousand spectators with a spectacular light show in the fields that culminated with the sun doing a swan dive over the horizon amidst a torrential rainstorm. She hasn't returned since, but hundreds of thousands still gather in Fatima every May 13 to parade her statue through town and hold a candlelight vigil at the Basilica.

* The Basilica of the National Shrine of the Immaculate Conception in Washington, D.C. contains some seventy chapels, oratories, and images honoring the Madonna, many

donated by religious orders from around the world. "When I sit here, I feel connected to women who lived centuries ago, and who will come centuries later," says motivational speaker Aliana Apodaca of El Paso, Texas. "It is a mystical place that honors the feminine. Whenever I am in D.C., I take a cab here to just sit and meditate for a while." Located at 400 Michigan Avenue in the northeast part of the city, the Basilica—the Western hemisphere's largest—can be reached via the Brookland-CUA metro station.

RECOMMENDED READING

Mary: A Flesh-and-Blood Biography of the Virgin Mary by Lesley Hazelton
A Woman's Path edited by Lucy McCauley, Jennifer L. Leo, and Amy G. Carlson

2 Egypt
Hatshepsut and St. Catherine

ANCIENT EGYPTIAN WOMEN WERE A FAIRLY LIBERATED BUNCH, possessing the right to both inherit and own property. But all were astonished when one of their own rose to the exalted rank of pharaoh and held it for twenty-two years. Born with a knack for self-promotion, Hatshepsut started spreading rumors at an early age that her father (the king) had chosen her—and not one of her half-brothers—as his successor. After seizing the regency, she acquired the symbols of her male predecessors (down to the fake beard) and was often portrayed as having no breasts. (Historians say this was her way of asserting her title as king and not some lowly wife or consort.) One of the most successful of all pharaohs, Hatshepsut is widely regarded as history's "first great woman," and is immortalized today in everything from a computer game (Civilization IV) to novels to a play by Betty Shamieh. Pay your respects at Deir el-Bahri, the sprawling complex of temples and tombs on the west bank of the Nile opposite Luxor, where her royal steward (and supposed lover) built the collonaded temple of Djeser-Djeseru (the Sublime of Sublimes) as a place of posthumous Hatshepsut-worship. Then walk down to the Valley of the Queens, the burial ground of the wives of the pharaohs. Only a few of its estimated seventy tombs can be visited, and that of Queen Nefertari—which has the most lavish reliefs—for just ten minutes, but the feminine energy is palpable.

After basking in Hatshepsut's glory, head on to Mount Sinai, the sacred mountain where God handed Moses the Ten Commandments. Follow the backpackers up the trail before dawn to watch the sun rise. Services are sometimes held on Sundays in the chapel up top, and a lamb is sacrificed once a year in the neighboring mosque. Then climb down to see the Monastery of St. Catherine, where Moses is said to have seen the burning bush. Now a museum, the monastery houses fifth- and sixth-century icons, chalices, mosaics, and other sacerdotal ornaments, as well  as the world's second largest collection of early codices and manuscripts. It also contains a rather sad-looking bush everyone claims to be the original.

St. Catherine's is named for a remarkable fourth-century woman who at age eighteen begged the emperor to stop persecuting Christians. Although she managed to convert his wife, as well as many pagans, authorities were sent after her. They attempted to torture her with the "breaking wheel," a device that slowly shattered every bone in the body, but it broke when Catherine touched it. Authorities beheaded her instead, and angels are said to have swooped down from heaven and carried her body off to Mount Sinai.

After contemplating the courage of St. Catherine, journey into the desert. Bedouin guides offer jeep rides to nomadic camps, where you can hike to the local watering source. The scenery here is dynamic, changing color with the sun, and shape with the wind. Arrange to visit Wadi Al-Zalaga (between the monastery and the Oasis of Ain Umm-Ahmed near Nuweiba) in mid-January, when tribes from southern Sinai converge to race dozens of camels in a chaotic 12.6-mile course. Celebrate the victories afterward with tea and *lebba* bread cooked right over the fire.

RECOMMENDED READING

Hatshepsut: From Queen to Pharaoh edited by Catherine Roehrig, Renee Dreyfuss, and Cathleen Keller

3 Lesbos, Greece
Sappho

PLATO CALLED HER THE TENTH MUSE. OVID INCORPORATED HER lyrics into his poetry, and Solon wanted to learn her work—and die. Fast forward many centuries and even TV's Wonder Woman cried out her name in times of trouble ("Suffering Sappho!"). While only a couple hundred samples of her work remain—totaling just four complete poems—she is a mandatory component of any classical education. She is, of course, Sappho: the Greek poetess and lyricist, and a modern-day icon for feminists the world over.

Born sometime between 630 B.C. and 600 B.C. to an aristocratic family, Sappho lived in great privilege until a violent coup sent her into exile. She later married a wealthy merchant and, according to some scholars, became the headmistress of a girls' finishing school. She dedicated so much of her sensual work to women, people assumed she had lesbian inclinations. (Indeed her birth island, Lesbos, is where the term "lesbian" comes from.) Sappho was the first Greek poet to write in the first person, daring to reveal her own interior rather than pontificate about the gods, as most of her colleagues did.

"Even when other poets do use the first person, there is still none of the 'freshness' and presence that Sappho conveys—her interior seems almost flammable in comparison to other stagey first-person speech," says Princeton instructor Sarah M.

Anderson. "As so many have observed, here surely is a woman speaking for and about herself for the first time."

Her poetry is also so melodic, it is nearly impossible to translate, and so erotic that the early Roman Catholic and Byzantine churches are said to have destroyed much of it. Remarkably, a poem she wrote 2,600 years ago was recently discovered on the wrapping of an Egyptian mummy. Scholars have interpreted it as a speech to young women that mourns the aging process:

> *...but my once tender body old age now has seized*
> *my hair's turned white instead of dark*
> *my heart's grown heavy,*
> *my knees will not support me,*
> *that once on a time were fleet for the dance as fawns....*

Sappho's modern-day admirers flock to Lesbos—Greece's third largest island—to soak in her muses. Mountainous and lush, Lesbos is covered with olive groves that produce some of the finest oils in the nation. Other offerings include Roman ruins, hot springs, museums, historical sites, and miles and miles of dusty brown beaches. Hiking here is a joy, with trails linking villages via dells lined with pink hollyhocks and wild pears. The half-mile path from Paleohori to Rahidi includes a fun pit stop at a *kafeneio,* or coffee house, open in the summer.

Poetry pilgrims especially enjoy Skala Eressos, a relaxed resort. An international community of lesbians has opened shops and cafes here, and women-only hotels abound. The Antiopi Hotel boasts an open-air Jacuzzi and massage studio, while the Mascot Hotel's rooms have private balconies overlooking citrus groves. Every September, the town throws a two-week

Women's Festival with open-mike nights, concerts, cruises, day trips, Silly Olympics, and workshops on everything from osteopathy to building space rockets (in Natalie's "Fly Me to the Moon Seminar").

Come back to me, Gongyla, here tonight,
You, my rose, with your Lydian lyre.
There hovers forever around you delight:
A beauty desired.

Even your garment plunders my eyes.
I am enchanted: I who once
Complained to the Cyprus-born goddess,
Whom I now beseech

Never to let this lose me grace
But rather bring you back to me:
Amongst all mortal women the one
I most wish to see.

—"Please," Sappho

RECOMMENDED READING

Sappho: A New Translation by Sappho, translated by Mary Barnard

TOURS

Sappho Travel offers women-only holidays, including a tour to the island of Lesbos (www.lesvos.co.uk).

4 Llanddwyn Island, Wales
Saint Dwynwen

SAINT DWYNWEN'S STORY DATES BACK TO THE FIFTH CENTURY. HER father, Wales' Prince of Brycheiniog, had twenty-four daughters, but she was fairest of them all. Along came a dashing lad named Maelon, who sought her hand in marriage. The Prince, however, had already hand-picked a husband for young Dwynwen. What happened next depends on which legend you believe: Some say Maelon raped his love in a fit of rage and left her crying to God for help; others say she sought God's assistance to remain chaste. Either way, He sent down an angel with a potion that turned Maelon into a block of ice. This was too much for poor Dwynwen, and she beseeched Him for three more wishes: to thaw her man, to enable her to forget him, and to give other lovers a collective break. All were granted, and she retired to Llanddwyn Island off the coast of Anglesey to pass the rest of her days in solitude. (Which isn't to suggest she wasn't happy here; indeed, Dwynwen is known for chipper proverbs like, "Nothing wins hearts like cheerfulness.")

In time, Dwynwen became revered as the patron saint of lovers. Pilgrims traveled to Llanddwyn to pay tribute to her and to test their own love at her holy well. Word has it, if you scatter breadcrumbs and lay out a handkerchief, an eel will peek out of its crevice if your lover is destined to be faithful. So many people left offerings at her shrine, a new chapel was built in her honor in the sixteenth century, alongside the ruins of her old one. Four centuries later, she was bestowed with a day of remembrance: January 25. The Welsh celebrate this day as Americans do Valentine's, with cards and chocolates.

Despite its name, Llanddwyn Island is attached to the mainland in all but the highest tides, so is technically not an island. It is, however, a romantic place with endless coastlines, rolling dunes, sea cliffs, salt marshes, and mud flats. Here and there are funny little geological formations known as "pillow lavas" formed during undersea volcanic eruptions. Wild ponies roam about the land and cormorants, shags, and oystercatchers soar through the sky. Soay sheep can ocassionally be spotted munching flower beds near Saint Dwynwen's chapel.

"There is something otherworldly about Llanddwyn that I can't really say," contends Nicole Fraser, an American paleontologist living in Wales. "It is just astounding."

Because it is so remote (the nearest train stations being Bangor and Holyhead), a car is essential here. Dickens fans will love the Ye Olde Bull's Head Inn on the opposite side of the island, near Beaumaris Castle. Enjoy a glass of ale over the views of the Menai Strait and Snowdonia, just as the author once did in 1859. (Every room at the inn has since been named for one of his characters.) Then drop in the upstairs restaurant for one of the best meals in North Wales: a Welsh beef fillet with red wine, shallot, seared belly pork, served au jus—seasoned with Anglesey sea salt—followed by warm Valrhona chocolate parkin with ice cream and a dark chocolate sauce.

www.bullsheadinn.co.uk

5 *Rouen, France*
Joan of Arc

THE EARLY FIFTEENTH CENTURY WAS A NADIR IN FRENCH HISTORY. A drawn-out war had induced great suffering among the people; the royal family was in shambles; the English and the Burgundians were seizing villages left and right. But then an illiterate maiden named Jeanne la Pucelle had a vision in which God implored her to help the motherland. Though only sixteen, she petitioned to visit the royal court and was soon leading troops into battle—and winning. In one famous skirmish, she even yanked out an arrow impaled in her own shoulder and kept on fighting. The French army felt empowered by her presence, and she soon became their touchstone.

But in 1430, Jeanne was captured by the English and thrown into prison. (They claimed her crime was heresy, but they just wanted to use her to discredit her king.) She tried to escape by jumping from her tower onto the dry moat below, but got dragged back inside, where she was nearly raped. (Thereafter, she wore men's clothing.) During the trial, Jeanne stunned the court by answering the trick question of whether or not she was in God's grace with: "If I am not, may God put me there; and if I am, may God so keep me." Nobody could think of a follow-up, and many began to fear she truly was a holy woman. But the Duke of Bedford sentenced her to death anyway. At her request, two clergymen held up a crucifix as the executioners tied her to a pillar, and she screamed out to Jesus as they set her aflame. The Duke had the body torched three times and then dumped in the River Seine so there would be no relics to collect afteward, but it was too late. Though only nineteen, she had already become Joan of Arc: martyr, heroine, and saint.

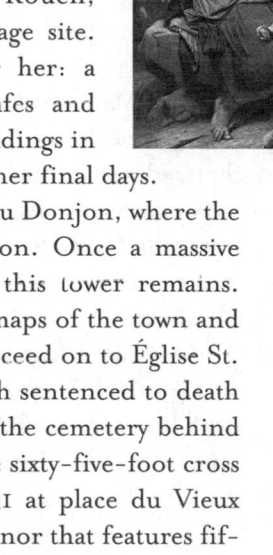

The town of Joan of Arc's death—Rouen, France—has since become a major pilgrimage site. Practically everything here is named after her: a bridge, a church, streets and squares, cafes and restaurants—even a cocktail. Many of the buildings in the medieval center have been around since her final days.

Start with La Tour Jeanne d'Arc on rue du Donjon, where the martyr was held prisoner until her execution. Once a massive chateau built by Philippe Augustein, only this tower remains. Climb its spiral staircase to see models and maps of the town and castle back in the early fifteenth century. Proceed on to Église St. Ouen on rue des Faulx. Joan of Arc was both sentenced to death and, twenty-five years later, rehabilitated in the cemetery behind this Rayonnant Gothic church. Next, see the sixty-five-foot cross that marks the spot where she died in 1431 at place du Vieux Marché. Nearby is a church named in her honor that features fifteen panels of Renaissance stained glass and a bronze statue of the young saint. Round out the tour at the Musée Jeanne d'Arc, where wax figurines (complete with false eyelashes) reenact major scenes of her life inside a cellar at 33 place du Vieux Marché.

RECOMMENDED READING

Joan of Arc: Her Story by Regine Pernoud and Marie-Veronique Clin

6 County Mayo, Ireland
Grace O'Malley

WHILE GROWING UP ON THE IRISH COAST IN THE SIXTEENTH CENTURY, Grace O'Malley had a dream: to sail the seas with her father. When he objected that her long hair would get tangled in the ropes, she chopped it off. That antic not only earned her a ticket aboard, but a reputation for fearlessness, and the nicknames Gráinne Mhaol (meaning Grace the Bald) and Granuaile. All served her well: for the next sixty years, O'Malley terrorized the coasts as a pirate, chieftain, lover, and mother, emerging as a great legend in Irish history.

O'Malley's first husband—with whom she bore three children—died young in battle, and she dealt with the loss by sailing back and forth between the Baltics and Spain for amber, silk, weapons, and wine (some of which she bought, much of which she stole). In time, she met "Iron Dick" Burke, owner of the swanky Rockfleet Castle, and after a brief courtship they married under Brehon law, which states "for one year, certain." They say she divorced him after the trial run and kept the castle. By then, she was an international outlaw, and authorities offered a handsome reward for her capture. In 1593, the British seized several members of her family as prisoners, and she sailed to England to petition Queen Elizabeth for their release. Though O'Malley refused to bow before Her Majesty—saying she herself was a queen, and furthermore, not an English subject—Elizabeth took a liking to her, and granted amnesty under the condition that the O'Malleys stop pilfering from Great Britain.

She agreed, but quickly resumed her pirate ways, albeit mostly against the "enemies" of England.

Commune with O'Malley's spirit in County Mayo, Ireland, an endless stretch of pristine beaches and islands that were nearly emptied during the Potato Famine. A seven-foot, four-inch bronze sculpture of the pirate queen was unveiled at Westport House a few years ago, and her Rockfleet Castle still stands near Newport (and is open to the public during the summer). Hop on a boat at a nearby pier and sail to Clare, the mountainous island she called home (as do about 200 people today). On the eastern edge of the island are the ruins of a tower house known as Grace O'Malley's Castle; near the southern coast is a small Cistercian abbey that contains the O'Malley tomb, that reads, "Invincible on Land and Sea."

Then enjoy exploring the rest of County Mayo, which is well off the beaten path (though that might change once O'Malley's life becomes the subject of a new Broadway musical called *The Pirate Queen*). Scuba divers will delight in the sea life: everything from squat lobsters and cuckoo wrasse to tompot blennies. The best time to visit the region is during the first two weeks of August, when locals throw a joyous festival called Scoil Acla that includes much singing and dancing on the rocky headlands of Achill Island. Then spend a few days at the world-class Delphi Mountain Resort and Spa, where you can dine on Killary mussels and sea bass after a long, hard day of tai chi and seaweed treatments.

www.delphiescape.com

RECOMMENDED READING

Granuaile: The Life and Times of Grace O'Malley by Anne Chambers

7 *Salem, Massachusetts*
Witches of Salem

THE HYSTERIA COMMENCED IN THIS MASSACHUSETTS VILLAGE IN 1692, when the daughter and niece of the local reverend were stricken with a medical condition "beyond the power of epileptic fits or natural disease to effect." After their family doctor failed to diagnose their illness, it was decided that the girls had been bewitched. A beggar, a bed-ridden old woman, and a slave from Barbados named Tituba, were the first to be accused in the infamous Salem Witch Trials. Although they were thrown into prison, the madness didn't stop there: the girls accused even more neighbors of practicing black magic and witchery. The jails soon swelled beyond capacity, and the governor called in a man trained in theology—not law—to serve as the chief justice of the court. During the outrageous trials that transpired, the girls pointed at the hapless prisoners and shrieked, "She comes to me at night and torments me! She afflicts me!" The courts tried and hanged the first woman within a week, and by the end, nineteen people had been senselessly killed—all but six of whom were women.

Interestingly enough, when Arthur Miller visited the town in the early 1950s to do research for his play *The Crucible,* no one wished to discuss this history. That changed in the 1970s, when the sitcom *Bewitched* shot a string of episodes in Salem and the city noticed a sizeable bump in tourism. Sensing the commercial possibilities, a few museums and self-proclaimed witches came to town. Today, Salem's high school mascot wears a conical hat and wields a broom, and witches are emblazoned on everything from police cars to the local newspaper's masthead—not to mention t-shirts, coffee mugs, keychains, and the like.

Start your tour with the Salem Witch Museum on 19½ Washington Square North, which brings the town's history to life with figurines, narration, and melodramatic special effects. A newer exhibit, "Witches: Evolving Perceptions," gives a good overview of witchcraft, from pagan midwifes to modern Wiccans. Then explore the clammy dungeon where Tituba and the others awaited trial in the Witch Dungeon Museum on 16 Lynde Street. The Witch House on 310½ Essex Street is the historical home of one of the judges of the trials.

www.broomcloset.com
www.crowhavencorner.net

They say more witches make their coven in Salem than anyplace else in the United States. The Broom Closet on 3 Central Street is a one-stop witch shop dedicated to bringing customers "the finest selection of ritual supplies and transformation tools for personal growth and self discovery." This includes Victorian Venetian capes, green glass rune sets, gazing balls, pentacle scrying mirrors, and a collection of Triple Goddess Wands. Crow Haven Corner, meanwhile, offers a bevy of services: everything from psychic consultations and tarot, palmistry, and pendulum readings, to "Wiccanings" (pagan-style baptisms) and cleansings (for your car, home, or person) at 125 Essex Street. They also offer hour-long tours "With Real Salem Witches!" to sites like Burying Point cemetery and the Essex County jail.

The best, albeit most crowded, time to see Salem is in October, when the city throws its month-long Haunted Happenings festival. In addition to "Hocus Pocus Walking Tours," haunted houses, and Bizarre Bazaar, the city hosts a children's costume parade and "Hawthorne's Annual Costume Ball." Seeking some aura photography, astrological guidance, or spirit mediumship and clairvoyance? Drop by the Annual Psychic Fair and Witchcraft Expo, held every day that month in the Museum Place Mall on 176 Essex Street.

Just five miles away, the town of Danvers is another good place for witch sightings. The Danvers Archival Center at the Peabody Institute Library on 15 Sylvan Street has an impressive collection of imprints related to Salem witchcraft, and the Witchcraft Victims' Memorial on 176 Hobart Street is a moving tribute to those who died. At 149 Pine Street, visit the seventeenth century home of Rebecca Nurse, the seventy-one-year-old mother of eight who was tried and hanged during the trials. When accused, she purportedly cried out: "…as to this thing, I am as innocent as the child unborn, but surely what sin hath God found out in me unrepented of that He should lay such an affliction upon me in my old age?"

"If it be possible no more innocent blood be shed…. I am clear of this sin."
—Mary Easty, hanged as a witch September 22, 1692

RECOMMENDED READING

The Salem Witch Trials: A Day-by-Day Chronicle of a Community Under Siege by Marilynnne K. Roach

TOURS

Salem Historical Tours offers daily witchcraft walks (www.salemhis-toricaltours.com).

8 St. Petersburg, Russia
Catherine the Great

PETER THE GREAT MAY HAVE BUILT THIS CITY, BUT CATHERINE THE Great made it sing. With its sumptuous museums and regal cathedrals, its wide boulevards and canals, St. Petersburg is Russia's most romantic city. Guidebooks call it a "Slavic Venice," but after a few days here, you'll agree that Venice is actually more of an "Italian St. Petersburg."

Born a German princess and educated by French governesses, Catherine the Great found her "in" to Russia's royal family by marrying the dreadful Grand Duke, Peter III (not "The Great"). Impotent and immature, Peter didn't consummate their union for twelve long years. Within months of his accession to the throne, Catherine had him overthrown and became Tsarina of Russia in 1762. Over the next thirty years, she added

200,000 square miles to Russian territory and made it a dominant power. An intellectual, she corresponded with Voltaire and Diderot and wrote memoirs, fiction, and comedies. She also founded the Smolny Institute for noble young ladies. Because of this, Europe considered her an "enlightened"

monarch, but at home, she was more of a tyrant, censoring publications and exiling her critics. She was also a brutal mother to
her sons, Paul and Orlov, preferring instead her eldest grandson, Alexander (who eventually became Tsar Alexander I). To
this day, wild rumors circulate about the cause of Catherine's
death—most of which involve her supposedly voracious sexual
appetite (and a horse). But historians say she merely had a stroke
while taking a bath and never regained consciousness.

One of Catherine's finest legacies is the Hermitage, whose
contents Russians rattle off like baseball stats: 117 staircases lead
to 350 halls with 1,057 rooms, in which 60,000 drawings and
15,000 paintings hang side by side, along with 12,000 sculptures and thousands of archaeological monuments. But even
those daunting numbers won't prepare you for wall after wall
covered in gold leaf and malachite, floors inlaid with marble,
and ceilings dripping with chandeliers. And then there's the art,
including classics by Rembrandt, Da Vinci, Michelangelo,
Renoir, Picasso, Gaugin, and Matisse. Peter the Great started
this unparalleled collection, but Catherine bought most of the
key paintings and built the Winter Palace to store them.

To really get a sense of Catherine the Great, visit her palace,
Yekaterininsky Dvorets, in nearby Pushkin. Every imperial family
from Peter the Great through the Romanovs spent their summers in this town, previously known as Tsarskoye Selo, or Tsar's
Village. Done in Russian baroque, the palace features a bright-
turquoise exterior that has white columns with gold moldings
and sassy garlic-shaped domes. Inside, one room is covered with
more than a ton of amber and glows in a dozen shades of yellow.
Also explore the gardens, which are landscaped with waterfalls,
ponds, pavilions, and bridges. The pyramid at the far end of the
pond is said to contain Catherine's beloved greyhounds.

Pushkin is located fifteen miles south of St. Petersburg; to get here, take the commuter train from Vitebsk Station or a minibus from Moskovskaya Metro.

After paying homage to Catherine, meet her descendants. Gone are the "wild east" days of the early '90s, when Mafiosi checked their guns in at the door, but fear not—Russian nightclubs still get rowdy. Hotspots change constantly, so it's best to read the *St. Petersburg Times* or, better yet, consult a Russian friend or expat. One nightclub of note is Tri El, quite possibly the first lesbian club in the nation's history. Late-night drag king shows are held here most nights of the week, along with live bands on Thursdays, and therapists offer free consultations. Tri El is located on No. 45, 5-aya Sovetskaya Ulitsa, near the Ploshchad Vosstaniya metro. Male friends can (and happily will) tag along on Thursdays and Fridays, and straight women will have fun, too.

RECOMMENDED READING

Catherine the Great by Henri Troyat, translated by Joan Pinkham

9 *Upstate New York*
New York Women

*"We hold these truths to be self-evident that all
men and women are created equal...."*

AND WITH THESE WORDS, THE WOMEN'S RIGHTS MOVEMENT WAS born in Seneca Falls, New York, in 1848. After just ten days of plotting and planning, feminist pioneers Elizabeth Cady Stanton, Lucretia Mott, Mary Ann M'Clintock, and three hundred other women (and a few good men, like abolitionist Frederick Douglass) held the first-ever Women's Rights Convention at Wesleyan Methodist Chapel. Back then, women were forbidden to study at university, own property, vote, or serve on a jury. Conventioneers listed these and fourteen other grievances in their monumental "Declaration of Sentiments" and then vowed to change them. Pay homage to these and other righteous ladies in the following locales:

* The Visitor Center of the Women's Rights National Historic Park displays exhibits and screens films about the historic convention, plus offers tours to sites like Wesleyan Chapel and the Elizabeth Cady Stanton House at 32 Washington Street. Born in 1815, Stanton grew up with her father's lament: "Oh my daughter, I wish you were a boy." By the time she was a thirty-two-year-old mother of three, she felt

like a "caged lioness." Perhaps this fueled her fire as a feminist, abolitionist, and staunch advocate for women's right to vote. End your tour at the Mary Ann M'Clintock house, where the convention organizers wrote the Declaration of Sentiments. Stanton later recalled that they "all seemed too tame and pacific for the inauguration of a rebellion such as the world have never before seen."

❀ The National Women's Hall of Fame was founded in 1969 to commemorate major contributions to women's history. Located at 76 Fall Street, this shrine honors writers like Harriet Beecher Stowe and Maya Angelou, activists such as Sojourner Truth and farm worker Dolores Huerta, Cherokee chief Wilma Mankiller, and entertainer Lucille Ball. Pay respects to your heroines or nominate a new one.

www.nps.gov/wori
www.greatwomen.org

❀ Just a twenty-minute drive from Seneca Falls is Auburn, Harriet Tubman's last town of residence. Known to her people as "Moses," Tubman not only helped deliver some three hundred slaves to freedom via the elaborate Underground Railroad system, she led African-American Union soldiers on raids during the Civil War. Her restored home is open for tours at 180 South Street, and pilgrims can also visit her gravesite and memorial.

❀ From Auburn, head east for four hours and then south to Hyde Park, where Eleanor Roosevelt resided at Val-Kill on Stone Cottage, 56 Val-Kill Park Road. Driven by a deep conviction that everyone deserves a fair shot at life, First Lady

Roosevelt spent her own life rallying for the poor and the oppressed. Her proudest achievement was convincing the United Nations General Assembly to adopt the Universal Declaration of Human Rights. "The future is literally in our hands to mold as we like," she once said, "but we cannot wait until tomorrow. Tomorrow is now."

"You gain strength, courage and confidence by every experience in which you really stop to look fear in the face. You are able to say to yourself, 'I have lived through this horror. I can take the next thing that comes along.' You must do the thing you think you cannot do."

—Eleanor Roosevelt (1884-1962)

10

Coyoacan, Mexico
Frida Kahlo

A TEQUILA-SLAMMING, DIRTY JOKE-TELLING SMOKER, THIS FAMOUS artist was bisexual and beautiful. She hobbled about her bohemian barrio in lavish indigenous dress and threw dinner parties for the likes of Leon Trotsky, photographer Tina Moddotti, poet Pablo Neruda, Nelson Rockefeller, and her on-again, off-again husband, muralist Diego Rivera. Although she staunchly supported Communism, the United States posthumously honored her with being the first-ever Latina featured on its postage stamp, and her paintings still fetch more money than any other female artist's. (Madonna is said to be an avid collector.) She is of course Frida Kahlo—cult icon extraordinaire—and a visit to her cobalt blue home in Coyoacan will be a highlight of any Mexican journey.

Much of Kahlo's life was tragic. Born in 1907, she was soon stricken with polio that shrunk one leg, making it difficult to walk without the clunky shoes she despised. Then at age eighteen, a bus she was riding crashed into a streetcar and she flew out—to be impaled upon an iron handrail that punctured her uterus and broke her back, leg, collar bone, and pelvis. Unremitting pain kept her from bearing children, which she mourned. She endured a stormy relationship with Rivera, who, though he loved her fiercely, could not keep his hands off the ladies (including Kahlo's sister). Kahlo retaliated with a few affairs of her own, including with Trotsky and actress Josephine Baker, but primarily assuaged her sorrows with the paintbrush. Tears run down her cheeks in many of her self-portraits.

> *"I paint self-portraits because I am so often alone,*
> *because I am the person I know best."*

—Frida Kahlo (1907-1954)

Touring through La Casa Azul, or Blue House, is like stepping inside one of Kahlo's fantastical paintings. The walls are awash with color and mosaics; a Day of the Dead altar yields pastries, flowers, candles, and papier mâché skeletons; the inner courtyard blooms with tropical flowers and cactus; and ceramic amphibians proliferate (in homage to Rivera, who swore he was as ugly as a frog). In the tiled kitchen, "Frida y Diego" is spelled out with tiny clay cups upon a wall. Most revealing is her four-poster sickbed, where a mirror hangs overhead (so she could better paint herself) and pictures of Lenin, Marx, and Mao are pasted at its foot. Many of Kahlo's personal effects are displayed throughout the house, including her embroidered dresses, pre-Hispanic jewelry, corset-like body cast, sketchbook diaries, and love letters to Rivera. And then there's her vibrant artwork, including her last completed painting (watermelons entitled *Viva la Vida,* or "live life") and some works-in-progress (a portrait of Stalin). You can buy everything from Frida t-shirts to computer mousepads to coffee cups in the gift shop, and sip a *café con leche* in the tranquil café. La Casa Azul is located on Londres 247 and reachable by the Coyoacan Viveros Metro Station.

Once you've gotten your Frida fix, walk two blocks to the bunkerlike home at 410 Churubusco where Trotsky spent the last year of his life. Its barren interior is a striking contrast to that of La Casa Azul, reflecting the inherent differences between a Mexican artist and a Russian revolutionary. Trotsky fled to Mexico after butting heads with Stalin, but despite Trotsky's home's high walls and armed security guards, the dictator had him murdered anyway, with an icepick to the head. The house is kept as Trotsky left it, with bullet holes in the door (from the first assassination attempt) and a crumpled copy of *Pravda* on the desk.

RECOMMENDED READING

The Diary of Frida Kahlo: An Intimate Self-Portrait by Frida Kahlo

TOURS

Andalé Mexico offers a six-day tour of Mexico highlighting the life of Frida Kahlo, among others (www.andalemexico.com).

11 Savannah, Georgia
The Lady Ghosts

OAK TREES DRAPED WITH SPANISH MOSS; GARDENS PERFUMED BY wild jasmine. Bed & Breakfasts with scandalous pasts; antique stores on every corner. Savannah is indeed an enchanting city, with twenty-one public squares built around statues, fountains, and gazebos. It is also the birthplace of many a powerful woman—the spirits of whom remain (some more viscerally than others).

* Known to her friends as Daisy, Juliette Gordon Low was an eccentric who lost much of her hearing to ear infections, one caused by an errant grain of rice thrown at her own wedding. She moved to Europe where she became impassioned with youth activism, eventually returning to the United States to found the Girl Scouts of America. She died of breast cancer and was buried in her Girl Scout uniform; 50 million young women have since joined her legacy. Visit her childhood home on 10 East Oglethorpe Avenue, now a shrine for troops.

* Born in Savannah in 1925, Flannery O'Connor was—in her own words—a "pigeon-toed only child with a receding chin and a you-leave-me-alone-or-I'll-bite-you complex." The author of such classics as *A Good Man Is Hard To Find* and *Everything That Rises Must Converge*, she won the prestigious O.

Henry Award for Best Short Story three times before dying of lupus at age thirty-nine. Her three-story childhood home at 207 East Charlton Street on Lafayette Square has since become a literary center offering seminars, readings, and films that celebrate not only her work but that of all Southern writers.

- Some blame the Civil War, which ravaged much of the state and piled up corpses in the process; others say the culprit is the Treaty of New Echota, which sent tens of thousands of Native Americans on a "Trail of Tears" from Georgia to Oklahoma. Whatever the reason, Georgia is fraught with ghosts—and in Savannah, they make themselves known.

There's Alice Riley, a servant indentured to a cruel man named Mr. Wise. Alice was washing his hair in a bucket one morning when his wandering hands got too frisky, and she drowned him. Her husband was promptly hung for the crime, but because she was pregnant, Alice got sentenced to a jail cell in the southwest corner of Wright Square for eight months until the baby was born and adopted. Then it was her turn. Deeming it improper to keep a woman's body hanging the customary three days, the authorities doubled the height of the scaffold so the trees would hide her. "To this day, no Spanish moss grows in those old oaks, as Alice is up there, looking for her baby," says Robert Edgerly, who gives late night Savannah tours.

Then there's Anna Powers, who at age fourteen flung herself from the roof of the 17 Hundred 90 hotel on President Street rather than marry an old man. She remains a poltergeist in room 204, slamming drawers, lifting the bed

www.hauntingstour.com

off the floor and crashing it down, turning the shower on and off, flushing the toilet, and making prank calls. "You answer it and hear a woman sobbing," says Edgerly. Couples in particular have reported sightings in the hotel, although Anna tends to leave businessmen at peace.

TOURS

Gutsy Women Travel offers a women-only six-day "Savannah's Style.
Charleston's Charm" tour which includes a Ghost Tour, among other things (www.gutsywomentravel.com).

12
Buenos Aires, Argentina
Evita and the Mothers
of the Disappeared

SPRAWLING BEFORE THE CASA ROSADA, OR PRESIDENTIAL PALACE, in downtown Buenos Aires is a massive square that has been the hub of women-led activism for the past century: the Plaza de Mayo. In the 1940s, María Eva Duarte de Perón (known to her supporters as Evita) gave eloquent orations on social welfare here; thirty years later, the mothers of Argentina's "disappeared" launched a potent protest that continues to this day. Come stand in this historic public space—also known as the Plaza de Protestas— to soak in their spirits or to witness their current struggles.

Nothing in Evita's early biography hints that she would someday become the most powerful woman in South America. An illegitimate daughter in a status-conscious society, she had neither a formal education nor any connections of note, and for several years scraped out a living as an actress in B-grade melodramas and radio soap operas. Struck by her beauty and verve, Colonel Juan Domingo Perón fell in love with her at a charity function, and, after a brief political imprisonment, married her right as he began to campaign for president. Evita rallied hard for her man, appealing especially to Argentina's *descamisados,* or impoverished, "shirtless" population, for their votes. After she became the nation's First Lady in 1946, she made good on her promises, creating the Eva Perón Foundation to offer services like food, clothes, hospitals, schools, and orphanages for the poor. She also helped secure the vote for women and created a women's branch to the Peronist party. But Evita is remembered most for her riveting speeches from the Casa Rosada balcony overlooking Plaza de Mayo. During one famed oration in 1951, she even conducted a spontaneous dialogue with a crowd of two million about whether or not to run for Vice President. (Her husband ultimately prevented her candicacy, but later gave her the title "Spiritual Leader of the Nation.") Cancer took Evita's life at the age of thirty-three, and Perón had her embalmed Lenin-style. Her corpse continued having adventures of its own—read Tomas Eloy Martinez's *Santa Evita* for a novelist's interpretation. Fans can visit her tomb in the posh Cementerio de la Recoleta, where one of the many epitaphs reads: "Don't cry for me, Argentina, I remain quite near to you."

After an extended period of exile, Perón ruled Argentina once more from 1973 until his death in 1974, a time of great social unrest. His new wife and Vice President Isabel Perón attempted to govern after him but was quickly overthrown by the right-wing military, led by a general who vowed, "As many people as necessary must die in Argentina so that the country will again be secure." In the so-called "Dirty War" that followed, some 30,000 political opponents, many of them left-wing students and workers, were forcibly "disappearred." (Most, presumably, were tortured and murdered by the military's death squads.) In an astonishing act of courage, a group of fourteen mothers entered the Plaza de Mayo one afternoon to demand the whereabouts of their children. Forbidden by dictatorial law from any kind of public assembly—including simply standing there—they walked around the plaza's main circle. They returned the following week and every week after, with more mothers joining in. Some wore white scarves to symbolize the diapers of their lost; others hung laminated photographs of their missing children around their neck. Although three of those original mothers soon disappeared as well, the others became renowned human rights activists who continue their protest today (although they've since added other issues to their reportoire, such as fighting globalization and the International Monetary Fund). Join them every Thursday afternoon for their weekly marches around the plaza.

"I have one thing that counts, and that is my heart; it burns in my soul, it aches in my flesh, and it ignites my nerves: that is my love for the people and Perón."

—Eva Perón

RECOMMENDED READING

Evita: The Real Life of Eva Perón by Nicholas Fraser and Marysa Navarro

13 *Washington, D.C.*
National Shrines to Women

THE U.S. CAPITAL PAYS HOMAGE TO MANY HEROINES OF AMERICAN history, from suffragettes to painters, war veterans to politicians. For an authentic D.C. experience, check in with groups like the National Organization of Women or Code Pink to review the major issues of the day before lobbying your elected officials. Then visit the following locales:

❀ In 1929, women's rights leader Alice Paul opened the headquarters of the National Women's Party at the Sewall-Belmont House at 144 Constitution Avenue, NE. There, she wrote the Equal Rights Amendment and rallied for its passage. Today, the museum offers hour-long tours of its extensive collection of women's suffrage memorabilia, plus a short video, *Equal Rights Amendment: Unfinished Business for the Constitution.*

❀ Every statistic about the Library of Congress astounds: the largest library in the world, it has more than 130 million items stacked on 532 miles of bookshelves. Its collection on the women's suffrage movement is exhaustive, including Susan B. Anthony's personal library and the three-volume *History of Women's Suffrage* penned by Anthony, Elizabeth Cady Stanton, and Matilda

WWW.
www.now.org
www.codepink4peace.org
www.sewallbelmont.org

Joslyn Gage. Be sure to visit the giant mosaic of Minerva, goddess of wisdom and knowledge, atop the grand staircase in
the library's main foyer. According to docent Amy
Schapiro, her feet follow you as you turn the corner!

* The Women in Military Service for America
  Memorial at the ceremonial entrance of
  Arlington National Cemetery pays respects
  to the 2 million women who have defended
  the United States since the American
  Revolution. At its heart is the register,
  where photos, oral histories, and stories
  can be accessed via the computerized database. Many are devastating in their simplic-
  ity: "[My most memorable experience was]
  befriending a young Korean boy in Seoul,
  Korea in 1975 for five to six months, only to
  find him frozen in a hole in the wall outside the
  compound," writes Joan Humes, an Army staff
  sergeant from Philadelphia.

  www.memory.loc.gov/ammem/collections/suffrage/nwp
  www.womensmemorial.org
  www.nmwa.org

* Wilhelmina and Wallace Holladay began collecting art by
  women in the 1960s, when scholars and historians were just
  beginning to debate their underrepresentation in museums and
  galleries. The National Museum of Women in the Arts was
  incorporated in 1981 and housed in a couple of offices before
  settling at 1250 New York Avenue, NW. The permanent collection now boasts more than three thousand works from the sixteenth century to the present, including selections by Frida
  Kahlo, Rosa Bonheur, Camille Claudel, Elaine de Kooning,
  and Käthe Kollwitz.

14 *Famous Women Writers and Their Creative Nooks*

WHERE WOULD WE BE WITHOUT OUR LITERARY SISTERS—THE ONES who shine light into our psyches and make sense of our souls? Pay tribute to some of history's greatest women writers in the following places:

* Born to a highly dysfunctional family in 1892, Russian Marina Tsvetaeva endured a conflicted life wrought with tragedy. She found her poetic inspiration as a teenager living in an artistic haven on the Black Sea, where she attracted many lovers—both men and women. However, she married a cadet who ran off to join the White Army in the Civil War following the 1917 Revolution. Tsvetaeva traveled to Moscow hoping to find him and got trapped in the war-torn city. Unable to care for her children, she sent one daughter to a shelter, where she starved to death. (The director, it turned out, was selling the food for profit.) This so devastated Tsvetaeva that she fled to Berlin, Prague, and Paris, only to despise being an émigré. Against her better judgement, she returned to Moscow in 1939, amidst the worst of Stalin's purges. Within a few months, both her husband and daughter were arrested (the former eventually shot); two years later, Tsvetaeva hanged herself (or so they say). Fans and relatives have since turned her Moscow residency on 6 Ulitsa

Pisemskovo into a museum. Though only one table and mirror are original, it is impressive to see her monkish study as well as the kids' room, where the family kept turtles, parrots, and squirrels as pets. The guides will recite her poetry if asked.

* The great Russian poet Anna Akhmatova also suffered terribly at the hands of Stalin. Two of her husbands were executed, and her son spent most of his childhood in the gulag. Although she had risen to prominence before the Revolution, she was repressed between 1925 and 1952, unable to publish anything but scholarly essays on Pushkin, some translations, and a few patriotic poems dashed off during World War II. *Requiem,* her masterpiece on living under Stalinist terror, wasn't published in Russia until after her death in 1966. Visit the Fountain House where Akhmatova lived for thirty years in St. Petersburg at Liteyny Pereylok 53 (near the Mayakovskaya Metro). The displays include old photographs, letters from lovers (including Boris Pasternak), and some writing that can only be read in a mirror. Buy a tape of famous Russian actors reading her work in the gift shop.

* History has never known a family as literary as the Brontës. Sisters Charlotte, Emily, and Anne published their first book (of poems) in 1846 under the pseudonyms Currer, Ellis, and Acton Bell. When it only sold two copies, they decided to give fiction a go. In the following year they published a novel apiece: *Jane Eyre, Wuthering Heights,* and *Agnes Grey.* All three were smash hits, but the sickly authors died before they could produce many more. (Fragments from Charlotte's notebooks were published posthumously as *Emma* five years after her death.) The sisters' home has since become a museum that

displays much of their original furniture and personal effects. Fans will particularly like the living room, where the sisters once paced around the table, reading aloud passages and calling out suggestions. It also contains Anne's favorite rocking chair and the black sofa upon which Emily died. The exhibition rooms showcase some of their earliest writings and poems, plus samplings of their paintings. The Brontë Parsonage Museum is located on Church Street behind the Parish Church in Haworth, West Yorkshire, England.

✿ Born to Transcendentalists with close ties to Emerson and Thoreau, Louisa May Alcott grew up in an impoverished family in the 1800s. An abolitionist and a feminist, she dabbled in teaching, sewing, and cleaning before taking up the quill and ink. Her early novels were deemed "blood-and-thunder tales" in the Victorian Era because they featured protagonists hell-bent on getting their way in life, and carried dramatic titles like *A Long Fatal Love Chase*. But Alcott is most famous for her wholesome novel *Little Women,* a semi-autobiographical account of growing up with her sisters in the Northeast. (The feisty character Jo, who chops off her hair and sells it to a wig shop so that her mother can visit their chaplain father off at war, is said to be based on the author.) Noting, "I'd rather be a free spinster and paddle my own canoe," Louisa never married, opting instead to care for her family. Visit their home, now a museum known as the Orchard House, at 399 Lexington Road in Concord, Massachusetts. Louisa is buried in nearby Sleepy Hollow cemetery, in the Authors Ridge. Honor her wish that her books be the "shabbiest" on the library shelf by visiting the Concord Free Public Library on 129 Main Street.

The gold that was my hair has turned
Silently to gray. Don't pity me!
Everything's been realized
In my breast all's blended and attuned.
—Attuned as all of distance blends
In the smokestack moaning in the outskirts.
And Lord! A soul's been realized:
The most deeply secret of you ends.

—Marina Tsvetaeva (1922)

RECOMMENDED READING

Selected Poems by Marina Tsvetaeva, translated by Elaine Feinstein

Earthly Signs by Marina Tsvetaeva, translated by Jamey Gambrell

The Complete Poems of Anna Akhmatova by Anna Akhmatova, edited by Roberta Reeder

Anna of all the Russias: A Life of Anna Akhmatova by Elaine Feinstein

The Brontë Myth by Lucasta Miller

The Brontës: A Life in Letters by Juliet Barker

Louisa May Alcott: Her Life, Letters and Journals edited by Ednah D. Cheney

15 *Women's Bookstores in the USA*

AS RECENTLY AS 1997, THERE WERE 175 WOMEN'S BOOKSTORES sustaining communities across the United States. Today, only about 30 remain in operation, due in part to the proliferation of mega-chains like Barnes & Noble and online outlets like Amazon. This tragedy is not only literary: women's bookstores have long served as gathering points to discuss issues ranging from pregnancy and motherhood to glass ceilings and sexual harassment. But while the remaining stores are struggling, they are kicking furiously, including the following:

* Founded in 1970, Minneapolis's Amazon Bookstore claims to be the oldest independent feminist bookstore in North America. The store is a worker-owned cooperative seeking to foster the "strength, wisdom, beauty, and diversity of women, girls, and their families." In addition to sponsoring meetings for book clubs as varied as Eclectic Dykes and Get Off Yer Ass & Do Something, Amazon sponsors movie nights, open-mike performances, and children's story hour. Visit them at 4755 Chicago Avenue South.

* Antigone Books at 411 North 4th Avenue in Tucson, Arizona builds community through such events as Stitch 'n' Bitch sessions where women gather to knit and, well, bitch. They also

sell gifts like bumperstickers, cards, stuffed animals, and jewelry, much of it crafted by local artists.

- Bluestockings on the Lower East Side of Manhattan has recently become more of an activist center than a women's bookstore, but still boasts an impressive selection of feminist titles and zines. It also hosts readings, film screenings, workshops, and discussions nearly every night of the week, and no one is ever turned away for empty pockets. Enjoy vegan and fair-trade treats in their café at 172 Allen Street (accessible by taking the F train to the Second Avenue stop).

  www. www.antigonebooks.com www.bluestockings.com www.ebookwoman.booksense.com www.milk-and-honey.com

- BookWoman has been supporting the women of Austin, Texas since 1975. Located at 918 West 12th Street, it offers 10 percent discounts for book club members and hosts a variety of events, including monthly Songwriters Circles.

- Milk & Honey on 123 North Main Street in Sebastopol, California specializes in women's spirituality. Here you will find everything from goddess statuary (for building your own sanctuary) and talismans to bodycare and aromatherapy products made by the store itself. Most of its books focus on healing and personal growth.

- A Room of One's Own Feminist Bookstore is a well-lit place on 307 West Johnson Street in Madison, Wisconsin. Monthly events include a Writergirrrls Writing Circle and a Shameless

Hussy Book Club. They also host receptions for events like WisCon, the feminist science fiction convention.

WWW.
www.roomofonesown.com
www.womenandchildrenfirst.com
www.litwomen.org/WIP/stores.html

● With 30,000 titles, Chicago's Women & Children First is one of the nation's largest feminist bookstores. It also carries music, videos, magazines, and pride products. They recently established a Women's Voices Fund to raise money to sustain their programming, which has focused on "women's lives, ideas, and work" since 1979. Visit them at 5233 North Clark Street.

Many of these booksellers can ship their items anywhere in the world, so consider placing your next order with them.

II

Places of Adventure

16 *Antarctica*

THE COLDEST, WINDIEST, AND MOST INHOSPITABLE PLACE ON Earth, Antarctica has captured the imagination of adventurers since its "discovery" in the early nineteenth century. Most nations operating bases here banned women until fairly recently (1969, in the case of the United States). Even today, women are a minority on the White Continent.

The best way to visit Antarctica is to land a job in your nation's base camp. In the United States, Raytheon Polar Service holds a job fair every April in Denver, Colorado. Take a stack of resumes and apply for anything you are remotely qualified for—including human resources, engineering, toilet scrubbing, or dishwashing. Jobs usually last four or five months, are well paid, and include all the equipment needed for surviving the climate.

Or just take a cruise. Tourist ships operate during Antarctica's summer, November to March, and are booked a good year in advance. Last-minute cancellations do occur, however, and if you spend enough time at the travel agencies of Ushuaia (the southernmost city of Argentina), you might get lucky enough to fill a space. A typical twelve-day cruise runs anywhere from $3,000 to $7,000 and includes a bed in a cabin, meals, lectures, and outings on the Zodiac boats that maneuver between the icebergs. Don't forget

www.usap.gov

the gear: rubber boots, waterproof pants, a windproof parka, an assortment of fleece and thermals, anti-UV sunglasses, and some serious anti-nausea drugs for the 600-mile journey through the turbulent seas of Drake Passage.

Antarctica has experienced a tourist surge since the release of *March of the Penguins,* and the film stars don't disappoint. "We went in January when the chicks were just a month old, and you would see them chasing after their moms crying 'Feed me, feed me!' and the mom would be like, 'I fed you already, leave me alone!' They were just a hoot. And if you sat down quietly, they'd come right up to you," says polar traveler Jackie Yang. Other wildlife include humpback, killer, Menke, and sperm whales; crabeater and leopard seals; albatrosses; and petrels.

Equally wondrous is the scenery: lichens and moss grow along craggy rocks and glaciated mountains cast reflections into icy pools. Jackie was particularly taken with Deception Island, where a volcano had spewed lava rocks across a black sand beach. "It was like walking on the moon," she remembers. "And in Pendulum Cove, the volcanic activity had made the water near the shoreline tepid, so we actually went swimming—in Antarctica!"

RECOMMENDED READING

Terra Incognita by Sara Wheeler

Swimming to Antarctica by Lynne Cox

TOURS

Antarctica tours can be arranged through Expedition Trips by Land and Sea (www.expeditiontrips.com) and Zegrahm & Eco Expeditions: Giving You the World (www.zeco.com).

17 *Africa Game Parks*

BIG GAME SAFARIS ARE NOT ONLY AN EXHILARATING ADVENTURE, but a meditative one as well. "You are finally looking outside of yourself and forgetting yourself, yet you are so connected with everything around you. It is the root of all life, Africa," says Puerto Rican poet and safari veteran Irene Perez.

There are two types of safaris: lodge-based or camping. Game lodges are often swanky—complete with five-star restaurants, massage therapists, and yoga studios—and can be fairly costly. Camping out is much cheaper, but be prepared for long-drop toilets, bucket showers, chores, and the possibility of unzipping your tent one morning to discover a wild hyena slurping from your water basin. (Lodges usually have electric fences that keep the animals out.) Budget travelers can rent jeeps and drive themselves around some national parks (like South Africa's Kruger National Park), but only official guides and trackers can go off-roading. Try to coincide your safari with a full moon, as their blood-orange rises and settings are extraordinary on the open plains. Be extremely cautious around all animals, especially hippos (which kill more tourists than any other animal—usually death by trampling), and don't hang lingerie outside to dry. Baboons have a penchant for stealing bras and panties.

Remarkable safaris can be taken in the following locales:

* About half of the world's mountain gorillas prowl around the primeval rainforests of Bwindi Impenetrable National Park in Uganda. Gorilla Forest Camp, a luxury tented camp in the heart of the park, offers tracking services. Irene's expedition involved a five-hour hike up a mountain with a tracker, a  guide who cleared the path with a machete, a porter, and two armed military soldiers (more for protection from guerrillas than gorillas). When they finally spotted a gorilla family, Irene experienced pure joy. "All my photos came out blurred because I was shaking so much from emotion and the tension in my muscles," Irene says. "The gorillas' eyes were just so intense, and the little ones looked straight at you." Bwindi is also home to 7 other species of primates, 200 kinds of butterflies, and a herd of the rare forest elephant.

* Giraffes, lions, cheetahs, hippos, and tens of thousands of elephants inhabit the lush green wetlands of Botswana's Okavango Delta, the world's largest inland delta. For a fun alternative to jeep travel, explore the lagoons in a mokoro, or dugout canoe, poled by a Bayei tribesman who will point out the African jacanas (a.k.a. Jesus Christ birds) skidding across the crystalline waters. Or catch an elephant taxi: elephant-back expeditions allow for greater proximity to the animals, as the elephants' scent overpowers your own.

* Home to some of Africa's most spectacular sights, including Mount Kilimanjaro (the continent's highest peak) and Ngorongoro Crater (at twelve miles wide, the world's largest intact caldera), Tanzania also boasts the famous Serengeti National Park. Come to watch 1.7 million white-bearded wildebeest migrate across 5,700 square miles of undulating grasslands and woodlands. A bird's paradise, Serengeti also hosts flocks of flamingoes, ostriches, raptors, and half a dozen types of vultures.

TOURS

Abu Camp offers an elephant camp and safari to Botswana's Okavango Delta (www.elephantbacksafaris.com).

Island-Safari Tours offers several choices to the Okavango Delta (www.okavango-wilderness-safaris.com).

18 *Surfing Sites*

FORGET THE ROCKS, THE REEFS, THE SHARKS, THE RIP TIDES. AS ANY surfer will tell you, paddling out to sea and riding back in on its waves is the closest we can get to nirvana on earth, and well worth the risk. Though it has been a male-dominated sport since its inception, more and more women are jumping aboard, thanks to world champion trailblazers like Margo Oberg, Layne Beachley, and Lisa Andersen. And the already initiated are delighted by it.

"Every time I meet a girl in the water, we say exactly the same thing: that we are so happy to see each other," says Aya Nakashima, who recently moved from Japan to California so she could surf every morning before school. "It gets lonely out here, being the only one in the ocean. Guys are always trying to tell me what to do just because I'm a girl."

Kristina Marquez and Sally Smith of Santa Cruz, California knew the feeling. They got so sick of being ignored, or worse, at surf shops, that in 1997 they decided to open one of their own: Paradise Surf Shop. They stacked their shelves with suits and tops that fit "real women," then created a clubhouse atmosphere with couches and piles of magazines and DVDs. Even their bathroom pays homage to female empowerment, with bumper stickers reading "Girls rip"

www.paradisesurf.com

and "Just because some designer cranked it out doesn't mean you have to wear it." They also got involved with the community, sponsoring forums on surfing safety and holding art shows and fundraisers for local non-profits. Women flock here from all over Northern California to check out the merchandise and hang out. You can, too, at 3961 Portola Drive.

Once properly outfitted in a new rash guard and booties, it's time to get stoked—or, at least, learn how to. In Hawai'i, Maui Surfer Girls offers both overnight surf camp and surf classes taught by women, for women (and girls), with a student/instructor ratio of 3:1. Visit them on Ukumehame Beach Park, five miles south of Lahaina. Surf Diva out of La Jolla, California offers two-day and five-day surfing clinics at both the beginner and intermediate levels, as well as weeklong Viva La Diva trips to the Nicoya Peninsula in Costa Rica. Drop by their office at 2160 Avenida de la Playa. For a luxury surfing experience, try Las Olas Surf Safaris for Women. Since 1997, they have been offering week-long retreats in oceanfront villas in Puerto Vallarta, Mexico that include morning yoga classes and sports massages in addition to daily, "women-specific" surfing instruction. (Depending on group interest, salsa lessons and henna body art parties can also be arranged.) As their motto so aptly says, "Las Olas—We make girls out of women."

www.mauisurfergirls.com
www.surfwomenonwaves.com
www.surfdivas.com
www.surflasolas.com

Then consider entering a contest or two. Girls and women ranging in age from seven to sixty-plus gather in Capitola, California each year to compete in the Women on Waves Festival. Throughout the long day, surfboards are raffled, bands play, the pros sign autographs, and all proceeds go to the local domestic violence shelter, a woman's cancer advocacy group, and a college scholarship fund.

TOURS

Surf Goddess Retreats offers tours to their Surf Goddess Sanctuary in Seminyak, Bali (www.surfgoddessretreats.com).

19 *Abseiling and Canyoneering Sites*

FIRST, SOME DEFINITIONS ARE IN ORDER. ABSEILING IS THE PROCESS of descending on a fixed—that is, secure—piece of rope. It is also known as rappelling, abbing, jumping, rapping, or snappeling, depending on which country you are in. As a technique, it is used by everyone from window cleaners and firefighters to rescue teams, but adventurers employ it for exploring the bowels of caves and valleys as well as the full expanses of mountains and waterfalls. Good equipment is essential: helmet, gloves, sturdy footwear, knee and elbow pads, a comfy harness, some hard-core rope that stretches about 2 percent under your body weight, and a descender (the safety device that lets out the rope in a controlled fashion).

Once you've mastered abseiling, graduate to canyoneering (also known as canyoning), a young but evolving "multi-disciplinary" sport that entails abseiling down ravines, swinging Jane-style over rapids, scrambling through caves, traversing over boulders, and finally—plunging from cliffs into pools of icy water. This is what Aron Ralston was doing in Utah before he got pinned behind a boulder and hacked off his own arm with a pocket knife to free himself, so in addition to the abseiling equipment, bring a buddy or two (along with a knife and perhaps a nice tourniquet).

Scared yet? Well, that's the first obstacle to conquer in extreme sports.

"Even after three years, there are still times when I sit on a ledge and cry and say, 'I can't do it, I can't do it,' and then I calm down and do it," says Shelley Buckingham, an avid canyoneer from Utah. "The first step is trusting your equipment and believing it will work, because it will. Then you start with small canyons and work your way up. It has been a great confidence booster for me, as well as a self-affirmation in overcoming my fear of heights."

The robust-of-heart can abseil and canyoneer in scenic spots in Spain, France, Scotland, and New Zealand, as well as the following:

❖ At the crossroads of the Colorado Plateau, Great Basin, and the Mojave Desert, Utah's Zion National Park offers 229 square miles of sculptured canyons that seem like hallowed ground. Indeed, the ancient Anasazi dwelled here for 700 years; the Paiute were so struck by its grandeur that they wouldn't even enter the Upper Canyon. Today, Zion is a pilgrimage site for canyoneers. Novices opt for the "Subway," which entails three abseils of up to twenty-five feet, hiking, and a bit of swimming; experts attempt Heaps Canyon, a strenuous two-day hike that includes at least thirty rappels—the last of which is a 280-foot, free-hanging descent over Emerald Pool. Zion Adventure Company offers outings for all levels as well as a three-day course for those who wish to canyoneer solo. Temperatures in the canyons can top 110 degrees so bring a tub of sunscreen and gallons of water. Also, be extremely cautious of flash floods in the narrower canyons: if the water turns murky or the clouds turn gray, seek higher ground immediately.

❀ Australia's Blue Mountains are named for their thick haze, created when sunlight ricochets off the eucalyptus oil hovering in the air from the gum trees. Based about ninety miles west of Sydney, High 'n' Wild Mountain Adventures offers training programs for all levels. In the Empress Canyon expedition, you'll work your way from ten- to thirty-three-foot drops into frigid water before the clincher: abseiling down a 100-foot waterfall into a deep rock pool. Sleep off the post-adrenaline crash at the Kanimbla View, an eco-lodge tucked in the bushland that offers overlooks of the canyons below. Soak away any soreness in the glasshouse spa before retiring to an adobe cottage complete with mud-rendered walls, solar lighting, composting toilets, and hemp bed sheets. Rise with the sun and do it all over again.

www.karimbla.com

TOURS

Zion Adventure Company offers rock climbing, canyoneering, and tours to Zion National Park (www.zionadventures.com).

High 'n' Wild Mountain Adventures leads daily adventures in abseiling, canyoning, rock climbing, and more in Australia (www.high-n-wild.com.au).

20 *The Amazon Basin*

A LUSH TROPICAL FOREST THAT ONCE COVERED 2 MILLION SQUARE miles, the Amazon Basin features the greatest biodiversity in the world. Thousands of its plants, insects, birds, and animals are not found anywhere else, and indigenous tribes still live deep within its terrain. Its unparalleled beauty make it a profoundly powerful place.

While Brazil is home to 60 percent of the basin and has a

highly developed tourist infrastructure, you are more likely to spot wildlife by floating down the slender waterways of northern Bolivia. Head to the town of Rurrenabaque and sign up for a $60-a-day animal-watching expedition. Pampas tours explore the wetland savannas while jungle tours motor up the Tuichi and Beni rivers for camping and forest treks. Common sightings include piranhas, anacondas, pink river dolphins, electric blue butterflies, three-toed sloths, toucans, and—if you're lucky—a jaguar or puma. Try to avoid the rainy season during the first months of the year unless you enjoy getting drenched. Bolivia also boasts a number of eco-lodges run by local indigenous communities that are highly worth supporting, including the following:

◉ Local families built the Chalalán Ecolodge abiding by a "minimum impact" philosophy on the edge of Chalalán Lake in Madidi National Park. The surrounding wilderness is phenomenally diverse, from cloud forest to dry tropical forest to savannah, and home to howler, spider, capuchin, and squirrel monkeys, plus tapirs and jaguars. On the night hike, don a headlamp and visit frogs and other nocturnal creatures. In La Paz, their office is at Calle Sagarnaga 189 at the corner of Murillo Street in the Michel Shopping Doryan building, 2nd level, office 35; in Rurrenabaque, go to Calle Comercio S/N in the Plaza Principal. The lodge itself is reachable by dugout canoe.

◉ Built, owned, and operated by the families of the Quiquibey River, MAPAJO Ecoturismo Indigena offers cabins well equipped with beds, mosquito nets, hammocks, and a deck, plus hot showers. Activities include arts and crafts, bow-and-arrow fishing, and treks down trails lined with ancient trees to visit nitrate and salt beds, macaw nests, and Moseten and Tsiman villages. Depending on the size of your group, MAPAJO charges $55 to $70 per person per day, which covers transportation, room, board, and guides. Drop by their offices on Calle Santa Cruz in Rurrenabaque.

www.mapajo.com
www.amazonwatch.org

The Amazon is slowly being pulverized by both local and international developers who are clearing, mining, and logging its land to pilfer its natural resources, polluting its waters in the process. Help fight the destruction by supporting organizations like Amazon Watch, which works with local groups throughout the basin to defend the environment, as well as the rights of communities.

RECOMMENDED READING

Running the Amazon by Joe Kane

The Last Forest: The Amazon in the Age of Globalization by Mark London and Brian Kelley

Travelers' Tales Brazil edited by Annette Haddad and Scott Doggett

21 Mountain Trekking Sites

THERE IS NOTHING LIKE A HARD CLIMB UP A STEEP MOUNTAIN TO test your limits, expand your boundaries, and—once you've reached the summit—bask in your physical prowess. In the past fifty years, Californian Betsy White has crested peaks on every continent but Antarctica and was in several instances the second woman in recorded history to do so. She offers the following tips to novice climbers: "Try out your gear on home territory first, especially your shoes. Packing lighter is better, but be prepared for emergencies with a parka, mittens, warm hat, and enough water and food to last an extra night. Trekking poles are also a good idea: they help the knees, are good for balance, and can fend off nasty dogs (or people)." The following are some of Betsy's all-time favorite treks:

* In Pakistan's remote Biafo-Hispar Traverse, the thirty-seven mile Biafo Glacier and the thirty-eight mile Hispar Glacier meet to form one of the longest glacial systems outside the arctic poles. Rocky, glaciated towers and virgin peaks pave the path and adventurous snowboarders can go sliding at 17,000 feet. It is home to Himalayan bears, ibex, markhors, and snow leopards, but almost no people (aside from the occasional shepherd). A good guide is essential, and Betsy swears by hers: Nazir Sabir out of Islamabad. A famed mountaineer

www.nazirsabir.com · WWW

who has climbed Everest and K2, Nazir can navigate his nation's political morass as well. The Biafo also marks a special spot in women's history: famed female mountaineer Fannie Bullock-Workman was the first to climb and document the region, along with her husband. "We camped in the same spot she did at the turn of the century. A group even found some of their trash a few years ago," says Betsy. "So in addition to the natural beauty, the Biafo offers a chance to hike in the footsteps of a remarkable woman mountaineer."

● The French Alps are always a pleasure, particularly in the south (although you might want to avoid the summer crowds around Chamonix). Mercantour National Park offers excellent trails up 10,000-foot peaks with spectacular views of lakes, Mediterranean olive trees, and fields of lavender and lady's slipper. Several thousand chamois live in the park, and herds can often be spotted charging up the rocky terrain. Ermines and wolves prowl around, too, but glimpses of them are rare. Archaeological sites abound, including Bronze Age-era petroglyphs etched at the foot of Mont Bego. Italy's nearby Alpi Marittime Natural Park is similarly lovely, and has *refugios,* or cottages, strategically placed along its trails, enabling hikers to walk high above the timberline for days without carrying a heavy pack.

● Dauntingly remote and fiercely windy, Patagonia offers peaks, lakes, forests, and glaciers to those who brave its elements. According to legend, the explorer Magellan named the region Patagão, or "The Land of the Big Feet," after the giants he encountered there—some of whom purportedly stood twelve feet high. (A few centuries later, historians re-estimated their height at a more probable, though still impressive, six-foot-six.) Big feet would certainly be helpful traversing the rugged terrain, much of which is covered with shingle. To reach this faraway land, fly into Punta Arenas, Chile, catch a bus to Puerto Natales, and then another to Parque Nacional Torres del Paine. Many hikers "Do the W," a four- to five-day circuit along the south side of the peaks of Torres del Paine (9,200 feet), the Paine Grande (10,000 feet) and Los Cuernos (7,900 feet). To avoid the thickest crowds, visit late in the fall or in March and April. The park offers lodging spaced a day's walk apart, but book in advance as they are popular.

RECOMMENDED READING

Trekking and Climbing in the Western Alps by Hilary Sharp
Lonely Planet Trekking in the Patagonian Andes by Clem Lindenmeyer and Nick Tapp

22 *Victoria Falls*

WITH MISTS VISIBLE FROM FORTY MILES AWAY, VICTORIA FALLS IS one of the most spectacular waterfalls on the planet. Spanning a mile, the waters of the Zambezi River cascade 400 feet into a gorge and then streak the sky with rainbows as spray leaps 1,000 feet back up into the air. European eyes first saw the falls in 1855,

when local tribesmen led explorer David Livingstone here by canoe. Although they already had the lovely name Mosi-O-Tunya (Smoke That Thunders), he coined them Victoria Falls after his Queen, and a nearby landmass that splits the falls in two was later pegged Livingstone Island in his honor. Despite being a serious tourist trap, both are worth a visit.

Two-thirds of Victoria Falls are in Zambia; the rest, in Zimbabwe. (While the latter is said to have the best views, many travelers avoid spending money there so as not to support the government of President Robert Mugabe. Among other things, his abhorrent policies and negligence have led to the shocking drop in life expectancy among Zimbabwean women from sixty-one years to thirty-four years—the lowest in the world.) Zambia has been investing heavily in its tourist infra-structure lately and features high-class resort hotels and lodges, including Tongabezi Safari Lodge and the Islands of Siankaba.

The adventurous will find no shortage of ways to charge their adrenaline at Victoria Falls, including bungee jumping from the century-old bridge spanning the Zambezi River, boogie boarding, tandem parachuting, gorge swinging, paragliding, canoeing, kayaking, and whitewater rafting through passages with daunting names like Ghostrider. If you have an extra $50 to burn, sign up for the fifteen-minute airplane ride over the falls—you'll swear you hear angels singing.

www.victoriafalls.com.za

23 *Places to Swim with Sea Creatures*

COMMUNING WITH ANY ANIMAL IN ITS NATURAL HABITAT IS MAGICAL; beneath the ocean, it is bliss. The following are some of the sea's gentlest creatures, and places where you can interact with them (but be careful—they can get protective of their turf!):

* Manatees, or "sea cows," are like twelve-foot, 2,000-pound puppies: delightfully curious and highly affectionate (when they're not napping). Completely herbivorous, they spend the bulk of their days grazing for plants along the sea floor. Their only nemeses are humans, who hunted them for flesh and oil until the Endangered Species Act intervened. Today, if they can steer clear of watercraft, fish hooks, and crab-trap lines, manatees can live up to sixty years. Approximately three thousand call the United States home. Crystal River, Florida fancies itself the Manatee Capital of the World and offers daily snorkeling trips to visit local herds. The cooler months, October to March, are best, but a small herd lives in the 72-degree Kings Bay year-round. They often swim right up to snorkelers and flip onto their backs for a good belly-scratch.

  www.manatee-central.com

* Early fishermen called them "devilfish," convinced they flew up from Hell to leap onto their boats with their "black

wings" and sink them. But modern divers have a different take on the manta ray. "They rub up right against you, kind of like a cat, but silky—and more sensual," says avid diver Svetlana Mintcheva of Bulgaria. Mantas can measure up to twenty-two feet from tip to tip and weigh 3,000 pounds—an impressive amount, considering they eat primarily plankton and krill. Unlike other rays, mantas have no stinging spine at the end of their long tail, which make them ideal swimming mates. In Ningaloo Reef Marine Park on the Western Australia coast, Coral Bay Adventures offers half-day boating tours with ample snorkeling opportunities. They also offer excursions to visit the biggest fish in the sea: the whale shark. The largest whale shark accurately recorded hit thirty-nine feet, but fishermen claim to have seen some pushing fifty-nine feet. For many a diver, spotting one is the ultimate dream, and for a fee, Coral Bay can make it happen. Only ten swimmers are allowed in the water with these gentle giants at any one time.

* The nurse shark can be found in almost any shallow, tropical water, particularly in the western Atlantic and eastern Pacific. They spend much of the day napping in caves or beneath reefs with as many as forty friends before heading off solo in search of crustaceans and stingrays. Nurse sharks generally swim away from humans and only attack if directly provoked. Encounters are possible via dive shops throughout Belize, which boasts the world's second largest coral reef. Caye Caulker-based Raggamuffin Tours offers spectacular snorkeling trips in the aptly-named Shark Ray Alley.

TOURS

Explorations in Travel can take you to Florida for the annual
Manatees and More! tour (www.exploretravel.com).

Coral Bay Adventures offers programs to swim with whale sharks
and manta rays plus whale watching in Western Australia
(www.users.bigpond.com/coralbay/index.htm).

Raggamuffin Tours offers a variety of tours along the coast of
Belize (www.raggamuffintours.com).

24 *Pearl Diving Sites*

FOR MUCH OF ITS HISTORY, PEARL DIVING WAS AMONG THE MOST brutal professions. Divers—often slaves—were forced to descend as deep as one hundred feet on a single breath to gather oysters from the ocean floor. Many fell victim to shark bites, jellyfish attacks, or decompression sickness, and of the thousands of oysters they brought to shore, only a few actually contained a pearl. Thanks to new technologies that implant particles in oysters to induce pearl formation, today's industry produces millions of perfect pearls a year. But the adventurous can still look for sea treasures the old-fashioned way in the following locales:

* A tiny archipelago in the Persian Gulf, Bahrain claims to have invented pearl diving 5,000 years ago. Their warm, shallow waters offer more than four hundred square miles of oyster beds that yield lustrous pearls. Start your tour at the Museum of Pearl Diving on Government Avenue in Manama, which showcases the industry's rich heritage, and ask for a recommendation of a travel agency that offers tours to pearl beds. A good one will include a history lecture as well as helpful tips on distinguishing the various types of oysters. Also consider a "wreck dive" to the ships, planes, and barges half-buried in the sea. Clown fish, turtles, rays, grouper, and barracuda are among the water's inhabitants,

and in the cooler months, manatees can occasionally be seen snacking on sea grass.

If all your oysters come up empty, other treasures can be found at Craft Centre on Isa al-Kebir Avenue. This artisan market presents traditional weaving, pottery, ironwork, and papermaking, and is operated entirely by women. Join them for a cup of coffee, reverently made with cardamom, saffron, and rose water, and ask about the 2002 constitutional amendment which finally gave Bahraini women the right to vote and run for political office.

❋ To watch divers in action, jet over to Jeju-do in South Korea. Known as the "Island of Three Abundances" for its rocks, wind, and robust women, Jeju-do is home of the venerated *haenyeo,* or women divers who, on breath alone, plunge deep into the cold waters of the East China Sea to gather shellfish, mussels, octopus, and seaweed that they later sell in the market. In some communities, such as Marado, traditionally they are the primary breadwinners and decision-makers of their households, since their husbands can't hack the cold. In the olden days, *haenyeo* dove in white cotton garments that were so revealing, men were forbidden by law to look at them. Nowadays, most wear full-sized wetsuits. They've become a bit of a tourist magnet in areas like Seogwipo, but in tranquil U-do, you can often spot a couple dozen working in the cove beneath the lighthouse. They stay underwater for an astonishing amount of time, then burst through the surface with a whistle.

If possible, arrange your trip during the Chilmeori Shaman Ceremony, when locals pray for the safety of the *haenyeo* as well as the fishermen on the first day of the second lunar month near Sarabong in Jeju City. Then take some time to explore this gorgeous island of beaches, forests, hot springs, lava beds, and mountains. Seogwipo is especially popular with honeymooners and lovers, who like to pose before the waterfalls. At night, duck into a restaurant for a hot bowl of *seonggyeguk* (sea urchin soup) or *jeonbokjuk* (rice porridge with abalone) and an order of grilled sea bream.

25 *Best Bungee Jumping Locales*

YOU KNOW THE DRILL: FASTEN AN ELASTIC CORD SOMEWHERE TO your body (your ankle, if you're daring), make a mad dash toward the edge of that bridge, cliff, or canyon before you, and plunge hundreds of feet until the cord stretches to its limits and (hopefully) snaps you skyward just moments before you smash head-first into that river, valley, or gravel pit below. It's called bungee jumping, and the craze began when the BBC aired footage of young men swan-diving off a high wooden platform with vines knotted around their ankles on Pentecost Island in Vanuatu. When some inspired English lads tried it out on Bristol's Clifton Suspension Bridge in 1979, they were promptly arrested, but not before the adrenaline addicted them. They went on to leap from the Golden Gate Bridge in San Francisco and Colorado's Royal Gorge, as well as from an assortment of mobile cranes and hot air balloons.

Then an enterprising New Zealander, A.J. Hackett, caught the bug. After illegally leaping from the Eiffel Tower in 1987, he began opening bungee-jumping operations around the world, including in Australia, Bali, Mexico, Germany, France, and the United States, and turned the reckless pursuit into a multi-million-dollar industry. Queenstown, New Zealand was the site of his first venture, at the Kawarau Suspension Bridge. Here, you can plummet 143 feet backward or forward, with or without another person, and either bob above the water or be fully immersed. Other exhilarating jumps include the night dives at Ledge Bungy and the 229-foot descents into the rocky gorge beneath Skippers Canyon Bridge.

According to Guinness World Records, the world's highest commercial bungee jump is off the Blaaukrans River Bridge, located twenty-four miles east of Plettenberg Bay in South Africa. Snap into a full-body harness and then walk along a specially-designed catwalk to the top of the bridge's arch 708 feet above the water and take the plunge. If that's too intense, they also offer a 656-foot cable slide (known as a "foofie slide" to South Africans) that will leave you buzzing for days.

Bungee operators adhere to rigorous safety standards, check-ing, double-checking, and even triple-checking all equipment prior to use. Body harnesses are usually employed as well, as back-up for ankle attachment. Yet accidents are not unknown—one of which occurred in 1997, when a young woman crashed head-first into the playing field of the Louisiana Superdome while prac-ticing for a Super Bowl half-time  show. Bungee jumping is not recommended for pregnant women or anyone with heart problems, epilepsy, or recently broken bones.

Still wondering why people do it? Amy Robben, a social worker from Portland, Oregon, asked herself this very question the afternoon she peered over the Pacific Northwest Bridge with a harness strapped to her body. She'd recently ended a difficult relationship, and wanted to do something significant to mark it.

Yet she was terrified to jump—until she realized that bungee jumping was the perfect metaphor for life.

"They have a rule against pushing people off the platform, so nobody can make you do this but you," she says. "It felt like everything challenging I'd ever done was physically there in front of me, and I had to let it all go to jump. The level of accomplishment felt even greater than para-gliding or rock climbing, because when you bungee, it's just you, strapped in all by yourself, with no one belaying you and absolutely nothing to hold on to—just like life."

TOURS

Thrillseekers Canyon Adventure Centre offers several bungee jumping opportunities in New Zealand (www.thrillseekers canyon.co.nz).

Overlanding Africa offers a Garden Route Tour that includes bungee jumping off Blaaukrans River Bridge (www.overlandingafrica.com).

26 *Alaska*

Searching for stories, fiction writer Jessie Sholl ventured to Alaska with a girlfriend the summer after college graduation to work at a fish factory. On the train ride from Seattle, they shared a beer with an Alaskan man who, when told of their plans, warned: "You'll definitely get raped. Probably killed." They took this foreboding in stride, and despite the daunting ratio of men to women, which to Jessie seemed like 10 to 1, they coveted their time there, playing kick-the-can in abandoned shipyards and sleeping in the wilderness. "I love Alaska," she says. "It is rugged, lawless, and beautiful."

Indeed, Alaska realizes the dreams of novelists and adventurers alike. Consider the following locales:

* At 20,320 feet, Denali (a.k.a. Mt. McKinley) is the tallest mountain in North America and seems even grander when you catch its reflection in the aptly-named Wonder Lake. It springs from the heart of Denali National Park & Preserve, a 6 million-acre stretch of subarctic tundra, glaciers, and deeply gorged valleys populated by black and grizzly bears, wolves, caribou, Dall sheep, and golden eagles. The sun shines between sixteen and twenty hours daily in the summer, and wildflowers carpet the forests. But winter brings its own joys, namely the sight of sled dogs tearing through the snow.

Alaskan huskies have been a fixture in the park since the early 1920s, when park rangers employed them to flush out poachers. Today, Denali's kennel keeps a team of about thirty dogs with names like Chulitna, Tikaani, and Pingo, and they conduct sledding demonstrations every afternoon. You can also take an eight-hour tundra wilderness tour from the boreal forests through the tundra to a scenic overlook of Denali. (Just don't look down: the sheer cliffs drop hundreds of feet around the edges.) Camping opportunities are plentiful, and each site is provided with a bear-resistant food container. When hiking, make a lot of noise and avoid berry patches. Should a bear pop out, wave your arms over your head and back away slowly, speaking firmly. If a chase commences, play dead: pull your knees to your chin, roll over so that your pack is on top, and cry as softly as possible.

❂ To catch Mother Earth's most acclaimed laser light show, visit Alaska between September and October or March and April. Head into a wide open field after 10 P.M. and behold the colorful spectacle above you. Known as Aurora Borealis or Northern Lights, this phenomenon occurs when electrons of energy collide with atoms of the upper atmosphere over a geomagnetic pole. (Or, according to Inuit legend, when the Great Spirits play football with a walrus skull.) A prime place to view the lights is Chena Hot Springs Resort, an hour drive from Fairbanks. Either sit in their Aurorarium, a heated look-out building with plate-glass windows facing northeast, or take their late-night "snow coach" to the top of a distant ridge for a completely unobstructed view (hot chocolate and cider await in the nearby yurt). Chena offers plenty to do during daylight as well, including a year-round ice museum. Constructed of 1,000 tons of ice and snow, it features a life-size chess board and a Stoli Ice Bar, where you can sip a martini from a sculpted ice glass. Other activities include soaking in its numerous hot tubs, snowmobile racing, snow shoeing, cross-country skiing, and "flight seeing" over the Arctic Circle in a prop plane. For an additional fee, you could also learn how to mush in a two-hour course that concludes with a "fun run" led by a team of four dogs.

www.chenahotsprings.com

- Still haven't gotten your mushing fix? If your datebook is clear in March, fly out to Anchorage for the annual Iditarod Trail Sled Dog Race. The journey to the finishing line in Nome is roughly 1,150 miles and marked with treacherous mountain passes, river crossings, and sub-zero temperatures with wind chills of −100 degrees Fahrenheit. The races usually last at least two weeks, with many mushers becoming so sleep-deprived, they start hallucinating. The dogs fare even worse: though mushers bring along a couple thousand pairs of booties, they often suffer from frostbite, pneumonia, strangulation in the towlines, and external myopathy from so much exercise. Animal rights groups fiercely protest the race, but it still brings in the crowds, with the top mushers assuming rock star status. Libby Riddles was the first woman to win the race in 1985; Susan Butcher snatched the purse in 1986 and held on to it for half a decade—longer than any other musher.

RECOMMENDED READING

Race Across Alaska: First Woman to Win the Iditarod Tells Her Story by Libby
Riddles and Tim Jones

Travelers' Tales Alaska edited by Bill Sherwonit, Andromeda Romano-
Lax, and Ellen Bielawski

TOURS

Adventure Women offers a women-only Alaska Safari and Bear
Viewing Tour (www.adventurewomen.com).

Women Traveling Together has an eight-day Alaska tour that features the Kenai Peninsula, Denali, and Fairbanks
(www.women-traveling.com).

III

Places of Purification and Beautification

27
Russia
The Banya

THE *BANYA* IS A SLAVIC EDEN: A STEAMY, WOMB-LIKE PLACE WHERE you take off all your clothes and snack on caviar and smoked herring. Russian *babushki,* or grandmothers, swear that frequenting these steam baths can tack years onto your life.

Try landing an invitation to your Russian friends' dacha, or countryside cottage. Many families build *banya* in their backyards, and they will likely join you inside, along with the requisite bottle of vodka (or two). That failing, visit a public *banya.* In Moscow, try Krasnopresnensky on Stolyarny Pereulok 7, near the Ulitsa 1905 Goda Metro, or the nineteenth century Sandunovskiye Bani on Neglinnaya Ulitsa 14. In St. Petersburg, there's the Mitninskaya Banya at Ulitsa Mitninskaya 17/19 near the Metro Ploshad' Vosstaniya, or Kazachie Bani on Bolshoy Kazachy Pereulok 11 near the Metro Pushkinskaya. Public baths are usually gender-segregated.

At the front desk, pay the fee and proceed to the changing room. Mischievous spirits called *bannik* are said to bewitch any clothing worn inside a *banya,* so strip all the way. Wrap up in a towel, slip on some flip-flops, and continue on to the showers for a rinse before entering the steam room, a wooden construction with a large furnace stove at one end. (Sometimes fragrances like pine oil, eucalyptus, or beer are added.) Spread your towel onto a wooden plank (the higher, the hotter) and observe the cultural phenomenon around you. Nothing wipes out class lines like nudity: Russian women of every income level will be perched upon those bleachers, massaging salt into each other's pores, swapping beauty secrets, and gossiping.

At some point, an attendant will lug in buckets full of birch and juniper soaked in water. Grab a branch and, starting with your feet, slap it against the full expanse of your body. This ritual is said to "bring the blood to the surface." *Babushki* will happily assist with any hard-to-reach places; just return the favor afterward. When the heat becomes unbearable, proceed to the pool room and jump in immediately. (Some are kept as frigid as 42 degrees; if you stick a toe in first, you might lose your nerve.) Get out before hypothermia kicks in and return to the steam room. Repeat as many times as you can: your skin will positively glow afterward. *S lyogkim parom,* may the steam be with you!

28 *Destinations for Holistic Spa Treatments*

IF YOU SIMPLY SEEK RESTFUL PAMPERING, JUST ABOUT ANY SPA WILL do. But for a systematic cleansing of the mind, body, and spirit, try the following:

- Tucked into a secluded stretch of Jamaican beach, Jackie's on the Reef is built in perfect accordance with its environment. Bamboo beds grace the polished tile floors of rooms with no radio, TV, or air-conditioning (although the latter isn't needed, thanks to the excellent ventilation system). The partly open-air bathrooms overlook hibiscus trees; the stone showers are furnished with sweetgrass soap. Ocean water fills the swimming pool, and red-billed hummingbirds and butterflies flutter about.

  Guests awaken each morning to New Age music and can join a meditation or yoga class. Breakfast—like every meal—is prepared over a wood-fire grill, and choices include banana pancakes topped with pineapple compote, homemade granola, and fresh yogurt. Spend the day napping in hammocks, reading from the self-improvement library, swimming in the ocean, or drawing on the veranda. Jackie's offers classes such as tai chi, African dance and drumming, and quilting, and guests staying a full week are asked to indulge in at least four spa services. The range is impressive: herbal body scrubs, aromatherapy, reiki sessions with crystals, deep-tissue or hot-stone massage, ear candling, live cell analysis (with nutritional counseling), and "astral travel" that facilitates encounters with angels and ancestors. Afternoon and evening meals borrow from Jamaican, Indian, Chinese, and Creole cuisines, and each concludes with a tea infused with herbs grown in the garden and sweetened with honey from a nearby hive.

"Jackie's is so serene, you really find yourself here," says Mercedes Gallego, a Spanish journalist who spent a week here after covering the war in Iraq. "It allows you to think and come up with some solutions for your life."

Jackie's on the Reef is a twenty-minute drive from the Negril airport; owner Jackie Lewis, an African-American model-turned-spa guru, will send a driver out to fetch you.

❀ Nestled in the meadows beneath a sacred mountain an hour's drive from San Diego is a spa that has been helping its guests "rest, renew, and redirect" since 1940: Rancho La Puerta. Built by a charismatic Transylvanian philosopher and his seventeen-year-old bride, the rancho became a hit with Hollywood celebrities and intellectuals who found pitching tents and eating legumes adventurous. It has since evolved into a 3,000-acre eco-resort that remains family-owned and operated.

Each week begins anew on Saturday, when up to 150 guests arrive. At any given time, there are seventy indoor or outdoor classes and activities to choose from. In addition to the usual suspects—Pilates, yoga, meditation, swimming, tennis—the rancho invites renowned speakers like Naomi Wolf, Erica Jong, and Bill Moyers to lead special sessions on topics of social or political importance. Famous artists and writers often do residencies here as well and hold workshops on their craft—be it

www.jackiesonthereef.com

memoir writing or still-life photography. Another favorite activity is hiking, particularly up the 3,885-foot Mount Kuchumaa, long revered by the local indigenous tribe, the Kumeyaay. Guided treks are offered every morning. Also worthy of exploration are the rancho's grounds, which consist of a labyrinth of brick pathways lined with cacti, oleander, and vines that hang heavy with grapes. Six acres of organic vegetable gardens and fruit orchards supply up to 90 percent of the rancho's produce in the summer, plus all of its olive oil and herbs (used not only for cooking but skin treatments and aromatherapy).

Rancho La Puerta's foremost goal is to nurture you, however, and saunas, massages, and herbal wraps abound. Two especially divine treatments are the hot-stone massage, done with warm stones from the nearby river, and the loofah salt glow, which exfoliates every inch of your body. Sun bins are available in the vineyard for private sunbathing and a 2,600-square-foot salon offers hairstyling and nail care. Then retire to one of eighty-seven rooms individually landscaped with outdoor patios. Leave the windows open to hear the coyotes howl at the moon.

www.rancholapuerta.com

"At Rancho La Puerta, you can exist in harmony, follow your inner voice, live in your own dharma," says Aliana Apodaca, a motivational speaker from El Paso, Texas. "It is all about allowing your soul to breathe."

Women-only weeks are generally held in August.

RECOMMENDED READING

Spas: Exceptional Destinations Around the World by Eloise Napier

29 Rio de Janeiro, Brazil
The Brazilian Bikini Wax

IN BRAZIL, SALONS ARE NOT A LUXURY, THEY ARE AN ESSENTIAL part of life. "It's where women go to replenish, rejuvenate, and renew," says Daphne Sorensen, an international aide worker from Rio de Janeiro. "Our stylists are our best friends. Everyone gossips, drinks coffee—always offered and always complimentary—and shares stories."

For generations, Daphne's family has been loyal to a salon called Makeup at Avenida Bartolomeu Mitre, 455 loja 103 in the Leblon neighborhood. Ask for Graça, resident master of cuticle-removal, or Teresinha for a cut and color. For a hair stylist in the Barra da Tijuca neighborhood, drop by Sonia Nesi in Shopping Barra Point and request Natan. In the Gavea neighborhood, try La Vie en Rose at the Shopping da Gavea mall and enjoy *folhado de queijo,* or cheese puffs, afterward in the divine Chez Anne, widely considered the best pastry shop in Rio.

Of course, a mani/pedi and cut/color is only half the salon experience in Brazil. To truly "go native," you must also get a bikini wax.

Any woman who prefers waxing to shaving will herald its benefits: a smoother finish that lasts for weeks and hair that not only grows back thinner but softer. But truth be told, the first waxing hurts. A lot. It helps to grow the hair out as much as possible. Take an aspirin (or two) an hour beforehand and chase it with a cold beer (or two). Also contemplate how much to wax: only up to the bikini line? Or something a bit more daring? The current rage is to sheer off all but a little *bigode,* or moustache, around the vagina, but you can also request stencil patterns of lightning bolts, stars, hearts, or—if you've met someone special—initials. (If the affair ends badly, you can always rip the letters off afterward.)

Once the waxing begins, relax the muscles, breathe deeply, and talk to the waxer. Think about it: What hasn't this woman seen—or heard? This is the perfect opportunity to gossip about men, sex, and whatever else comes to mind while contorting your body into highly intimate positions as you lay nearly naked on a table.

30 *Japan*
The Onsen and Sento

WORRY NOT WHEN THE CONTROLLED CHAOS OF JAPAN TAKES ITS toll. There are two marvelous antidotes, both of which entail stripping down to nothing and roasting in a tub: the *onsen* and the *sento*.

First, the *onsen*. Because Japan stretches across active volcano fault lines, many of its springs are naturally heated and rich in minerals. Japanese have enjoyed taking *kamiyu,* or divine baths, in these healing waters since ancient times, and families, friends, and colleagues still spend long weekends in the countryside together, sipping cold sake in steamy *onsen.* The significance of this activity cannot be overstated: the *onsen* is one of the few public spaces in which Japanese diverge from their carefully heeded social formalities. Here they can truly speak their mind—and do they!

Many *onsen* feature several baths, each offering a different temperature or mineral composition (and thus, different healing properties). Women and men generally soak separately, and those offering coed pools will almost always have a women-only option as well. Keep in mind that personal hygiene is sacrosanct. People watch foreigners closely, and will be extremely offended if you hop in the tub any less than squeaky clean. Even if you showered at home beforehand, carefully wash and thoroughly rinse off again. Soap is generally provided, but why stop there?

This is a prime opportunity to pamper yourself: break out those pumice stones and fancy creams and lotions. Then take a deep breath, fling open the door, race out to the pool, and plunge in.

"As I lean back to enjoy the view of the sky through the bamboo leaves and watch my fingers pucker like raisins, I cannot help but observe my older fellow *onsen* denizens. I start thinking, 'so *that's* what I'm going to look like when I'm eighty,'" says Debby Katz, who spent two years soaking wet in Kyushu. "And because we're all naked and sitting in the same tub of water, we start talking. 'Where are you from?' they all want to know. 'Do you like *onsen*? Hot as hell in here, isn't it?'"

A popular *onsen* is Dogo, a spa center in Matsuyama, Ehimeken on Shikoku Island. The "Bath of the Spirits" includes hot tea, sweet bean-paste dumplings, and a coveted resting spot on the tatami mats on the veranda outside. Free *ashi-yu*, or footbaths, can be found at the nearby hot spring, Tsu Baki-no-yu Onsen. Another great option is the onsen at the base of Mount Fuji, a 12,390-foot volcanic cone located forty-four miles south of Tokyo. Go in May, when the azaleas are in bloom, and linger until sunset. These hot springs are said to cure everything from stress to rheumatism.

Then there's the *sento*, or neighborhood communal bathhouse. They came into vogue in the Edo period of 1600-1868, when Japan began to urbanize, but have declined in recent years, as most apartments now have their own bathrooms. They can still be found in some residential neighborhoods, however. *Sento* tend to be utilitarian: a simple room with a tall barrier separating the sexes. The women's entrance is usually red and says woman in kanji (, *onna*); the men's, meanwhile, is blue (, *otoko*). Store your shoes in the locker and—as in the *onsen*—make a production of deliberately cleansing your entire body. Then hop in.

"The *sento* are a good way to get to know your neighbors, check in on each other, get the elderly out of the house, etc.," says Marie Doezema, a Tokyo-based journalist. "I go to mine about once a week to hang out with the old ladies and boil myself silly. The last time I went, a total stranger offered to scrub my back for me because I couldn't reach."

Visit Marie's *sento,* Rokuryu, at 3-4-20 Taito-ku in Ikenohata, Tokyo.

RECOMMENDED READING

The Japanese Spa: A Guide to Japan's Finest Ryokan and Onsen by Akihiko Seki and Elizabeth Heilman Brooke

31 *Free Body Culture Sites*

IS ANYTHING AS LUXURIOUS AS NAPPING IN THE SUNSHINE, WITH NARY a bikini strap to disturb you? Nudism (or naturism) is not merely a physical state, but a mental one as well—a return to the truest, purest, and freest self. Plus, as Katherine Mansfield famously pointed out, "Why be given a body if you have to keep it shut up in a case like a rare, rare fiddle?" Perverts are one reason we shield our fiddles, but the following locales are reputed to be women-friendly and peeping Tom, Dick, and Harry free:

❀ World-famous for its naturist resorts, Croatia takes pride in the fact that about 15 percent of its tourists (mainly hippies from Germany, Austria, Italy, and the Netherlands) travel here just to slip off their clothes and bask in the sun. At Koversada Naturist Park, this tradition is said to have begun when international playboy Giacomo Casanova plunged into the sea without a stitch before an admiring audience in the eighteenth century. Two centuries later saw the rise of Freikörperkultur, a German social movement that heralded "free body culture," and by the 1960s, Koversada was an entirely nude islet. Today, there are dozens of naturist camping grounds along the Adriatic Coast, usually marked by "FKK" (short for Freikörperkultur). Near Dubrovnik, try Lokrum Island's FKK Beach, a ten-minute walk from the harbor on the far eastern tip of the island; the Sunj Naturist Beach on Lopud Island (reachable by boat from Gruz harbor); and the Betirina naturist beach in a secluded cove close to the fishing village of Mlinj. To experience naturism at its finest, you can't beat Koversada, though. Spread over one hundred hectares, it offers nearly two thousand camping units set beneath olive and pine trees, plus activities like bocce, beach volleyball, tennis, and miniature golf. You can also rent boats and surfboards. Single women are warmly welcome on these beaches, as are couples; single men generally must show an International Naturist Federation Members card before gaining entrance.

* Ask your Spanish friends about their naturist beaches: they are sure to rave about them. Astrophysicist Amaya Moro-Martín, for instance, swears she could happily spend the rest of her life in Playa de Torimbia in Eastern Asturias. "Its cliffs are high, its beaches are white, its coast is green, and there's no sign of construction anywhere," she sighs. Journalist Mercedes Gallego, meanwhile, prefers Caños de Meca near the Strait of Gibraltar, claiming it is completely unspoiled and surrounded by thick pinewoods. Families rent seaside bungalows for weeks at a time here. With its 2.5 miles of golden sand and crystalline waters, Bolonia is another fine choice. Smack on the coast of Cadiz, its nudist section straddles the southernmost tip; facilities include bars and restaurants, showers, and plenty of hammocks.

www.cronatur.com
www.wilburhotsprings.com

* California earth mamas (and papas) adore Wilbur Hot Springs, a two-and-a-half-hour drive northeast of San

Francisco. Set in an 1,800-acre nature preserve of wildflower valleys and meadows, it features a coed and clothing-optional bathhouse with several hot tubs. Help prepare a communal dinner and then pass the night making music with your fellow bathers (guitar, piano, and bamboo flutes provided) before crashing in the turn-of-the-century hotel. Go river-rafting the following morning in nearby Cache Creek Canyon (though you might want to put on a swimsuit for that). Jaybirds also flock to Orr Hot Springs, a dozen miles west of Ukiah, California on 12201 Orr Springs Road. A rustic resort with vintage décor, Orr offers hot tubs, saunas, massages, an English garden, a communal kitchen, and endless hiking trails through hilly woods of eucalyptus and redwood trees. Leave the razors at home: Orr celebrates the hairy human condition. Also keep in mind the wise words of novelist Heidi Julavits: "Casual eye contact (and eye-body contact) is encouraged, if only because you quickly realize that refusing to register a person achieves the same alienating, even rude, effect as ogling. There is, thus, a certain enjoyable freedom at Orr, to be accepted for who you are: an unexceptionally naked stranger."

32 Lago Atitlán, Guatemala

DEEP IN THE GUATEMALAN HIGHLANDS IS A MYSTICAL VILLAGE THAT has beckoned hippies and backpackers for decades: San Marcos La Laguna. The scenery is reason enough to visit, with its three active volcanoes (Toliman, Atitlán, and San Pedro), wild orchids, ancient Mayan communities, and Lago Atitlán, a collapsed volcanic cone filled with water 1,000 feet deep. But New Agers are drawn by the belief that San Marcos spans a powerful vortex of energy (thus the meditation centers and massage and yoga studios lining the cobblestone pathways too narrow for cars).

The first stop on many a list is Las Piramides meditation center, where every standing structure is shaped like a pyramid and oriented to the cardinal directions. Yoga classes are held at dawn and meditation, tarot, and channeling courses throughout the day. The four-week Full Moon Course is popular with yogis, while those seeking a hard-core cleansing opt for the 40 Days of Silence supplemented with juice fastings. Nonlethal scorpions prefer the dormitory, so bring a mosquito net. Casa Azul, meanwhile, offers reasonably priced massages and organic snacks. Other options around town include *reiki,* reflexology, cranial-sacral massage, and homeopathy.

Food and accommodations are another highlight in San Marcos. For breakfast, head to El Tul y Sol to enjoy its lakeside view over a hot plate of fried plantains, black beans, eggs, and fresh cheese. Vegetarians will love the falafel plate at Moonfish, while the decadent chicken *mole* platters at Paco Real will make any omnivore cry. Sleep off those three-hour lunches at the cliffside Hotel Aaculaax. Its prized room is the  tri-level Mirador, which has glass window walls and a bathroom sprawled across an outdoor terrace with remarkable views.

"There is a lot of camaraderie among the travelers in San Marcos, as though we are all sharing a great secret," says Irene Carranza, owner of an eclectic earth store called Yin Yang Fandango in Corpus Christi, Texas. "We gather here to appreciate the tranquility of the lake and to focus on our own nurturing. This is R&R in its purest sense."

Once you've reached your holistic threshold, get out and go day-tripping. Party-seekers will like San Pedro, a ten-minute boat ride or thirty-minute pick-up truck joy-ride away. On Fridays, head to Santiago Atitlán for their colorful markets. As in all Latin American countries, Semana Santa, or Easter, is the best time to visit, when Mayans create works of sawdust art on the ground and hang effigies of red-eyed devils called Machimon.

For a memorable night, check into the Casa del Mundo Hotel and Café near Jaibalito. Accessible only by boat or on foot, it is built on a secluded cliff surrounded by gardens and offers hot tubs and swimming holes with views of Lago Atitlán. In the morning, rent mountain bikes or kayaks; in the afternoon, take a tour to a nearby village. All meals are served family-style at Casa del Mundo, and conversations last late into the night.

www.lacasadelmundo.com

IV

Places of Indulgence

33 *Amsterdam, Netherlands*

AMSTERDAM IS EITHER THE WORLD'S MOST PROGRESSIVE OR DEPRAVED city, depending on your perspective. Whether drawn by its hedonism, liberalism, or stacks of *pankoeken* served piping hot at every diner, you'll likely fall for it—hard.

Serious shopping abounds in this city. Stroll down P.C. Hooftstraat—a.k.a. the Dutch's Fifth Avenue—for designer clothing, jewelry boutiques, and art galleries. On Sundays, head out to Westerstraat in the Jordaan (near Centraal Station) for a bustling market that sells vintage clothing styles you'll later find in H&M at twice the price. For a treat, stop by a *stroop* stall for a waffle sandwich drowning in syrup. Then amble over to Albert Cuyp, a market that stretches nearly a quarter-mile and peddles everything from fresh seafood, Indonesian curry, and cheeses to jewelry, books, and shovels. If tulips are your vice, steal to the city of Aalsmeer for the world's largest flower auction, held weekday mornings in a warehouse the size of nine football fields.

Pub crawling is a national pastime, and many Dutch chase their *jenever*—a potent gin—with beer. The rowdy Nol Cafe on Westerstraat 109 can usually be counted on for a fun time, especially if you enjoy sing-alongs to American '80s hits and Dutch folk songs. Lux bar at Marnixstraat 403 near the Leidseplein blends classic Dutch brown (those century-old bars lining the canals) and Euro chic, and is jam-packed with artsy locals and bohemian expats. Spend enough time here and you might score an invitation to their late night lock-ins, where you can lounge until nearly sunrise.

Amsterdam's "coffee shops" tend to serve their joe in bongs or space cakes, and you can catch a residual high just by walking through the front door. Connoisseurs should head to De Dampkring at Handboogstraat 29, the winner of several prestigious *High Times* Cannabis cups. Abraxas at Jonge Roelensteeg 12 is good for multitasking: You can check your email and play chess or backgammon while waiting for those funky cakes or shakes to take effect. With its ambient music, soft lighting, and comfy seating, you might never leave Global Chillage at Kerkstraat 51. Fortunately, their staff is accommodating (and DJs spin on weekends).

The infamous Red Light District on De Walletjes is worth a visit, if only for anthropological purposes. Although it is lined with sex shops, sex shows, and a sex museum offering five floors of "enjoyment and arts," you're more apt to bump into curious couples and drunk frat boys than sketchy old men in raincoats. The sex workers—who have been unionized since 1984—await their clients behind rose-lit windows, but are more likely to be filing their nails or reading a magazine than anything else. For a voyeur trip, check out the Theater Casa Rosso. According to the Coalition Against Trafficking in Women, about 80 percent of sex workers in the Netherlands are from other countries, and many are victims of sex trafficking. For more information, drop into the Prostitution Information Center at Enge Kerksteeg 3.

"The road of excess leads to the palace of wisdom."
—William Blake

34 *Champagne, France*

ACCORDING TO LEGEND, CHAMPAGNE WAS DISCOVERED IN THE seventeenth century by French Benedictine monk Dom Pérignon, who purportedly cried out "I am drinking stars!" after taking a sip. The French insist that only bubblies produced in their Champagne-Ardennes region and that meet a lengthy set of requirements can be authentically labeled "champagne."

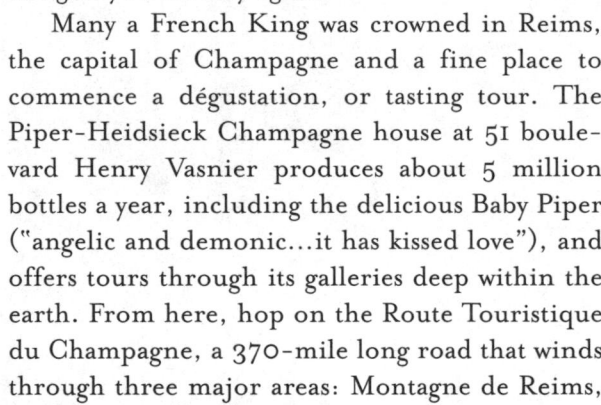

After touring the bountiful cellars of their local villages, you'll likely agree.

Many a French King was crowned in Reims, the capital of Champagne and a fine place to commence a dégustation, or tasting tour. The Piper-Heidsieck Champagne house at 51 boulevard Henry Vasnier produces about 5 million bottles a year, including the delicious Baby Piper ("angelic and demonic...it has kissed love"), and offers tours through its galleries deep within the earth. From here, hop on the Route Touristique du Champagne, a 370-mile long road that winds through three major areas: Montagne de Reims, Côte des Blancs, and Vallée de la Marne. Not to be missed is Épernay, which features France's most famous champagne houses (which boast some 200 million bottles between them). De Castellane at 64 avenue de Champagne has an informative museum and a forty-five-minute tour of its facilities; climb its tower for a panoramic view of the town. The exquisite Moët & Chandon at 18 avenue de Champagne is another excellent choice for tours and tastings.

Connoisseurs can visit the picturesque village of Hautvillers and pay homage to the monk Dom Pérignon, whose tomb is adjacent to the altar of the abbey church, Église Abbatiale. Long ago, this church ordered Pérignon to get rid of the bubbles in his magical concoction, as they were believed to be the reason so many of the (improperly pressurized) bottles exploded—and thus the "work of the devil."

TOURS

Arblaster & Clarke leads wine tours worldwide, including a Champagne Weekend in France (www.winetours.co.uk).

35 Best Bazaars and Boutiques

AFTER HITTING THE FOLLOWING SHOPS, YOU CAN KISS YOUR SHRINK goodbye forever:

* For the Saudi princess look, jet over to the gulf nations. Dubai proudly calls itself the "Shopping Capital of the Middle East," boasting among other things two of the world's largest (and tax-free!) malls and a Shopping Festival between January and February where prices are slashed up to 75 percent. For designers like Donna Karan, Cartier, and Tiffany, head to the BurJuman Centre on Trade Centre Road; for Armani, Gucci, Prada, and Jimmy Choo shoes and handbags, try the Emirates Tower Boulevard on Sheikh Zayed Road. Dubai is most famous, however, for its Gold Souks, which have surely broken records for the most bling per cubic inch. The shops on Old Baladiya Street in Deira are simply dripping with earrings, necklaces, bracelets, and pendants in 18-, 21-, 22-, and 24-karat gold. In the unlikely event you don't find the perfect design, draw your own. For silver, visit Aries Trading in the Old Gold Market, opposite the main

entrance of the souk. For something tailor-made, choose your favorite silk or chiffon at the Meena Bazar off Al Fahidi Street and take it to Dream Girl Tailors opposite Emirate Bank International.

* For the Penelope Cruz look, zip over to Barcelona, Spain, home to tens of thousands of malls, shops, and chichi boutiques, many situated on a three-mile, mostly car-free shopping line that stretches from the top of the Ramblas to Avenida Diagonal. Spend time in Eixample for stores like Jean-Pierre Bua at Avenida Diagonal 469 (which can fulfill any Marni or MiuMiu needs) or Spanish designer Antonio Miró's minimalist boutique at Calle Consell de Cent 349. The Barri Gòtic, meanwhile, features Argentine designer Daniela Yavich at Calle Escudellers 56; a terrific remainder store offering end-of-line clothing by Josep Font and Purificación García called Stockland at Calle Comtal 22; and everyone's favorite outlet for catwalk castoffs, Zara, at Avenida Portal de l'Angel 32-34. For shoes, hit up Muxart on Calle Rosselló 230 in Eixample, and Rouge Poison at Calle Flassaders 34 and U-Casas at Calle Espaseria 4, both in Born. When the packages get too heavy, hop aboard the TOMBUS, a special bus service that shuttles shoppers back and forth along the route.

* For the Bollywood bombshell look, head to India, where women's clothing has been celebrated since the days of ancient Tamil poetry. Most saris measure five to six yards in length (although some Brahmin women opt for nine) and are wrapped around the waist and then elegantly draped over the shoulder. (Prior to colonization, some saris left the

upper body exposed, but the British put a fast end to that practice.) Many are lavished with beadwork, embroidery, tiny mirrors, and even pearls or precious stones.

"Just go up to the clerk and say what you want, like a red silk sari, and they will show you every shade of red imaginable and give you fifty different types of silks," Trina Chattoraj, an Indian-American from Maryland, says of her family's favorite emporiums, which include the following:

In Kolktata (Calcutta) try Gourisaria Sarees at 10-A Shakespeare Sarani; Adi Dhakeswari Bastralaya in Gariahat Market; and Adi Mohini Mohan Kanjilal, India Silk House, and Benarasi Kuthi in the College Street Market area. In New Delhi, visit Ushnak Mal in the South Extension and Nalini Sarees in the Defence Colony for saris and *salwars;* Sethi Collections in Latpat Nagar Central Market for *bindis* and bangles; and Tribhandas Zavery in Connaught Place for jewelry. In Mumbai (Bombay), Rajkamal in New Marine Lines is excellent for saris, while Minawala Jewelry in Hira Panna Shopping Centre, across from Haji Ali, has the best gold bangles and jewelry.

❋ For the Frida Kahlo look, fly to Oaxaca, Mexico where you'll be greeted in the street by women carrying mounds of *rebozos,* or shawls, slung over their shoulders, each handwoven on a backstrap loom. The *tienda* that beats the rest is Mujeres Artesanas de las Regiones de Oaxaca (The Regional Association of the Women Artisans of Oaxaca), or MARO for short. This cooperative was founded by a group of women who wanted to eliminate the "middlemen" who travel from village to village, buying arts and crafts at the lowest possible prices and then selling them in the capital for high markups.

Today, the work of some three hundred women is sold out of a two-level shop that moonlights as a museum of indigenous crafts. The range of items is extraordinary: fine leather purses, satchels, and sandals; delicate gold and silver jewelry; a room full of *huipiles*—robe-like dresses—hand-embroidered by Triqui and Zapotec Indians; an entire wall festooned with shawls and scarves; and a side room of traditional Oaxacan wedding dresses, jewelry, and those lace headpieces Frida Kahlo wears in some of her self-portraits. No bargaining is allowed, and while you'll find cheaper prices elsewhere, you'll never match MARO's quality. Visit them at 5 de Mayo 204, just three blocks south of Santo Domingo, any day from 9 A.M. to 8 P.M.

RECOMMENDED READING

The Fearless Shopper: How to Get the Best Deals on the Planet by Kathy Borrus

Born to Shop Guides by Suzy Gershman (various locales)

TOURS

Chic Shopping Paris offers ten different shopping tours (www.chicshoppingparis.com).

Artisans of Leisure offers over a dozen shopping tours around the globe (www.leisure.com).

36 *Famed Chocolate Sites*

GENEEN ROTH SUMMED IT UP BEST WITH: "YOU DON'T LIKE chocolate. You don't even love chocolate. Chocolate is something you have a love affair with." Indeed, chocoholism is an international affliction, and you can get your fix in nearly every corner of the planet.

* Residue found in an ancient Mayan pot suggests that indigenous Mexicans were drinking chocolate 2,600 years ago. Their modern-day successors still reign superior when it comes to chocolate creations, especially *chocolate* (hot chocolate) and *mole,* a sophisticated concoction of chili peppers, chocolate, and as many as thirty other ingredients that is thick as bisque and can be poured over anything. For the best of both, head to Oaxaca, the culinary capital of Mexico. Mercado 20 de Noviembre sells dozens of brands and you can watch (and smell) the chocolate being mixed in enormous vats. Buy some packages and a *molina* (decorative wooden whisk) and then stop by a food stall for the real thing.

* Many a cacao slave bows before Belgium. In Brussels, Mary Chocolatier at 73 rue Royal displays its regal chocolates like

Tiffany's does its pearls. But true devotees head straight to Bruges, which not only features the Choco-Story Museum at Wijnzakstraat 2 but more than forty shops that sell nothing but confections.

* The Dutch swear by the puccini bonbons at 17 Staalstraat in Amsterdam. Some are sated with liquor (gin, Cointreau, cognac, port, rum), others with spices (anise, lemongrass, nutmeg, thyme). There are fruity bonbons, like plum, cranberry, raspberry, and fig-marzipan, as well as old-fashioned favorites like vanilla and caramel. Heaven.

* The creator of many a palatable delight, Italy also makes a fierce piece of chocolate. Perugia, a hill town in Umbria, hosts the ten-day Eurochocolate every October; offers tours through Perugina Chocolate Factory; and is the birthplace of the legendary Baci, or chocolate "kisses" with hazelnut filling, wrapped in love notes. Chocoholics should also visit Museo del Cioccolata Antica Norba at Via Capo Dell' Acqua 1 in Norma, which includes a visit to the Antica Norba factory and a drink from a chocolate fountain.

  www.puccinibomboni.com
  www.divinechocolate.com

* London's Divine confectioners not only live up to the name, they have a big heart. Organic and shade-grown, these fair trade sweets guarantee that farmers and harvesters receive fair wages for their back-breaking labor. Their products include chocolate bars, drinking chocolate and cocoa, fair trade fruits and nuts enrobed in chocolate, and seasonal treats.

RECOMMENDED READING

Essence of Chocolate: Recipes for Baking and Cooking with Fine Chocolate by
    John Scharffenberger and Robert Steinberg
The True History of Chocolate by Sophie Coe and Michael Coe

TOURS

inTrend International conducts Travel's Chocolate Lovers'
    Paradise Tour to Belgium, which can include chocolate and
    pastry cooking classes (www.intrend.com).

RESOURCES

Chocosphere is the site for buying chocolate online
    (www.chocosphere.com).

Český Krumlov, The Czech Republic

A FAIRYTALE RIVER TOWN 113 MILES SOUTH OF PRAGUE, ČESKÝ Krumlov is the kind of place that poets and painters dream about. The medieval buildings that line its winding, cobbled passageways pay homage to Renaissance, Baroque, Gothic, and Rococo traditions; church spires and red-tiled roofs clutter its skyline. Artisan shops display handcrafted treasures like amber jewelry, Czech crystal, and the regional specialty: Bohemian glass, used in everything from beads to perfume bottles and carafes. And towering above it all is Krumlov Hrad, the second-largest castle in the republic, which contains a Baroque theater so historic, it only holds one performance a year: an opera lit only by candles. Be sure to try the following:

* Everything you've heard about Czech *pivo*, or beer, is grossly underexaggerated; it tastes even better, and Czechs drink it a whole lot more. (According to one set of statistics, 42 gallons per capita per year. Canadians, by contrast, down just 18 gallons.) Beer brewing dates back to the fourteenth century in Český Krumlov. Within two centuries, every eighth house in town was a tavern, and by 1630, the Eggenberg Brewery had been established at Latrán 27. It's been churning out brew ever since. Touring the brewery is a must, as is sampling its five offerings: grade 8 and 10 draft beer, three types of lager,

and a beer with reduced sugar content (for diabetics). As the Czech proverb goes: "Wherever beer is brewed, all is well. Wherever beer is drunk, life is good."

* Have a taste for the macabre? The Museum of Torture is your place. Located in the cellar of Town Hall, smack on the main town square, this museum chronicles corporal punishment in the Middle Ages, down to the grizzliest detail. The cost-conscious aristocracy found it cheaper and more effective to torture someone—say, by whipping them senseless and branding them with a hot iron—and set them free, rather than keep them locked in prison for weeks on end, where they had to be fed and cleaned. So jailers got creative—nailing their prisoners to the wall so that only their head could move, stretching them until their joints popped, tying them to a chair full of spikes. Spinsters and other women who defied convention often got hauled in and examined for "marks of the devil," such as unusual birthmarks or oddly-shaped moles. If found, they were submitted to a water test: if their bodies floated, they were a witch; if they drowned, they were innocent.

* The Czechs are a celebratory people, and Český Krumlov throws the greatest fests. It is well worth planning your summer around the Festival of the Five-Petaled Rose, held during the summer solstice. For three days, downtown is closed to traffic as locals and travelers dressed as medieval queens and kings, maidens and knights, peasants and jesters fill the streets in drunken merriment. Jousting, fencing, ballroom dancing, and theater are staged throughout town, and late at night firecrackers explode

above the castle. Book a room weeks in advance (the closer to the river, the better), and bring a costume.

RECOMMENDED READING

Travelers' Tales Prague and the Czech Republic edited by David Farley and Jessie Sholl

TOURS

Krumlov Tours, located in the heart of Český Krumlov, offers independent travelers a variety of guided tours through the city and its environs (www.krumlovtours.com).

38 Eminent Ice Cream Parlors

ICE CREAM IS SO UNIVERSALLY LOVED, EVERYBODY CLAIMS TO HAVE invented it. Persians contend that their royalty was chilling and eating rose water with vermicelli on hot summer days back in 400 B.C. Arabs say they were not only the first to add sugar to icy concoctions, but had ice cream factories in the tenth century. The Chinese, meanwhile, insist they were selling iced fruit juice in the Song Dynasty, 960–1279. The truth is, food historians still haven't traced its exact origins, but connoisseurs agree that the following parlors are among its finest creators:

* At twenty-three liters per capita per year, U.S. citizens are the world's leading ice cream consumers—perhaps because they have such tasty parlors to choose from. Princeton, New Jersey takes its ice cream as seriously as its academia, offering not one but two famed shops. Thomas Sweet at 179 Nassau is an old-fashioned parlor that specializes in blend-ins: your choice of ice cream with up to three kinds of fresh fruit, candies, cookies, or nuts whirled in. (There are also locations in New Brunswick, New Jersey, and Washington, D.C.). The Bent Spoon at 35 Palmer Square West, meanwhile, is an "artisan ice cream and good-ingredient bakery" that uses

hormone-free dairy and mostly organic produce in its gelato-style treats. The esoteric menu changes daily, but regulars include ginger cardamom, white chocolate with lavender, avocado spiked with blood orange juice, and coffee varieties made with fresh pots of joe from Princeton's favorite coffeehouse, Small World, on 14 Witherspoon Street.

Any Midwesterner will resolutely declare that Graeter's is the greatest. For well over a century, this family-owned chain has been serving their famed dessert French pot-style, continuously folding their secret mixture of egg custard and fresh cream into itself, so that no air is whipped in. (While a typical pint of ice cream can weigh as little as eight ounces, Graeter's weighs nearly a pound.) Their all-time bestselling flavor is black raspberry chip, with black raspberries from Oregon and giant shards of chocolate. Try it in Ohio, Indiana, and Kentucky.

www.graeters.com
www.amysicecreams.com

Texans, meanwhile, crave Amy's Ice Cream, founded by a pre-med student who wrote a hot check for her parlor's first lease in the mid-'80s. The servers wear zany hats and sing as they serve their 300-plus flavors, which include pumpkin cheesecake, bourbon chocolate walnut, honeyed brandy, and—for the truly Texan—Shiner Bock beer. Amy's has ten shops in Austin, two in Houston, and one in San Antonio.

✹ A year wouldn't be long enough to sample every *gelaterie* in Italy, but it would be fun to try. Most offer *frutta* (fruit-based) and *crema* (cream-based) ice cream, as well as *sorbetto* (dairy-free *gelato*), *granita* (semi-frozen coarse ice), and *grattachecca* (shaved ice flavored with fruit syrup and chunks of fresh coconut and lemon). Romans claim that Il Gelato di San Crispino is not only the best in their city but the free world. The branch near Trevi Fountain at Via della Panetteria 42 is the most popular, but purists head out to the suburbs for the original shops, at Via Acaia 56 and at Via Bevagna 90. In Florence, the best shops are said to be Vivoli on Via dell'Isola delle Stinche and Perche No? on Via dei Tavolini.

* Mexicans also scream for ice cream (although they call it *helado*). The nation's best hails from a mountain village near Mexico City called Tepoztlán. Known as *tepoznieves,* it has flavors ranging from tropical fruits like *guanabana,* mamey, and *tuna* (the fruit of a cactus) to concoctions like Queen of the Night (three types of chocolate plus chopped fruit and sesame seeds) and Rose Petals (flowers roasted with honey and butter cream). Practically every village has at least one Paleteria La Michoacana, that sells fruity *paletas* (popsicles) that are either blended with milk (*paletas de leche*) or with water and sugar (*paletas de agua*). The most traditional flavors are melon, strawberry, lime, and chocolate, but they also do innovative flavors like *pepino con chile,* which consists of cucumber, watermelon, fresh lime juice, and powdered chili peppers. Paleterias La Michoacana have recently popped up in U.S. cities with significant Latino populations as well, including San Antonio, Texas and Brooklyn, New York.

* The most appreciated parlor on the planet is undoubtedly Coppelia, a spaceship-looking structure plopped in a park near the Hotel Habana Libre in the Vedado district of Havana, Cuba. Opened in 1966 as the country's first democratic ice cream emporium (meaning blacks and the poor

were welcome), Coppelia routinely serves about thirty thousand customers a day. Before the so-called "Special Period" (or time of rationing brought about by the collapse of Cuba's Soviet sugar daddy in 1991), Coppelia offered sundaes and more than twenty-four flavors. Nowadays, they sell only a couple of flavors at a time and lines can be more than an hour long. Yet, it is always delicious and you'll likely make new friends while waiting.

"Ice cream is exquisite—what a pity it isn't illegal."

—Voltaire

TOURS

Ice Cream University offers seminars plus an annual gelato tour (www.icecreamuniversity.org).

39 *Culinary Class Destinations*

RAISE YOUR FORK IF YOU TRAVEL FOR THE FOOD! THE BEST PART OF exploring a nation through its culinary tradition is that—by taking a class or two—you can bring the journey home to share with family and friends.

* The author of *The Foods of Greece* and the *Mediterranean Pantry,* chef Aglaia Kremezi offers five-day classes in her kitchen and gardens in Kea, Greece. A typical day could include workshops on the art of grape leaves (from selecting and blanching to rolling and baking), how to fillet and marinate an anchovy, and the tricks to making twice-baked savory biscotti. Aglaia also takes her students on outings to ancient archaeological sites and secluded beaches, as well as vineyards and goat farms for wine and cheese tastings. Evening feasts are always held in different locales, such as hilltop villas overlooking the Aegean Sea. Aglaia warns in advance that all prospective students must love garlic, seafood (including octopus), and dogs (which will be underfoot, not on the table).

* You could spend a fat and happy lifetime studying the intricacies of French cuisine. Dozens of courses abound, some

specializing in pastries, others in regions, still others in seafood or cheeses. A fun (and inexpensive) course to whet your appetite is in the Paris kitchen of chef Françoise Meunier. In just three hours, students will prepare, devour, and clean up after a three-course, wine-fueled meal. A sample menu includes goat cheese pancakes, lamb stew with spring vegetables, and pineapples doused in Bourbon vanilla caramel sauce. Drop by at 7 rue Paul-Lelong, near the Bourse or Les Halles Metro.

- You haven't experienced Mexican cuisine until you've dined in Oaxaca. This southern state boasts such specialties as *tlayuda* (giant tortillas with more toppings than a pizza, folded in half and grilled crisp) and *tamales oaxaqueños* (chicken tamales doused with *mole negro* and steamed in a banana leaf). Several restaurants offer classes, including the popular El Naranjo located in a courtyard one block west of the *zocalo* at Trujano 203. Although locals consider her a heretic for refusing to use lard, owner Iliana de la Vega is much loved by her students, who enjoy her poetic musings about the souls of chili peppers. In her six-hour course, you will make a full meal, including an appetizer, soup, dessert, fruit drink, two different salsas, and, of course, one of Oaxaca's seven prized *moles*. The class concludes with a guided tour of Mercado Benito Juarez. Book ahead, as classes can fill up fast.

www.keartisanal.com
www.fmeunier.com
www.elnaranjo.mx

RECOMMENDED READING

The World Is a Kitchen: Cooking Your Way Through Culture edited by Michele
Anna Jordan and Susan Brady

Cooking in Paradise: Culinary Vacations Around the World by Joel and Lee
Naftali

TOURS

A comprehensive website for culinary schools, classes, and tours is
available online at www.worldisakitchen.com.

40 *Zanzibar, Tanzania*

ZANZIBAR. THE VERY WORD CONJURES WHITE SAND BEACHES surrounded by turquoise waters, a tropical paradise paved with coconut and mangrove trees. Yet Africa's Hawai'i is a surprisingly complex place, its heritage dipping into Persian, Portuguese, Arab, Indian, and English as well as native Swahili cultures. These influences are highly pronounced in everything from the architecture, music, and food, to the festivals.

This autonomous island-province is best reached by ferry from mainland Tanzania. You'll know you're near when the white sails of wooden dhows, or sailboats, appear on the horizon. The first stop will likely be the capital Stone Town, a Middle Eastern-style city of bazaars and markets, ancient Omani palaces and manors. Stroll through the labyrinthine passageways until the sun grows too intense, then relax in the shade in the Forodhani Gardens along the waterfront. Follow the footbridge at the southeast corner of the garden to the Zanzibar Orphanage to donate books, toys, or games. (To volunteer time, check in with the Department of Social Welfare first; the orphanage's headmaster can provide directions.) Return to Forodhani at night for some of the freshest (and cheapest) cuisine on the island. Locals set up charcoal stoves and oil lamps and can whip up seafood or goat meat, both liberally doused in chili sauce. Be sure to try *mantabali,* or Zanzibar pizza—a chapati stuffed with anything the cook can grab hold, plus melted cheese and a fried egg. Wash the meal down with tamarind juice and top it off with some grilled bananas dipped in chocolate.

Stone Town is a shopper's dream, but prepare to haggle. Darajani Market on the west side of Creek Road outside the city bustles with fish mongers, spice sellers, produce vendors who arrange their fruits by shape, and the random bicycle, lamp, or Pokémon hawker. Behind the Omani Fort and House of Wonders is Gizenga Street, which has a wide range of funky shops offering Arabian antiques, brass-studded chests, second-hand jewelry, and palm-leaf baskets and mats. Drop in the Duka la Uwazi on Mizingani Road for handicrafts by local women's groups, or to get your hands (or feet or belly) tattooed with henna.

Cooks and gardeners will love the half-day spice tours offered by many travel agencies. These guided plantation tours provide not only sniffings and tastings of fresh herbs and spices, but detailed descriptions of their uses—both culinary and medicinal. Sucking on cloves, for instance, is said to help recovering alcoholics lose their cravings. Jasmine balm and vanilla pods, meanwhile, are effective aphrodisiacs. Take it easy with the nutmeg, though—infusing a cup of water with just half a ground nut could leave you hallucinating for days!

For diving and snorkeling, journey on to the island of Pemba. Visibility here is spectacular—up to 230 feet during incoming tide—and you'll likely see barracudas, dolphins, marine turtles, manta rays, sharks, and the enchanting Spanish dancer, a foot-long sea slug with an undulating red "skirt." In September, whales can be heard but generally not seen. Swahili Divers in the Old Mission Lodge in Chake Chake

www.swahilidivers.com

offers PADI-certification classes and camping trips to uninhabited islands.

Zanzibar is pelted with rain from March to May and October to December; the rest of the year is steamy hot. Avoid visiting during Ramadan, as many stores and restaurants will be closed. Malaria can be a problem, so take a course of prophylactics prior to departure and bring some heavy-duty repellent.

RECOMMENDED READING

Tanzania & Zanzibar (Cadogan, 2nd Ed.) by Annabel Skinner

TOURS

Tanzania Adventure offers a one-day spice tour through Zanzibar (www.tanzania-adventure.com).

Zanzibar Excursions operates a spice tour, dolphin tour, and city and forest tours, among others (www.zanzibarexcursions.com).

41 *Sexiest Lingerie Shops*

EVERY WOMAN SHOULD HAVE AT LEAST ONE FABULOUS PIECE OF lingerie tucked inside her drawers—even if there's no one around to show it to. (Slipping on a chiffon babydoll and dimming the lights is, after all, the surest way to turn a lonely TV dinner into a romantic dinner-for-one.) Here is where to buy it:

* In London, Agent Provocateur's name says it all. Their satin Diva corsets feature traditional boning and back lacing for great access (...um, control) while a naughty line of bras has stitched-in peepholes (pasties not included). Feeling extra daring? Ask for their limited edition Viv knickers, made of translucent tulle with mohair detailing and gold chain, ring, and safety pin finishing. Visit their premiere location at 6 Broadwick Street, Soho.

* There will never be a better time to incorporate the "when in Rome..." traveling philosophy. Start with Demoiselle at Via Frattina 93 (at the corner of Via Belsiana), where you can search for luxurious La Perla sleepwear and sexy Missoni swimwear by chandelier light. Nearby Brighenti at Via Frattina 7, meanwhile, offers satin-and-lace selections by high-fashion designers like Dior and Nina Ricci, all displayed in a traditional Roman boutique with art nouveau light fixtures.

- Not into frills and bows? Neither is Jean Yu. For a sampling of her "minimalist" approach, check out 37=1 at 37 Crosby Street in New York City, where bras are nothing more than two triangles and string. No outrageous colors here either—just the wide spectrum of human flesh. *New York Magazine* voted this boutique the best place to buy lingerie in 2005.

- If you really want to spice up the lingerie drawer, catch a flight to Paris, where they claim to have invented it. Herminie Cadolle went down in fashion history for "freeing" women by slicing the stifling corset in two in 1889, thus creating the world's first bra. Even today, her Parisian boutiques—currently run by her great-great-granddaughter—remain among the finest places to purchase one. Cadolle specialties include Victorian corsets, bodices, and a broad collection of hand-sewn brassieres, but to truly treat yourself, make an appointment for a satiny, made-to-measure something at 255 rue Saint-Honoré (Metro: Concorde or Tuilleries). For her ready-to-wear collection, visit the location at 4 rue Cambon.

  www.agentprovocateur.com
  www.cadolle.com
  www.fifichachnil.com

  You know you're in good hands with a designer whose motto is: "The main function of the underwear we choose every morning is to turn us into a good mood." Indeed, Fifi Chachnil has been delighting Parisian women (and, presumably, men) with her silk chiffon negligées and high-cut

panties with froufrous chérie for years at 26 rue Cambon
(Metro: Concorde). Pick up a pack of her day-of-the-week
lace undies.

V

Places of Celebration and Womanly Affirmation

42 *Belly Dancing Sites*

BELLY DANCING DATES BACK TO PRE-BIBLICAL TIMES, WHEN IT WAS performed as a fertility cult. In ancient Arab tribes, midwives assisted women in labor by dancing around them, rolling their stomachs to imitate the contraction of the uterus. It was also performed as entertainment throughout the Orient by and for women who stayed home while their husbands were out. In addition to being a great physical workout, modern belly dancing is a way to bond with other women and get in touch with your earthy self.

Belly dance communities can be found in every corner of the United States. Performances are generally participatory events: when a dancer does a sensual move, join the crowd in making a snakelike noise, "*Ssssss.*" A complicated move, meanwhile, should be cheered with a hearty (Greek), "*Opa!*" When she takes her final bow, let out a *zaghareet*—pressing your hand against your upper lip, cry out "*yalalalalalalalalah!*" Most shows culminate in an open dance. If you feel inhibited, down a glass of wine (the best hip lubricant around!) before kicking off your shoes and joining in.

www.abda.org

The following are dance communities of note:

* The belly dancing capital of the Southwest—Austin, Texas—features shows nearly every night of the week; check in with

the Austin Belly Dance Association for the schedule. (Note: a performance by Z-Helene is not to be missed!) If in town on a full moon, call Lucila Dance Productions and ask if she's hosting a Hafla that night. Held outside of her studio in the heart of Texas Hill Country, Lucila's Haflas are an eclectic gathering of dancers and drummers who snack on hummus and grape leaves as they dance barefoot beneath the moon and stars.

❋ San Francisco, California is home to Fat Chance Belly Dance, one of the most renowned tribal dance troupes in the country. Take a class and load up on their instructional videos, booklets, CDs, costumes, and accessories at their studio and resource center at 670 South Van Ness Avenue.

❋ With its vibrant Middle Eastern and artistic and dance communities, New York City offers myriad performances, seminars, and events. Take a class with legendary teacher and scholar, Morocco, of the Casbah Dance Experience, or tribal specialist, Sarah Johansson Locke, of Alchemy Performance. Then catch a show by Kaeshi and Amar Gamal of Belly Queen.

www.fcbd.com
www.casbahdance.org
www.alchemyperformance.com
www.bellyqueen.com

❋ For complicated social and economic reasons, it is difficult to find quality shows or teachers in the birthplace of the dance, the Middle East, on your own nowadays. In Istanbul, Turkey, the Orient House at Tiyatro Caddesi 27 near the Grand Bazaar hosts a good—albeit touristy—show. Your best bet is joining Morocco of New York City on one of her dancing tours to the Middle East.

RECOMMENDED READING

Belly Dancing: The Sensual Art of Energy and Spirit by Pina Colucia, Anette Paffratha, and Jean Pütz

43 *Museum of Menstruation*

THE WORLD'S FIRST AND ONLY MUSEUM OF MENSTRUATION NO longer has a physical address—but not for lack of effort. Its director, an American bachelor named Harry Finley, came up with the idea while working as an art director in Germany. Intrigued by the ways different cultures promoted menstrual hygiene in their magazines, he started clipping advertisements. Upon his return to the United States, some public relations departments sent him ads of their own, along with samples accumulating dust in their archives. By 1994, Harry had such a collection, he opened the museum in his basement in Maryland. Over the next four years, some 1,500 guests dropped by, 95 percent of them women.

"Total strangers would sit together on the couches and trade stories for hours," Harry remembers. "More than one told me afterward that they had never talked to anyone about it before in their life."

Alas, the rigors of museum maintenance gradually took a toll. Since it was only open on weekends, Harry could never take a vacation, and missed whole seasons of NFL football. His gender was also a hindrance: more than a few prospective visitors quickly drove away upon realizing the museum was located in his basement. With regret, he closed shop and focused his attention on building a web site that today offers an exhaustive retrospective of menstrual history. Among other treasures, Harry has scanned in the puberty booklets that companies sent schools back in the 1920s to educate young ladies (while hooking them on their products). There are photos and critiques of the genesis of menstrual products, from rags to belt-and-pads, sanitary panties, tampons, washable pads, and reusable menstrual cups; home remedies for discomfort (yoga; ginger, chamomile, or red raspberry leaf tea; milk thistle tablets; heating pads); and Q&A's with medical professionals on topics like douches (short answer: don't use them). He has also posted menstrual-inspired art, poetry, cartoons, short stories, and impassioned replies to on-line polls like "Would you stop menstruating if you could?"

WWW. www.mum.org

While the site is wildly successful, Harry still dreams of reopening his museum in a major public space some day. "I just wish that one woman out there would, instead of buying an impressionist painting for her own private collection, give the money to establish something like this for all women."

Harry envisions a museum with a menstrual hut that visitors could actually sit in; a permanent exhibit on the history of menstrual products; and revolving displays on women's health, such as estrogen supplements and breast cancer. He'd also like an accompanying bookstore, gift shop, garden, and café with plenty of couches for women to gather and share. Drop him a line at hfinley@mum.org.

RECOMMENDED READING

Our Bodies, Ourselves by Boston Women's Health Book Collective

44 Brazil
Candomblé and the
Sisterhood of Good Death

Like Santería in Cuba and Voodoo in Haiti, Candomblé is a vibrant religion born from the tragedy of slavery. During three centuries of colonial rule, Portuguese planters enslaved five million Africans to work the sugar cane fields of Brazil, and forcibly converted them to Catholicism in the process. The slaves noticed many similarities between this new faith and their own native religions, including the worshipping of supreme beings who created and maintained the world, and the use of intermediaries to talk with them. Over time, the slaves fused them all together, with every Catholic saint corresponding to an African *orixá*, and created a new syncretic religion called Candomblé. It is a passionate faith, and respectful travelers are often welcome to partake in its rituals.

One particularly revered Orixá is Iemanja, the goddess of the sea, often associated with Mary. If you're lucky enough to spend New Year's in Rio, stop by the Copacabana beach that evening to watch white-clad practitioners float little boats to her, proffering gifts of flowers, mirrors, and candles along with their wishes for the new year. If she accepts the gift, she'll sink the boat; otherwise, she'll return it. Iemanja's official feast day, February 2, is marked with music and offerings throughout the nation, but festivities are especially grand on the beaches of Rio Vermelho in Salvador da Bahia.

The colonial town of Cachoeira in the state of Bahia is considered Candomblé's spiritual center. Ask a local or someone at the tourist office on Praca da Aclamaca for a schedule of the week's ceremonies. Most start late in the evening and end around midnight: wear all white and leave the camera behind. Women generally stand on one side of the room and men on the other. Several hours of drumming will transpire as the all-female *maes-de-santo* (or priestesses) ask the Orixás to come forth and possess them. One by one, they do—often dramatically. It is usually possible to tell who has possessed whom, as assistants give the *maes-de-santo* the corresponding Orixá's paraphernalia, such as their trademark headpiece, crown, or club. At this point, the drumming is very intense, and the energy—frenetic. Once the Orixás finally take their leave, everyone sits together for a communal feast. "It is mesmerizing, from the unceasing drum rhythms to the physical intensity of each Orixá's arrival," says Latin American historian Victoria Langland. "When it's over, you know you've experienced something profound."

A great celebration of the New World's African diaspora is the Festival of the Boa Morte in Cachoeira. Held in mid-August, it is organized by the Irmandade da Boa Morte, or Sisterhood of Good Death, a society of women that dates back to the days when abolition and escape routes were discussed in whispers in slave quarters. For three days, their descendants dress up in traditional Bahian fashion—full, ankle-length skirts, turbans, shawls, and yards of shell-and-bead necklaces—and parade through the streets with an elaborately dressed Virgin (to symbolize her Assumption). They also cook up a storm and offer a great samba. The festivities draw enormous crowds, particularly of African-Americans wearing "Black Pride!" t-shirts. Indeed, for many, the Boa Morte embodies Brazil's flourishing black empowerment movement.

RECOMMENDED READING

Sacred Leaves of Candomblé: African Magic, Medicine, and Religion in Brazil by Robert A. Vocks

TOURS

Sankofa Tours offers a Good Death's Festival Tour in August of each year (www.sankofatours.net).

45 *Havana, Cuba*

FEW COUNTRIES ARE AS COMPLICATED AS THIS BEAUTIFUL ISLAND nation. To be sure, Fidel Castro's ruthless policies have induced wide-scale suffering, but the 1959 Revolution has also made significant strides in many arenas, including race relations. Racism still rears its ugly head now and then, but Cuba overall has achieved a racial harmony that seems light years ahead of other nations in the Americas.

"As soon as I am in Cuban airspace, I start feeling more comfortable in my own skin," says African-American journalist Lori Robinson. "There is a respect for African people and culture and heritage here that I don't experience anyplace else."

Despite the hardships, smiles are vibrant in Cuba. Gaits are fluid. Movements are rhythmic. Theirs is a sensuality that transcends physical appearance. It is an attitude, it is infectious, and it is most viscerally experienced in a rumba club.

Born in slavery and raised on the streets of poor black neighborhoods by musicians possessing little more than a cardboard box, a bottle, and a stick, rumba derives from the verb *rumbear,* which means to party and have a good time. In clubs throughout the island, you'll find musicians pounding away on *bata,* bongo, and conga drums while revelers undulate on the dance floor. On Monday nights, drop by Dulce Maria Baralt's place on the third floor of Calle San Ignacio 78 between

O'Reilly and Callejon del Chorro in Habana Vieja. During her Sweet Maria's gatherings, a band plays old rumba songs as the crowd passes around communal bottles of rum and beer. Another group to catch is Las Mulatas del Caribe, an all-female band that performs at Calle Obispo 213A.

You'll know you've arrived at Callejon de Hamel when a whirl of reds, yellows, greens, and blacks suddenly streaks across the neighborhood highrises like a comet and explodes in a mural blur of eyes and roots and feathers. Artist Salvador Gonzalez Escalona hosts rumbas every Sunday afternoon in his gallery, located between Aramburu and Hospital streets near the Hermanos Almeijeiras Hospital in Centro Habana. Come to dance, meet locals and backpackers, and view the Santería-inspired artwork.

Then head over to Cementerio Colon to visit La Milagrosa, or the Miracle Lady. According to legend, a young woman named Amelia Goyri de Hoz died in childbirth in 1901 and was buried with her baby snug at her feet. When keepers opened her tomb a few years later, however, they found Amelia cradling her daughter in her arms. Locals have called her the Miracle Lady ever since, and consider her a protector of pregnant women. If you knock three times on her tombstone and make a wish, she'll grant it—as long as you don't turn your back on her as you leave. Hundreds of grateful pilgrims have left small plaques and tablets around her gravesite, thanking her for their *milagros*. Visit her at the corner of Calles 3 and F.

RECOMMENDED READING

Dreaming in Cuban by Cristina Garcia
Travelers' Tales Cuba edited by Tom Miller

46 Places to Dance the Tango and the Texas Two-Step

SEEKING A NIGHT OF COURTSHIP AND BODILY CONTACT? TWO suggestions: tango dancing and the Texas two-step. No matter if you haven't got a partner, just hover near the dance floor and smile.

● Born in the impoverished neighborhoods of Buenos Aires in the late 1800s, tango quickly spread throughout the city, thanks to street barrel-organ players, before catching on in Paris, London, Berlin, and New York City. Its music fuses African rhythms and European melodies with a South American twist, and its dance is at once passionate and elegant.

"I'm not graceful in my normal life at all—I'm always bumping into things and cutting myself—but tango forces me to hold my posture and be graceful," says Sylvia Smullin, a physicist studying the dance in New Jersey. "It's also incredible to have someone pay such close attention to me, and to in turn be focused on a very tender and intense physical communication with him."

Buenos Aires breathes tango, from its glitzy shows in classy hotels to its packed night clubs, known as *milongas*. Café Tortoni holds shows in its upstairs salon nearly every night of the week at Avenida de Mayo 829. To learn a few moves, head to Centro Cultural Torquato Tasso on Defensa 1575 (near

Lezama park) or Confiteria Ideal on Suipacha 384. Some 175,000 addicts gather each spring to watch the pros at the Buenos Aires Tango Festival and you can study with them as well. Free classes are available for beginners, with seminars for intermediate and advanced students. No worries if you're traveling solo—there's a database to find the perfect partner. You can also satiate any shopping lust at the Tango Fair, which sells everything from dancewear and footwear to photographs, music, and books.

www.tangofestivals.net

- ❋ Whoever says chivalry is dead has never been two-steppin'. Known in Texas as "kicker dancin'," it entails two quick steps followed by two slow ones, gliding your feet just above the wooden floor (a.k.a. boot scootin'). Once you've got the moves down, slide on your tightest pair of jeans, spruce up your bangs with hair spray or smash them flat with a Stetson, and find yourself a cowboy. The best nightclubs feature live bands like the Derailers, the Mad Cowboys, and Kelly Spinks, but a good rule of thumb is to search for the parking lot packed with the most trucks. In Austin, check out the Broken Spoke at 3201 South Lamar Boulevard, or Dallas Night Club (a.k.a. the cheapest watering hole in town) at 7113 Burnet Road. In Fort Worth, try Pearl's Dancehall & Saloon at 302 West Exchange, which boasts poker nights and $1.50 Longnecks and $1 draft beer. In Dallas, you can't beat Cowboys Red River at 10310 Technology Boulevard. If nature has endowed you, enter their Dolly Parton Look-alike Contest; otherwise, try your luck at the mechanical bull-riding contest. Yee-haw!

47 *Florence, Italy*

FROM ITS SUMPTUOUS ART AND SHOPPING TO ITS ADORING MEN who whistle from every street corner, Florence, Italy celebrates the feminine. Grab a pair of designer sunglasses, tie on a silk scarf, and go!

Florence is awash with paintings and sculptures that honor the voluptuousness of women. "After a few hours of strolling through these museums, you realize that it is O.K. to be curvy, to have a little *chicho,*" says Natasha Lycia Ora Bannan, a Latina from the Bronx. "In fact, it makes you feel beautiful!"

Start with the Uffizi, keeper of the luminous *Birth of Venus* by Sandro Botticelli. Painted in the late fifteenth century, this masterpiece depicts the Goddess Venus emerging from the sea as a full-figured woman atop a seashell (which, in classical antiquity, is a metaphor for the vulva). Some scholars say that Venus and the other female figures in the painting represent a trinity of Mother, Daughter, and Holy Spirit. Next, visit Titian's *Venus of Urbino.* This controversial piece depicts a young woman reclining nude on a bed while gazing straight at you, her left hand coquettishly covering her pubic area. A dog, symbolizing fidelity, is fast asleep in the background while maids dig through a chest, presumably for something for Venus to wear. Mark Twain may have called her "the

www.uffizi.com

foulest, the vilest, the obscenest picture the world possesses," in his travelogue, *A Tramp Abroad,* but Venus still packs in the crowds, 500 years and counting. The Uffizi is located at Pizzale degli Uffizi 6. Advance booking is often required.

After drinking in the female form, move on to the Galleria dell' Accademia at via Ricasoli 60 to behold the male. Here stands Michelangelo's most heralded piece: *David.* Carved from a 19-ton block of marble, this exquisite statue lends credo to the artist's claim that the body is "a divine creation; a beauty without peer." But for years, *David's pisello,* or rather his lack of one, has attracted the bulk of the attention—just 5.91 inches on a 14-foot man! In 2005, however, the Dutch Institute for Art History deemed this size "normal" for someone fixing to take on Goliath.

Shoe fiends should then head to the newly renovated Museo Salvatore Ferragamo, accessed via Piazza Santa Trinitá 5. The eleventh of fourteen children, Ferragamo is said to have made his first pair of shoes at age nine, after learning his parents couldn't afford shoes for his sister to wear at Communion. He went on to craft functional works of art for princesses and movie stars, including Audrey Hepburn, Rita Hayworth, Sophia Loren, and Bette Davis. Prance up the red carpet staircase to the museum on the second floor, which showcases Ferragamo's grandiose collection that dates back to 1927.

By now you must be ready to shop for your own art. Florence has great taste, with boutiques specializing in everything from cashmere-lined leather gloves to glass-beaded jewelry—and many items are handcrafted in century-old workshops nearby. For handmade paper, drop into the mother-and-daughter-owned bookbinding company, Il Torchio, located at Via dei Bardi 17. The Farmacia Santa Maria Novella at Via della Scala 16 sells cologne and other potions made from recipes concocted by seventeenth-century Dominican monks. If you prefer your fragrances custom-made, stop by Lorenzo Villoresi's laboratory at Via dei Bardi 14. Italian readers should visit the Libreria delle Donne, a terrific women's bookstore at Via Fiesolana 2/B. Find a job, tutor, or roommate on their community board.

48

Andalucía, Spain
The Art of Flamenco

IT IS THE PERFECT EXPRESSION OF WOMANHOOD: GRACEFUL AND elegant, yet fiery and passionate. Some dance historians trace its origin to the mass exodus of the *gitanos,* or gypsies, from Punjabi, India more than a thousand years ago. These nomadic people migrated across North Africa and up into Southern Spain, picking up musical and dance influences along the way (particularly from the Moors and the Jews) before being forcibly herded into *gitanerias,* or ghettos. There, they say, the dynamic song and dance known today as flamenco flourished. While it is performed in studios and venues throughout the world, it is best experienced in its birthplace, Andalucía, Spain.

The spontaneous days of singers and dancers seizing bars and clapping, stomping, and twirling til dawn have largely passed, but you can still catch great shows in Seville. Try the Sala Teatral Sol Café Cantante at Calle Sol 5, which features new talent Wednesday through Saturday at 9 P.M. La Sonanta at Calle San Jacinto 31 in Barrio Triana (home of the *gitanos* until the 1960s) holds shows on Thursdays. Teatro Central brings in prized dancers for its annual Flamenco Viene del Sur program: Be on the lookout for superstars like Adella Campallo, Manuela Carrasco, Eva Yerbabuena, Cristina Hoyos, and Sara Baras. Travel agencies push *tablaos,* which include live performances with dinner and drinks, but they are less than authentic. Still, if only in town for the night, try Los Gallos on Plaza de Santa Cruz 11, which hosts shows at 9 P.M. and 11:30 P.M.

If you're inspired to learn some fancy footwork, Seville offers excellent classes and workshops. Fundación Cristina Heeren de Arte Flamenco at Calle Fabiola 1 has trimester-long courses in singing, guitar, and dancing plus an intensive four-week program in July that includes 106 hours of instruction. Three scholarships are available a year for students from the United States. Taller Flamenco holds classes in guitar, dance technique, *compás y palmas* (rhythm and clapping), plus the Spanish language at Calle Peral 49. Before you descend upon those tapas bars to show off your moves, hit the shops. Calzados Mayos has been handcrafting flamenco shoes, boots, *castañuelas,* and those fabulous frilly skirts since 1940. Visit them at Plaza de la Alfalfa 2. Mantilla Feliciano Foronda sells Andalusian shawls at Calle Alvarez Quintero 52, and Casa Rubio sells traditional fans at Calle Sierpes 56. For music, try Compás Sur at Calle Cuesta del Rosario 7-F.

WWW. www.flamencoheeren.com www.tallerflamencc.com www.calzadosmayo.com www.bienal-flamenco.org

Aficionados plan their travel itineraries around the Bienal de Flamenco, hosted in Seville in September of even-numbered years. Performances are held in venues like the Alcázar every night of the week for a solid month. Equally incredible is the Feria de Abril held after Easter in a temporary tent city on the far side of the Río Guadalquivir. For six sherry-fueled nights, dancers and their musical accompaniment pack into tents and perform from sunset to sunrise. Festivals in other regions of Andalucía include the Festival Torre del Cante (one long night in June in Alhaurín de la Torre near Málaga), Festival de Jerez (two weeks in February-March), and Gazpacho Andaluz (August at the Morón de la Frontera bullring). *¡Olé!*

RECOMMENDED READING

Travelers' Tales Spain edited by Lucy McCauley

49 *Women's Gatherings in the USA*

MAYBE YOU'RE GOING THROUGH A DIVORCE, OR A REALLY BAD break-up, and you need the sort of support only women can provide. Or you work in an office full of men and are seeking some sisterly company. Or you want a partner of the same gender. Or you just need a jolt of female empowerment. Whatever the symptoms, a women-only gathering is the antidote.

* Sue Ellen Cooper bought a bright red fedora at a thrift shop one day, for no reason other than she thought it "quite dashing." When she later stumbled upon Jenny Joseph's poem "Warning," she was struck by the line: *"When I am an old woman I shall wear purple/ With a red hat that doesn't go and doesn't suit me."* She gave a vintage hat and copy of the poem as a birthday present that year, and it was so well-received, she made it her calling card. Before long, so many friends had crazy red hats that she organized a tea outing to show them off, and it was such a hit, they founded the Red Hat Society. The rest, they say, is herstory. Today, this "dis-organization" boasts more than 1 million registered members in 40,000 chapters in the United States and twenty-five other countries. Its mission: "to gain higher visibility for women in our age group [fifty and above]

www.redhatsociety.com

and to reshape the way we are viewed by today's culture." Its maxim: you really must wear purple, and top it off with a big red hat (unless you're under fifty, in which case it's lavender and pink hats). Regional gatherings called "Funventions" are held several times a year, and the official Red Hat Society day is April 25.

● Las Comadres Para Las Americas was founded in Austin, Texas in 2000 by two Latinas seeking to build their community of *comadres*, or close female friends. They invited some women to their home for a potluck *comadrazo*, and it was so successful they made it a monthly event. Today Austin boasts more than one thousand members, and the movement has spread to nearly fifty cities across the nation. Any woman who is either Latin-identified or who is married to a Latino can join. In addition to the *comadrazos*, Las Comadres throws national Fiesta Conventions every other year and maintains a list-serv where members post information about jobs, scholarships, and the like. There are no dues, rules, or officers, but Austinite Nora de Hoyos Comstock holds down the fortress.

WWW
www.lascomadres.org
www.michfest.com

● In 1976, three concert-loving women decided they'd had enough of watching female musicians get demeaned both on- and off-stage. So they created a safe space of their own where artists like Tracy Chapman made their debut: the Michigan Womyn's Music Festival. Every August, some four thousand women gather to build a mini-city of camps, stages, and community centers on 650 acres of remote woodlands. Everyone is required to contribute eight hours of labor, and in exchange receives three vegetarian meals a day plus free access to childcare, health care, open-air showers, and all the festival's activities, including forty musical performances, hundreds of workshops, dozens of films, and a thriving Crafts Bazaar. The festival's "womyn-born womyn only" policy has stirred controversy in recent years, however, and some transsexual women and their allies now hold "Camp Trans" outside the gates, where they debate sexual inequalities over the distant sounds of folk music.

* Nearly every autumn since 2002, some five hundred women have gathered at the Omega Institute in New York's Hudson Valley to "take a bold look at the obstacles that mute the feminine voice" and explore the necessity of womanly power. For three days they attend workshops, sing and dance, and hear keynotes by such luminaries as actors Jane Fonda, Susan Sarandon, and Sally Field; authors Maya Angelou and Alice Walker; and activists Gloria Steinem and Eve Ensler. The Omega Institute provides cabins and primarily vegetarian meals as well as morning yoga classes; designer Eileen Fisher offers full scholarships to young women of color. Be forewarned that this "Women and Power Conference" fills fast. If no space is available, sample the other programs offered by Omega's Women's Institute, including "Enlightened Power: How Women Are Changing the Way We Live" with activists like Yolanda King (daughter of Dr. Martin Luther King, Jr.) and Loung Ung of the Campaign for a Landmine-Free World.

www.eomega.com

* Around Labor Day each September, the Black Rock Desert of Nevada is home to an experimental community of 35,000

people seeking something radically different in life. Dressed in outrageous costumes (if anything at all), they build elaborate theme camps and psychedalic art installations on the ancient lake bed, then roam about, performing guerrilla street theater and swapping gifts for necessities (as no cash exchanges are allowed on premises, save for coffee and ice). And at the height of festivities, they torch a giant wooden man—hence, the gathering's name: Burning Man.

"This is a place where, whatever you are seeking, you can find," says Jenni Peskin, a four-time Burner from Bend, Oregon. "There is a respect and an honesty and an openness here that you can find nowhere else on the planet. And it's so much fun."

While Burning Man is open to anyone, its greatest event is women-only: the Critical Tits bike ride. At 4 P.M. on the festival's third day, thousands of women hop on bikes, rip off their shirts, and tear through the makeshift village, baring their breasts to the adoring male public, who line up on either side of the route to cheer them on and cool them off with squirt bottles. After touring the camps, the massive bike parade ends at a zone marked-off for women, where a giant party is thrown in celebration of their glorious bodies.

www.camptrans.squarespace.com
www.burningman.com

WWW

RECOMMENDED READING

A Woman's World edited by Marybeth Bond

VI

Places of Struggle and Renewal

50 *New Orleans, Louisiana*

NOT LONG AGO, THE BIG EASY WOULD HAVE TAKEN FIRST IN BOTH the "Places of Indulgence" and "Places of Celebration" categories. This was, after all, the city that invented jazz in its famous red-light district and nurtured delta blues and zydeco in its outskirts. It welcomed tens of thousands of international revelers with its balls, parades, and parties in the weeks preceding Lent, and delighted tens of thousands more with live shows during its Jazz Festival. And it dazzled tastebuds with Creole delicacies like étouffée and jambalaya; sea platters like giant crawfish and Gulf oysters on the half-shell; po'boys and Italian muffalettas; coffee laced with chicory and piping hot beignets. New Orleans was the city of sex shows and underage drinking; of funerals that turned into fiestas; of red beans and rice every Monday night; of infectious *joie de vivre*.

But then, in August 2005, along came Hurricane Katrina. Severe government negligence and the fiercesome force of nature coalesced into one of the worst natural disasters in U.S. history. Four of New Orleans's protective levees collapsed, drowning more than 80 percent of the city in twenty feet of toxic water and sludge. Fifteen hundred people lost their lives; tens of thousands, their homes. Libraries lost their books; musicians, their instruments; artists, their canvases. And on Katrina's first anniversary, neighborhoods like the Ninth

Ward, Lakeview, and New Orleans East still looked as though she had just pulverized through. Heartbreaking bus excursions by groups like Tours by Isabelle now drive by these obliterated neighborhoods as well as key sites like the London Avenue Canal Breach and the Superdome.

Yet, the City that Care Forgot refuses to face defeat. Some two hundred thousand gathered for its 2006 Jazz Festival, and while Bruce Springsteen and Bob Dylan graced the stage, the show-stoppers were the city's own gospel, blues, and folk singers. Though only a third of its restaurants have re-opened, those include favorites like Napoleon House at 500 Chartres; Clancy's at 6100 Annunciation Street; Parkway Bakery & Tavern (best roast beef po'boy in town!) at 538 Hagan Avenue; and Café du Monde the in French Market. The hotel industry has rebounded, as have legendary music venues like Preservation Hall and House of Blues. And Pat O'Briens on Bourbon Street is still serving up its renowned drink.

"I understand how wrong it can feel to binge Hurricanes when so much of the city lies devastated, but life goes on in New Orleans," says writer Stacy Aab, who has conducted more than one hundred interviews with Katrina survivors as part of an oral history book project. "Residents eat out, drink, and get merry. They have always known how to celebrate, even in the worst of times, so why not join in?"

Stacy suggests that tourists earmark part of their vacation to volunteer projects—of which there are many. Since December 2005, for instance, Emergency Communities serves 1,300 meals a day at its Made with Love Café and Grill in the parking lot near St. Bernard Parish in the residential neighborhood of Chalmette. They also offer first aid and herbal medical care,

WWW.

www.emergencycommunities.org

52 *Benin*

Traveling in West Africa can be empowering for women—precisely because it is so difficult. You must utilize every available resource to make it through each day. When you finally find that market or village you are seeking, it is like unearthing rubies. "The real trick is learning when to say yes, and to not be afraid," says Suzanne Kratzig, who lived here as a Peace Corps volunteer. "You might end up sleeping with a family in the middle of nowhere beneath the stars, but that's great." The warmth and hospitality of its people make Benin a particularly welcoming destination for female travelers. The following are some highlights:

* So many millions of men, women, and children were shackled and sold as slaves to the New World in the sixteenth century, that this part of West Africa became known as the "Slave Coast." In Ouidah, ask around for Martine da Souza, who gives tours of their final days in the native land. After being sold in the market, the slaves-to-be were led around the Tree of Forgetfulness (so they wouldn't miss Benin as much) and the Tree of Return (so their spirit would return here after they died) and finally to the shoreline, where they were dragged onto ships. La Porte du Non Retour, or the Gate of No Return, is now a deeply moving memorial to Africa's lost sons and daughters.

❁ Some 65 percent of Beninese practice voodoo, a belief that natural forces like rain and wind have spiritual forces behind them. Practitioners build shrines out of small mounds of earth and offer their gods alcohol, flowers, food, and the blood of animals sacrificed in their honor. January 10 is National Voodoo Day, and a vibrant festival is held in Ouidah, where you can partake in dancing fueled by copious amounts of *sodabe,* a local palm liquor that will make you go blind if you're not careful (or so the locals say). Look out for the Mami Wata worshippers, who dress in white and adorn themselves with baubles and beads. Mostly women, they are considered very powerful.

❁ For some relaxation, head out to Grand Popo, a beach surrounded by fishing villages about two hours from Cotonou. The Awalé Plage area is a bit more upscale, with European-style cafes and cabana bars; to camp out with Rastafarians, go to Coco Beach.

❁ Upon arrival to any Beninese town, visit the mayor's office and ask for the local women's group. With luck, a guide will take you to the town's textile or craft cooperative, where you can buy directly from the artisans. Another great way to interact with Beninese women is to sit with them in the market, help collect water at the well, or join in the daily pounding of yams with a pestle and mortar. "Stay there until you lose your fear, until you are comfortable, until you realize there is no difference between there and here—that when any group of women gets together, they gossip about neighbors, children, men, life," says Suzanne. "They'll probably laugh at you, because Beninese laugh at everything, but they will appreciate your attempt to get to know their culture."

53 *Cambodia*

THERE IS TRAGEDY, AND THERE IS CAMBODIA. COLONIZED BY THE French, occupied by the Japanese, and bombed by the United States, it was then terrorized by an internal communist revolution that attempted to turn its clocks back to "Year Zero." Anywhere from 1 to 3 million Cambodians (out of a total population of 8 million) are believed to have perished in the madness of the Khmer Rouge's brutal regime, which officially ended in 1979 but maintained a guerrilla presence until 1996. Yet, within a few days in this recovering nation, you'll see why it has become a favorite of intrepid travelers: ancient historic sites, stunning landscapes, a cuisine straight out of the trees and sea, and a people who radiate beauty.

* Prior to your departure, brush up on the history of the Khmer Rouge, starting with the 1984 film *The Killing Fields.* Then take a deep breath and visit the Tuol Sleng Genocide Museum in the nation's capital, Phnom Penh. The Khmer Rouge used this former high school as a prison and interrogation center between 1975 and 1979, and many thousands were slaughtered with machetes and pickaxes (as bullets were too coveted to waste). Photos of the prisoners line the walls. Then visit Choeung Ek, located about ten miles south of the city. Some eight thousand bodies were tossed into mass graves

here, and bits of their bones still protrude through the mud. Thousands of human skulls fill a nearby Buddhist stupa, and the entire area exudes profound sadness.

* If your stomach can handle food after that, head over to the Lotus Blanc for some badly-needed cheering. Founded by the French organization Pour un Sourire d'Enfant (For the Smile of a Child), this restaurant hires its  employees from the nearby Stung Meanchey garbage dump, where thousands of families make their living sifting through trash. Since 1996, about five thousand of these children have received schooling, vocational training, and health care from the organization, and many now work as cooks, bakers, and waiters at the Lotus Blanc. The food is Pan-Asian/French (mango cream cakes!) and the atmosphere is uplifting. Similar restaurants include Le Rit's between Phlauv 51 and Norodom Boulevard, which works with women; and Friends by the National Museum, which aids street children.

* Nothing can top the majesty of Angkor Wat, but Banteay Srei comes closest. Located forty minutes from Siem Reap, this Hindu temple is dedicated to Shiva and is coated with carvings so intricate, many say it was built with the nimble hands of a woman (thus its nickname, Citadel of Women). Solar eagles and monkeys stand guard at the entrance while celestial nymphs dance with abandon. At certain points of the day, the entire temple glimmers pink from the red sandstone.

● For outdoor adventures, head to Rattanakiri, or the Hill of the Precious Stones, a densely forested province near the Vietnam border. The capital, Ban Lung, offers elephant tours to neighboring villages, rubber plantations, and waterfalls like Ka Tieng, where you can swing from a vine. Nearby Virachay National Park is the largest protected area in Cambodia and home to elephants, leopards, and tigers, among other wildlife.

● French colonists lived extravagantly in Kampot at the turn of the twentieth century, gambling, carousing, playing water sports. But then the Khmer Rouge dismantled and the Vietnamese looted their resorts, leaving behind skeletal towns that are strangely fascinating. (You'll beg the crumbling walls to talk at the abandoned casinos in Kep.) Stop by the Kampot Traditional Music School in the evenings, where orphans and disabled children give music and dance performances. Then dine on fresh crab at one of the beachfront restaurants and settle in for a shiatsu massage at Seeing Hands, where all the masseurs are blind.

TOURS

Three Land Travel has ten different tours available to Cambodia from six to thirteen days in length, all-inclusive (www.cambodia.threeland.com).

54 *Ethiopia*

SYNONYMOUS WITH FAMINE IN THE '80S, ETHIOPIA IS SLOWLY being recognized today for what it has quietly been all along—a gem of a nation. At the crossroads of Africa and the Middle East, Ethiopia offers historical and archaeological wonders, a gorgeous people, and a reverent coffee culture.

* Ethiopians call their nation The Land of the Queen of Sheba and her legends proliferate. She left her country only once during her long reign to visit King Solomon in Jerusalem, and he was so taken by her beauty that he seduced her. The Queen (known to her descendants as Makeda) gave birth to a son named Menelik, who became the first Emperor of Ethiopia. At some point, Ethiopians say, Menelik took from his father the sacred Ark of the Covenant (the gold-and-acacia container that Moses built to store the Ten Commandments) and it remains hidden in the treasury of the Ethiopian Orthodox Church in Axum. While you can visit the ruins of Queen Makeda's palace in the fields of Axum, only the highest of religious leaders can peek at the Ark.

* At the National Museum of Addis Ababa, pay respects to Lucy, the oldest and most complete skeleton of a hominid (the link between humans and apes) ever discovered. She was named

after the Beatles song "Lucy in the Sky with Diamonds," which anthropologists played in honor of the remarkable find near the River Awash. Then head to the main campus of Addis Ababa University, where the Ethnological Museum offers an overview of the cultural, religious, and musical traditions of the nation's sixty-plus ethnic groups. In the likely event you covet their textiles—handspun white cotton with colorful borders—drop by the Sheromeda Market and start haggling.

- The eleven churches of Lalibela are said to have been carved out of a single monolith in the thirteenth century at record speed, thanks to the angels who covered the night-shift. All Ethiopian Christians make at least one pilgrimage here before they die; January's Timket celebrating the baptism of Jesus is a particularly extraordinary festival. The monasteries in the islands of Lake Tana, the headwaters of the Blue Nile, are also worth the journey.

- Joining in the green movement sweeping across Africa, Ethiopia is rapidly building eco-lodges out of natural resources using traditional techniques. Try the lovely Bishangari Lodge on Lake Langano, which runs on solar power and offers every activity from horseback riding to hippo-spotting.

www.bishangari.com

- According to legend, an Ethiopian goatherd discovered coffee when his animals got extra spunky after chewing on some leaves and berries. A monk perfected the art of roasting and brewing, and the beverage quickly spread to the Middle East and then throughout the world. Ethiopians serve their coffee with the same reverence of the Japanese at tea time. As frankincense burns, the host roasts the beans and then swirls them before the guests so they can inhale the rich fumes. After a blessing, three cups are poured for each guest over the course of an hour (or two); if any is spilled, it means that spirits have joined you.

TOURS

Journeys International presents a nineteen-day Ethiopia Cultural Explorer with Timkat Festival each year (www.journeys-intl.com).

55 *Cartagena, Colombia*

IN A NATION PLAGUED BY GUERRILLAS, PARAMILITARIES, AND NARCO-traffickers, Cartagena is considered a safe haven—an oasis amidst the violence. This is somewhat ironic, considering its own precarious beginnings. As a way station for treasure pilfered from Indians, this seaside town once featured a thriving slave market and an inquisition center that saw hundreds of "witches" and other heretics tortured and executed. Pirates raided it half a dozen times in the sixteenth century alone, and the Spanish retaliated by building forts and a high wall around the entire town, much of which stands today.

Modern Cartagena is a monument to Spanish colonial architecture, with narrow streets that wind through plazas, monasteries, and palaces. The houses are vividly painted—red houses with orange trim; blue houses splashed with green—and draped with bougainvillea and hanging potted plants. Strolling guitarists serenade diners at the outdoor cafes in the Parque de San Diego, while Plaza Santo Domingo hosts art exhibitions. For indigenous crafts like hammocks or replicas of pre-Columbian jewelry, try Galeria Cano on Plaza de Bolivar.

Cartagena's fruit juices and smoothies are the tastiest in the Caribbean. Any respectable street stall will blend passion fruit, *guanabana, lulo,* and *zapote* together with milk or yogurt and heaps of cane sugar. Look out for *arepa* vendors, too: these cornmeal pockets can be stuffed with your choice of cheese and egg or chicken, and are hot, cheap, and delicious. Then hit the restaurants for some Afro-Caribbean/Latin specialties, like seafood poached in *sancocho* with a side of fried yucca.

Now for the day trips. From Mercado Bazurto, take a bus to Cienaga del Totumo, which looks like a stunted volcano but spews mud instead of lava. Climb the stairs to the top and leap into the crater: it's like swimming in cocoa (and *las viejit*as rave about its therapeutic properties). Rinse off in the lagoon, dry in the sun, then do it all over again (it only costs $1!). To achieve a truly vegetative state, head to the Rosario Islands next, a two-hour boat trip from Cartagena. These small coral islands are peaceful, and children will adore the open-sea Oceanario, where dancing dolphins steal the spotlight.

56 *Beirut, Lebanon*

FOR DECADES, BEIRUT WAS KNOWN AS THE "PARIS OF THE MIDDLE East." Travelers flocked here from all over the globe to gamble in its casinos, lounge on its sunny beaches, and shop in its trendy boutiques, until a fifteen-year civil war broke out in 1975. Bombs and shellings nearly razed the city, but by the turn of the millennium, Lebanese Christians and Muslims were again living in harmony as five-star hotels rose above the rubble. Tragically, in July 2006, war broke out once again when Hezbollah guerrillas in southern Lebanon kidnapped two Israeli soldiers, and Israel responded tenfold. This frightening conflict was unresolved as of press time, and it will likely be a while before travelers can safely return here. But return we must, as Beirut is unquestionably one of the region's most spectacular cities.

Any Lebanese morning is best commenced with a cup of Arabic coffee—order *sadah* for no sugar, *wassat* for a bit, and *hilweh* for a lot—and a pastry, the freshest of which can be found on rue Bliss. Then explore the downtown area, which straddles the infamous Green Line that once separated East Beirut from West (and thus Christians from Muslims). Many of its Ottoman and French buildings, mosques, and churches were obliterated during the civil war, but thriving commerce has taken their place, including Beirut's greatest sweet shop, Rafaat Hallab & Sons on rue al Maarad. (You haven't had *borma* until you've tasted it here!)

Then visit the museums and galleries. Local artists are showcased at the Agial Art Gallery at 63 rue Omar Abdel Aziz. Drop in Al-Badia at 78 rue Makdissi to buy dresses, shawls, and scarves made by refugee Palestinian women living in Lebanon.

Then hit the Corniche, the promenade along the Mediterranean. Here, you'll find families and friends pole-fishing, rollerblading, playing backgammon, and otherwise strolling about. Snack on hot nuts from a pushcart, and when the sun sinks into the horizon, take a few puffs on a nargileh (a.k.a. hookah, hubble-bubble, or water pipe). Cherry is particularly flavorful, but as any Arab will tell you: it's not what's in the pipe but who you share it with that counts. The most scenic site for nargileh is the Bay Rock Café's outdoor terrace, which overlooks the Pigeon Rocks rising out of the sea beneath the cliffs of Rouché.

Lebanese dine late. For a special treat, consider Al Mijana at rue Abdel Wahab El-Inglizi, set in an Ottoman house with indoor and outdoor seating. Chez Andre on rue Hamra has a more bohemian flair. Then check out the listings in the *Daily Star* and spend the night bar crawling and club hopping along rue Monot. If it still exists after the 2006 conflict, peek into the war-themed 1975, where waiters in combat fatigues serve nargileh made of old ammunition cases to customers seated on sandbags. If that's too surreal, drop by the Gemmayzeh Café instead on rue Gouraud for some live music (usually a singer and oud player). October sees the Beirut International Film Festival, which includes outdoor screenings in Freedom Square.

www.baalbeck.org.lb

Fifty miles northeast of Beirut is the ancient Sun City of Baalbek, home to the grandest Roman ruins in the Middle East (including a temple to Venus). In late summer, it is also site of a major arts festival that brings in world-class acts. Deep Purple, the Dizzy Gillespie All-Star Big Band, and the Boris Eifman Ballet Theatre of St. Petersburg are among those who canceled in 2006 because of the war; let's hope they can return some day soon.

57 *Places That Cannot Be Forgotten*

THE ARMENIAN MASSACRE. THE HOLOCAUST. CHERNOBYL. Hurricane Mitch. The Kashmir Earthquake. All were acts of extreme violence committed by the hands of man or the whims of nature upon an innocent populace. As global citizens, it is imperative we visit the memorial sites, however shattering, so that they are not forgotten—or repeated.

* In the early morning of August 6, 1945, a U.S. B-29 bomber named *Enola Gay* (after the pilot's mother) hovered above Hiroshima, Japan. World War II had been raging for years by that point, but at 8:15 A.M., it radically changed course when the plane dropped an atomic bomb carrying 13 kilotons of TNT over the city. Some 75,000 people perished instantly, and another 65,000 died from its effects soon after. Three days later, the United States dropped a second bomb over Nagasaki, killing roughly 74,000. Japan promptly surrendered (and the war ended thereafter) but the bombings still haunt its people—especially the 260,000-plus surviving *hibakusha,* or "explosion-affected people" (many of whom face grave discrimination due to societal ignorance about radiation).

    In Hiroshima, you can witness the bomb's frightful force at the Atom Bomb Dome, a former industrial building that stood almost directly beneath the explosion. A skeleton of its former self, it has been preserved in its ruined state and is floodlit at night. Across the river, Peace Memorial Park contains shrines as well as an eternal flame that will not be extinguished until the last nuclear weapon on earth has been destroyed. One statue is based on Sadako Sasaki, a little girl who believed her radiation sickness would fade away if she folded 1,000 paper cranes. Millions have since been folded in her honor and sent here from schools around the world.

In Nagasaki, visit the Atomic Bomb Museum, which shows live footage of the blast as well as testimonies from survivors. It ends with a sobering tally of the world's nuclear weapons, plus predictions on the mass destruction they could bring. Join locals in their annual anti-nuclear protest on August 9.

- Relations between the Hutu and Tutsi in Rwanda, Africa had always been fiery, but in early 1994, they ignited. During the horrific 100 Days of Madness, Hutu death squads, militia groups, and common citizens went on a rampage, massacring every Tutsi (and moderate Hutu) in sight and then looting and burning their neighborhoods and businesses. Corpses— hacked to bits by machetes—quickly piled up under the watchful eyes of the media, but the international community did shamefully little to stop the violence (as in 2006 Darfur). By the time Tutsi rebels finally overthrew the Hutu regime in mid-July, 1 million people had been slaughtered. Two million Hutus then fled the country, fearing retribution.

  Capital Kigali is a remarkably functional city, considering how recently this occurred. Viewers of the 2004 film *Hotel Rwanda* will appreciate a visit (or stay) at the four-star

Hotel des Mille Collines, where a sympathetic Hutu manager protected more than one thousand refugees by bribing militia officials. Then spend an afternoon at the Kigali Memorial Centre, which screens video testimony from victims' families. The museum's upper level documents survivors of other genocides, including Armenians, Jews, and Cambodians. Outside, pay respects at the rows upon rows of mass graves, where families leave fresh flowers and other mementos.

"It is powerful beyond words," says Neda Farzan, a medical student in San Francisco. "From the room filled with victims' family photos and wedding pictures, to the personal items at the mass graves, like Superman bedsheets and little kids' t-shirts—it is just gut-wrenching."

✸ One of modern history's deadliest disasters occurred the day after Christmas in 2004. Just before eight that morning, the earth began to rumble beneath the sea off Sumatra, triggering tsunamis that destroyed coastal communities throughout Southeast Asia, including Indonesia, Sri Lanka, India, and Thailand. Thousands of homes and hundreds of hotels got swept out to sea, and nearly 230,000 people vanished—tens of thousands of whom have yet to be found. Due to their lesser ability to hold on tightly to trees and other structures, four times more women died than men, and approximately one-third of the victims were children. Because many of the regions were poor to begin with, recovery has been exceedingly slow: in some parts of rural Sri Lanka, it seems that the waves just washed through.

WWW.

www.kigalimemorialcentre.org
www.lonelyplanet.com/travel_ticker/tsunami
www.tsunamivolunteer.net

A few heroines emerged from the calamity, including a ten-year-old British girl who was vacationing with her parents on Mikhao Beach in Thailand when the tsunami struck. Thanks to a recent geography lesson, she recognized the rapidly receding seashore as a sign of impending doom, and her family helped evacuate the beach of nearly one hundred people. The tsunami has also been credited with inspiring the peace agreement between separatists and the military in Aceh, Indonesia, a highly volatile region.

The most profound way to assist with recovery efforts is to plan your next vacation here. Cram extra clothes, toys, medicine, and tools into your suitcases and contact local schools, hospitals, or non-governmental organizations to see who needs them. In the Thai tourist hub of Khao Lak, where sixty hotels got sucked into the sea, try the Tsunami Volunteer Center. Created with the objective of "restoration through empowerment," they need helping hands in such areas as childcare, small business development, and environmental restoration.

"For us, genocide was the gas chamber—what happened in Germany. We were not able to realize that with the machete you can create a genocide."
—Boutros Boutros-Galli

VII

Places of Inspiration and Enlightenment

58 *Mount Kailash, Tibet*

SHANGRI-LA. THE ROOF OF THE WORLD. THE PLACE OF THE GODS. Tibet is widely considered a vortex of energy, a center of spirituality. You'd be hard-pressed to find a more peaceful people anywhere, despite the violence they've endured since China invaded a half century ago. Their spiritual leader, the Dalai Lama, was forced into exile in 1959 and by 1970, an estimated 100,000 Tibetans had joined him. Thousands who stayed perished under stringent Chinese rule. Yet the faithful continue to light their yak butter candles and meditate with their prayer beads, confident that this era, too, shall pass; and at least once a lifetime, they make a pilgrimage to their Precious Jewel of Snow: Mount Kailash, the most sacred mountain in Asia.

At 22,028 feet, Mount Kailash is believed to be the core of the cosmos by Buddhists, Hindus, and Bons (practitioners of Tibet's indigenous religion). For the past 1,000 years, devotees have traveled here to perform the *kora* (or *parikrama,* if they're Hindu), a thirty-two-mile circumambulation of the mountain, in the footsteps of the Sakyamuni Buddha. Partaking in this reverent experience can be challenging logistically. The easiest way is to take an organized tour with a reputable company, such as World Expeditions. Otherwise, fly to Tibet's capital, Lhasa, buy a permit, and hire a trustworthy driver/guide with a Land Cruiser. The four-day drive travels along the northern spine of the Himalayas and runs about $725 a person. Bring a good tent and sleeping bag, as accommodations can be hard to find. Once at Mount Kailash, spend the night in the village of Darchen and set out the next morning. Most foreigners complete the trek in three days, starting with the twelve and a half-mile trail from Darchen to Dirapuk Monastery. Along the way, you'll pass the thirteenth-century Chuku monastery, which was demolished during China's Cultural Revolution but has since been restored. Amidst the *thangkas,* prayer flags, and prayer wheels is a marble statue that is said to talk when so inspired. Pass the night in the guesthouse of Dirapuk Monastery if there's room, or pitch a tent. Consider hiking out to the Kangkyam Glacier if your feet are up to it, or relax at the tea house. The next morning, hike to Zutulpuk Monastery eleven miles away, passing by the rocky expanse of Shiva-tsal. Pilgrims are said to undergo a symbolic death here, and leave behind clothing, hair, and other personal items to represent their previous life. The most devout prick themselves for a blood offering. Spend the night at Zutulpuk and complete the eight and a half-mile journey back to Darchen the following day.

This itinerary will take you clockwise around Mount Kailash, the direction of choice for Hindus and Tibetans. Those traveling in the opposite direction are likely Bon. Extremely dedicated Tibetans prostrate the *entire* way of the journey, which takes about three weeks—and many do it more than once. A single circuit around the mountain only wipes out the sins of *this* life time; it takes 108 to clean the slate for *all* your lives. Thirteen circuits is generally considered a happy minimum, as this enables you to visit special detours that are off-limits to other trekkers.

If possible, coordinate your trip with the Saga Dawa festival, held during the full moon in late May/early June. In this ceremony, lamas lower the enormous Tarboche flagpole at the base of the mountain and remove its hundreds of fading prayer flags. Then pilgrims walk around it, praying and attaching new flags they brought from home to the musical accompaniment of horns and cymbals. Hours later, everyone gathers to help the lamas raise the pole again. The instant it stands perfectly erect, pilgrims toss "wind horses," or colorful slips of paper with scriptures scrawled across them, into the air and cheer. You can almost feel the prayers explode into the universe.

TOURS

World Expeditions offers several different tours and treks to the Himalayas (www.worldexpeditions.com), as does Himalayan Kingdoms (www.himalayankingdoms.com).

59 *Sacred Native Spaces*

IT IS ONE OF PREHISTORIC NORTH AMERICA'S GREAT MYSTERIES. Between the first and fifteenth centuries, the Anasazi civilization flourished in the southwestern United States, building marvelous sandstone houses as many as four stories high, developing sophisticated irrigation systems, and creating solar and lunar observatories that marvel modern astronomers. But then, for no traceable reason, they suddenly abandoned these communities and vanished into history. All that remain are their remarkable ruins, which are considered sacred spaces by indigenous communities today. Visiting them is a mind-expanding experience.

* The Anasazi outdid themselves in New Mexico's Chaco Canyon. Between A.D. 850 and 1250, they created an urban center here of roads, ramps, and dams as well as 100-room structures with subterranean ceremonial chambers called *kivas*. Even more impressive is how meticulously they aligned the buildings with the cardinal directions. Sunlight spills through the main window of one major *kiva* just one day a year: the summer solstice. During the spring and fall equinoxes, meanwhile, the sun rises and sets in perfect alignment with the east-west wall of Pueblo Bonito. And then there is Fajada Butte, which rises 377 feet above the canyon floor on Chacra Mesa. Behind three slabs of rock on the

butte's eastern side are two spiral petroglyphs. At 11:15 A.M. on the summer solstice, the sun shines between the slabs, creating a dagger of light that bisects the larger spiral down its center. Light cuts through the smaller spiral during the spring and fall equinoxes. Unfortunately, this magical butte has been closed to the public for some time now. Some say it's because of She Who Dries You Out, a ghost who lives high on the butte. (On full moons, she likes to call out to lonely men and lure them into her lair.) The Anasazi abandoned Chaco Canyon so abruptly, they left behind beads and pottery. You'll likely find shards as you explore the grounds, but locals say that your hand will swell if you touch them. Park rangers are forever receiving mailed-back packages of pilfered pottery, along with sad letters of bad karma.

* One of the longest continuously inhabited places in North America, Arizona's Canyon de Chelly housed the Anasazi from the eighth to mid-thirteenth centuries. They left behind cliffside dwellings made of sun-dried clay and stone, along with the finest rock art in the United States. The Navajo moved in a few centuries later and named it Tsegi, or Rocky Canyon. Several hundred remain here today, working as farmers and jeep guides on the "shake and bake" tours of the 130 square miles of ochre- and salmon-colored sandstone, Russian olive groves, creeks, and grazing horses. The canyon not only offers heart-stopping views, but is filled to the brim with myths and legends. Spider Rock, the 800-foot spire jutting from the canyon floor, is thought to be the ancient home of the Spider Woman, who taught the Navajo how to weave. Massacre Cave, meanwhile, commemorates a surprise attack by the Spanish, during which a Navajo woman

fought off a soldier so fiercely, the two fell off a cliff to their deaths. To hear more, coordinate your visit with the Navajo Nation fair in September, when tens of thousands of Native Americans and visitors gather in Window Rock for a week of gourd dancing, drumming competitions, crafts markets, and livestock and rodeo shows. Find some old-timers and savor their stories.

60 *Bhutan*

ONLY SINCE 1974 HAVE TRAVELERS BEEN GRANTED PASSAGE INTO the Land of the Thunder Dragon tucked deep in the Himalayas. Before then, Bhutan was the epitome of isolation: a hermetic kingdom with no roads, airport, television, or telephones, reachable solely by a month-long mountain trek from India. Then its pragmatic king, Jigme Singye Wangchuck, decided that high-end tourism could bring in some badly-needed capital, and opened the doors to a select number of tourists each year (generally between 5,000 and 9,000). Bhutan has since become the destination of choice for the rich and famous as well as the intrepid traveler willing to part with big bucks for a unique opportunity.

First, the rules: travelers are almost never permitted to venture off on their own in Bhutan. You must book a trip through an agency. The government charges a daily tariff of $200 in the high season; $165 in the low season. While steep, this fee includes everything from transportation and guides to basic room and board. (You can, of course, spend more: some resorts charge $900 a night.) Smoking has been banned in public spaces since 2005 and it is illegal to sell tobacco. Marijuana grows wild everywhere, but the Bhutanese mainly use it to feed their pigs (who are noticeably fat and happy). It is also forbidden to swim in lakes or climb mountains, out of respect for the deities residing within.

Locals have rules of their own to obey, including a strict dress code in schools and public offices. Women wear *kira,* or brilliantly colored dresses and short jackets adorned with brooches, while men wear *ghos,* or knee-length robes with white silk cuffs. Though not without their faults, such regulations have enabled Bhutan to preserve its rich ethnic and cultural identity. Ninety percent of the population are subsistence farmers who live as they have for generations, and the king keeps careful tabs on their "Gross National Happiness."

The landscapes of Bhutan are a knock-out: rivers saturated with rainbow trout, terraced rice fields, dense forests, cloud-kissing mountains. Most temples and monasteries can only be reached by foot, and it is always worth the effort. A favorite is Taktshang Goemba, or Tiger's Nest, a monastery perched on a rocky cliff with a 4,000-foot drop into the valley below. Legend has it that the Guru Rinpoche flew here on the back of a female tiger from Tibet and spent three months meditating in a nearby cave before converting the entire valley to Buddhism. Hike through some rice paddies to the ancient temple Chimi Lakhang, said to be highly auspicious for women wishing to conceive. Ask for a blessing if you're contemplating motherhood. Animal lovers should also visit the Jigme Dorji Wildlife Sanctuary, home to such endangered species as the snow leopard, red panda, blue sheep, and the straight-out-of-*Star-Trek* takin.

Like most Buddhists, the Bhutanese are festival-happy; you're bound to catch one with a thousand-year-old history. Also attend an archery match. Though forbidden to compete, women play the critical role of loudly cracking jokes about the opposing team's manhood as a means of distraction. Bhutanese aren't bashful with sexuality. The king himself has four wives (all sisters), and many families paint penises on the sides of their

houses to ward off evil spirits. This tradition dates back to a fif-
teenth-century saint known as the Divine Madman, who purportedly tied sacred ribbons around his penis to attract women.

A monsoon climate means Bhutan is in a downpour for half
the year, so consult the weather before booking your trip. Allow
plenty of time to acclimatize upon your arrival, as the altitude
can wipe you out. Medical care is totally free in Bhutan—even for
tourists—but they might not have the medicine you need, so
bring a full first aid kit.

RECOMMENDED READING

Beyond the Sky and the Earth by Jamie Zeppa

TOURS

Adventure Women offers a women-only Bhutan tour titled
"100,000 Dakinis" (www.adventurewomen.com).

RESOURCES

Festival Calendar of Bhutan
(www.tibet-travels.com/bhutan_festival.php)

61 *Whale Watching Destinations*

IS ANY SIGHT SO STRIKING AS THE TAIL OF A WHALE CRESTING ABOVE the sea line? Fortunately, whale-watching expeditions are offered throughout the globe:

* Forget SeaWorld: if you want to see Shamu, head over to Vancouver Island, British Columbia, which hosts about 200 orcas—or killer whales—from late June until winter. The largest member of the dolphin family, these regal creatures can reach up to thirty feet in length and weigh about nine tons. Stubbs Island Whale Watching offers three-hour, $75 expeditions through Johnstone Strait and Blackfish Archipelago on vessels equipped with underwater microphones that allow passengers to eavesdrop on the latest orca gossip. Approximately 90 percent of outings find orcas, but if yours is ill-fated, the bountiful dolphins, porpoises, sea lions, seals, and minke, gray, and humpback whales will surely compensate. Bird watchers might even glimpse a bald eagle.

  www.stubbs-island.com

* Every year, some eighteen thousand gray whales swim in a conga line from the icy, nutrient-rich waters of northern Alaska to the warm breeding lagoons of Baja California, Mexico and back—11,000 miles in all. Dozens of chartered

cruises and flights are available along the route, but it is also possible, and perhaps even preferable, to watch the whales migrate while picnicking on the seashore. An organization called Whale Watching Spoken Here stations volunteers at thirty sites along the Oregon Coast during peak whale-watching weeks to help spot the whales.  The National Park Service also offers free services at Point Reyes Peninsula in California. Jutting ten miles into the Pacific Ocean, the peninsula's headlands allow views of whales as close as a few hundred yards away. Late April to early May is the best time to see mothers with their calves. Bring a warm jacket and a good pair of binoculars (7x35, 7x42, or 8x40 are best).

* Beluga whales—known fondly to their fans as marshmallowheads—can also be viewed from ashore in Cunningham Inlet on Somerset Island, Nunavut, Canada. From mid-July to August, they swim right up to the mouth of the Cunningham River to molt and nurse their young in the warm river water. Nearby lodging—along with adventures like sea kayaking and polar bear watching—is available at Arctic Watch Lodge.

www.whalespoken.org
www.nps.gov/pore
www.canadianarcticholidays.ca

62 *Buddhist Retreats*

When life and its discontents wear you down, take a break and meditate. Buddhist centers offer rejuvenating retreats for women and men of every religious persuasion (including those who do not subscribe to any religion). Powerful centers pop up in the least likely of places, such as the following:

● Situated on the Beara Peninsula of southwest Ireland, overlooking the Atlantic Ocean, is the Tibetan Buddhist retreat center of Dzogchen Beara. Guests can take daily meditation classes and, on Saturday evenings, watch video teachings by the center's spiritual director, Sogyal Rinpoche, author of the *Tibetan Book of Living and Dying*. A farmhouse hostel is open year-round and offers two dormitories, a family room, fully-equipped kitchen, and communal living room. Dzogchen is remote: the nearest grocery store is about five miles away, and no bus can take you there. (Most retreats provide lunch and supper, however.) Yet many visitors thrive on this isolation.

> "It feels ancient and beautiful, and you really get a profound sense of being a part of nature here," says Lila Rose Kaplan, a playwright who stumbled upon the center while on a writing retreat. "It is the perfect place to seek out your wisdom."

www.dzogchenbeara.org

❋ Hidden deep within the Wood Valley of the Ka'u District of Big Island, Hawai'i is a magical place called Nechung Dorje Drayang Ling, or The Immutable Island of Melodious Sound. Built by sugarcane workers in the early 1900s, this center sits amidst twenty-five acres of eucalyptus, bamboo, and palm trees. Jasmine and ginger blossoms permeate the air, and wild peacocks strut among the tropical flowers. Nechung is an ideal place to study the tenets of Buddhism. Tibetan Lama Nechung Rinpoche has been teaching here since 1975 and guest lecturers have included the Dalai Lama. Practice their teachings or create some of your own in the upstairs meditation hall, which is dedicated to Tara, the female Buddha of Compassion. The local guest house can accommodate up to fifteen people at a rate of $50 a night. Stay three weeks and the fourth is free.

www.nechung.org
www.taramandala.org

❋ Tucked in the Four Corners area of southwest Colorado is a Buddhist retreat center with a feminine link: the Tara Mandala. Its founder is an American Tibetan Buddhist nun named Tsultrim Allione, who at fifteen received her first book on Buddhism from her grandmother. After working with Mother Teresa in Calcutta, she went on to study in the Himalayas, learning Tibetan as well as various meditation practices. A mother and a feminist, she wrote *Women of Wisdom* as a way of introducing the role of enlightened women in Tibetan Buddhism. Her Tara Mandala sits on 600 acres of medicinal plants and rugged wildlife in the San Juan Mountains. In addition to Buddhist training, the center offers seminars on subjects like deep ecology, natural medicine, conflict resolution, and exploration of the sacred feminine. The facilities are quite basic (even the office lacks electricity) and all meals are vegetarian. Visitors must bring their own tents and camping gear, and are asked to conduct daily karma yoga (chores). Prices are based on a sliding scale and scholarships are available.

"The mind, the Buddha, living creatures—
these are not three different things."

—Avatamasaka Sutra

RECOMMENDED READING

Women of Wisdom: The Mandala of the Enlightened Feminine by Tsultrim Allione

63 *Australia*
The Outback

THE DEAD HEART. THE GHASTLY VOID. THE NEVER-NEVER. ALL are fitting nicknames for the Outback, Australia's unforgiving interior, yet they betray the landscape's vast beauty—or, in the case of Uluru-Kata Tjuta National Park, its majesty. Here resides the world's largest monolith, a rock so massive (2.2 miles long, 1.5 miles wide, and 1,141 feet high) it was once thought to be a meteorite. (Geologists have since identified it as a single piece of arkrose, aged 700 million years.) Its color changes with the sun, from ocher to burnt sienna to orange to blood red to finally—at sunset—a deep purple that sends visitors racing to the parking lot to climb atop the roofs of their cars and snap photos like crazy.  When night falls, the monolith becomes a mammoth void that blocks the rising moon and the stars. Some swear it awakens then.

The monolith has a few nicknames of its own—The Rock, Ayers, and Uluru—and, like the Outback itself, the term you use says something about you. Those who come to climb call it Ayers Rock, after a nineteenth-century South Australia governor who never actually visited it. Local Aboriginal tribes, meanwhile, say Uluru, a name of reverence. Known as Anangu, or "the people," these Aborigines are believed to have lived alongside Uluru for the past 20,000 years, but a British explorer is credited with "discovering" it in 1872. After years of tension, control of the monolith was returned to the Anangu in 1985. Among other things, they now determine its hours of operation, so ensure it is open before heading out, as anything from strong winds to special ceremonies can inspire a shut-down. The Anangu also request that visitors not climb Uluru, due to its spiritual significance.

A great way to visit the park's hidden treasures, such as cave paintings and sacred watering holes, is with Anangu Tours, a company owned and operated by local tribes. The guides hold demonstrations on ancient bush skills like starting a fire without matches and carving wooden tools out of stones, and share traditional legends of figures like the Blue Tongue Lizard Man. You might even get a tasty bush snack. Drop in the Maruku Arts & Crafts Center afterward, as it sells music sticks, bowls, boomerangs, spear throwers, and desert animals carved from river red gum root. During Australia's summer, November to March, temperatures at Uluru regularly break 100 degrees; to escape the heat, go between June and September (but bring a sweater, as it grows chilly at night).

Two hundred and eighty miles from Uluru is Alice Springs, home of the National Pioneer Women's Hall of Fame. In addition to its artifacts and reference library, the museum is actively gathering stories and photographs of pioneering Australian women for its "Herstory Archive." Add an entry about your favorite Aussie heroine.

www.pioneerwomen.com.au

TOURS

Anangu Tours offers several types of guided tours of Uluru (www.anang12waai.com.au/anangu_tours/).

64
Varanasi, India
The Holy Ganges

IF IT'S TRUE THAT SOME PLACES DEFY DESCRIPTION, THE GANGES tops the list.

Every day, some sixty thousand people sweep through the ancient streets of Varanasi (a.k.a. Benares) to the ghats (paved steps leading to the river), where they partake in the full range of human experience. They eat, they cut each other's hair, they defecate, they wash their clothes, their bodies, and their buffalos. They spit out blood-red betelnut juice and sing. The sadhus, or wandering holy men, shake out their dreadlocks and tell stories. Beggars beg and karma-seekers give. Pilgrims raise their hands toward the sun in reverent puja. And Untouchables haul in dead bodies atop bamboo stretchers, build wooden funeral pyres around them, and set them ablaze.

"You really have to release your Western concepts of order at Varanasi, because all those rules are broken here," says Kavitha Rao, who spent two years traveling the globe as a correspondent for The Odyssey: World Trek. "It makes you laugh at yourself, to see there is order in chaos that you can't understand."

In Hinduism, the River Ganges is depicted as a goddess holding an overflowing vessel that symbolizes the fertility sustaining the universe. Hindus believe that bathing in her will wipe away the sins of a lifetime, and that dying in her mother city, Varanasi, will allow them to circumvent the tiresome cycle of birth, death, and rebirth, and leap straight into *moksha,* or enlightenment. Sadly, the river suffers from severe environmental degradation. No less than thirty major sewers discharge into the Ganges, as do a number of leather and carpet factories. Then there are the daily dumpings of human ashes and even entire corpses. (People who have died from leprosy, chickenpox,

or snake bites are generally weighted down with stones and submerged.) This is particularly unfortunate given that, at 1,557 miles, the Ganges supports about one in every twelve people on earth.

The best way to see the Ganges is to rise before the sun, hire a boat from the main steps of the Dasawamedha ghat, and head toward Harishchandra ghat to see pilgrims perform the *surya pranam* at dawn. Also monitor the water, as virtually anything could pass by: a freshwater dolphin, a fleet of palm-frond boats filled with candles and marigolds, a bloated corpse. Ghats of particular interest are the Manikarnika ghat, which is considered the most auspicious ghat in which to be cremated, and the Ahilyabai ghat, named after the legendary Queen Ahilyabai of Indore.

Hinduism isn't the only faith that reveres Varanasi. Soon after achieving enlightenment, Gautama Buddha is believed to have given his first sermon about the Four Noble Truths in nearby Sarnath. Today this sacred site is a major Buddhist pilgrimage center and contains a stupa that dates from A.D. 500. It is also the birthplace of two spiritual leaders of the Jain religion and home to a sizeable Muslim population. The great Gyanvyapi Masjid mosque has minarets towering 230 feet above the Ganges and is an integral part of the city's skyline. Varanasi is also home to a major backpacker scene, which means cheap hostels, internet cafes, and scams of every variety. Only use official guides from the India Tourism Office, and beware that local men can be aggressive with foreign women. Consider traveling with a man or in a group, not only here but anywhere in northern India.

Many foreigners are so taken with Varanasi, they stay a spell. A couple thousand study Indian culture, philosophy, and Sanskrit at Benares Hindu University; others take sitar or tabla lessons at the International Music Centre Ashram near Dasaswamedh ghat. The International Yoga Clinic and Meditation Center near the Man Mandir ghat receives glowing reviews, and offers classes in hatha, *pranayama,* and *kriya* yoga.

RECOMMENDED READING

Travelers' Tales India edited by James O'Reilly and Larry Habegger

TOURS

PanTours of Australasia has four tours to India, including a Northern India Spiritual Tour (www.pantoursindia.com).

65 *Jerusalem and Bethlehem, Israel*

THE GREAT ISRAELI POET YEHUDA AMIHAI SUMMED IT UP BEST: "The air over Jerusalem is saturated with prayers and dreams.... It is hard to breathe." This is truly hallowed ground, sacred to Jews, Christians, and Muslims alike. For this same reason, Jerusalem has long been a battleground, but its riches ensure that no journey here is in vain.

For Jews, no place is holier than the Kotel ha-Ma'aravi, or Western Wall. As the only structure left standing after the

Romans destroyed the revered Second Temple in A.D. 70, it reduces many of its pilgrims to tears (thus its gentile nickname, the Wailing Wall). A popular custom is to write a prayer on a piece of paper and slip it into a crack. The wall has incited controversy in recent years due to an ultra-Orthodox mandate forbidding women from organizing prayer services here. A group called Women of the Wall is currently fighting this archaic law, and on the first Shabbat of every month (known as Rosh Chodesh), they defiantly gather here to pray, despite the dirty looks and hisses.

Christians, meanwhile, come here to follow the Via Dolorosa, or Way of Sorrow, that traces Jesus' final walk to crucifixion. Fourteen incidents that occurred along the route are marked with a chapel, known collectively as the Stations of the Cross. The 6th Station commemorates the moment when Veronica wiped the blood and sweat from Jesus' face, and found his image emblazoned on her handkerchief. The 8th Station—now a Greek Orthodox Monastery—is where Jesus consoled the city's weeping women. Other major Christian sites are the Church of the Dormition, where Mary is believed to have died, and the Tomb of the Virgin, where she was buried (along with Queen Melisande and Saint Anne).

Muslims travel to Jerusalem to pray in the Al-Aqsa Mosque, which can accommodate up to five thousand worshippers. If visiting during Ramadan, come by for Leilat Il-Qadr, or the Night of the Moon, when Muslim women arrive to pray by the busload. (Only Muslims are allowed inside the mosque, however.)

After beholding Jerusalem's ancient treasures, enjoy a few contemporary ones. Widely considered the best bakery in Israel, La Cuisine at Yad Harutzim 4 (or 32 Gaza Street) makes sweet breads stuffed with dates or chocolate chips, chocolate caramel tarts, and an exquisite lemon pie with half a foot of meringue piled on top. Another local favorite is the Cinemateque near the Old Train Station, which features documentaries, artsy flicks, dramas, and gay and lesbian films. Not to be missed is their Jerusalem International Film Festival, which shows 200 films on human rights and Jewish themes over a ten-day period. It opens with an outdoor movie screening in the Sultan's Pool amphitheater by the Old City walls.

www.jer-cin.org.il/jff.php

The nearby city of Bethlehem is best known as the place where Mary gave birth to Jesus (now the Basilica of Nativity). Virgin devotees will enjoy the nearby Milk Grotto Church, where the Holy Family hid during their escape to Egypt. Some of Mary's milk is believed to have splashed onto the rocks here, forever turning them white (hence the church's name). Women with fertility problems come here to pray and receive tiny packets filled with white dust that symbolizes the Virgin's milk, and generations of grateful mothers have returned to pin photos of their plump babies on the wall. Jews will want to visit the Tomb of Rachel, considered the third holiest site in Judaism. Described in Genesis as "beautiful of form and beautiful of appearance," this favorite wife of Jacob died while giving birth to his twelfth son, Benjamin. They say she wept for the Jews from inside her grave when they were later banished into exile. Located near the intersection of Manger Street and Hebron Road, her tomb is now a major pilgrimage site for women unable to conceive.

Most people travel to Bethlehem as a quick day-trip from Jerusalem, but try to spend more time here to learn about Palestinian culture. At a minimum, visit the Heritage Center near Rachel's Tomb on Manger Street, which sells traditional crafts like carpets and teapots made by women from the town and nearby refugee camps. Locally-made tablecloths and placemats can be purchased from the Arab Women's Union at the Bethlehem Museum off Star Road.

66 Japan
The 88 Sacred Temples

SOME ONE THOUSAND YEARS AGO, THE GREAT BUDDHIST KOBO Daishi achieved enlightenment by walking across the island of Shikoku in Japan. His descendants have been retracing his footsteps ever since in an 870-mile pilgrimage to the 88 sacred temples. Some Japanese make the trek to pay homage to their ancestors and affirm their cultural identity; others do it as an act of faith. For everyone, the pilgrimage is a rare opportunity to reflect on the beauty of the world, as the trail passes through forests, mountains, and valleys along the sea.

The first decision every *henro,* or pilgrim, should make is her mode of transportation. Options include bus, car, motorcycle, and bicycle, but the truest way is to do as Daishi did, and walk. This can take anywhere from one to two months, depending on your speed and whether you follow the Japanese example of traveling from the 1st temple to the 88th and then back again to the 1st, to complete the circle.

Then come the preparations. Practice taking long hikes up steep hills with all of your equipment several months in advance. Pack sparingly, but don't forget foot care products, pain medications, rain gear, and a good map. Special *henro* equipment can be purchased at Ryozen-ji, the first temple on the route. This includes the white robe that will identify you as a *henro* to others; name cards; a *nokyocho,* or stamp book; a straw hat; and a walking stick inscribed with: "Homage to Kobo Daishi. We two—pilgrims together." As it represents Daishi, this stick should be treated with respect. Wash its base every night.

Legend dictates that once a *henro* walks through the gates of Ryozen-ji, she is committed to completing the pilgrimage—even at risk of death. Upon arriving at each new temple, say the Hannya Shingyo, or Heart Sutra, one of the oldest chants in Japanese Buddhism. Then light some candles and add a few prayers of your own. Next, write either your name or that of a loved one on a name card and deposit it in the bin. (These cards will later be set aflame in a special ceremony so that the deities can learn of your intentions.) On your way out, ask a clerk to write the name of the temple's deity in your *nokyocho*. This stamp is said to contain the deity's spirit, so that you can carry it with you to the next temple.

When dusk falls, there are several sleeping options. Most temples offer accommodations, although those busloads of Japanese retirees zipping by tend to reserve them far in advance. Traditional inns and guesthouses are a better choice, as is camping. Locals recognize the sacrifice involved in being a *henro* and will treat you accordingly. Feel free to ask anyone for help: they will likely be glad to. Some might even offer *o-settai*, or a small present.

The pilgrimage passes through four prefectures of Shikoku Island: Tokushima, Kochi, Ehime, and Kagawa. Two highlights:

- Before giving birth, women visit Gokuraku-ji about a half-mile west of Ryozen-ji. The enormous cedar tree here is said to have been planted by Daishi himself. Say a prayer with your hand on her trunk.
- Yakuo-ji, or the 23rd sacred temple, is believed to ward off bad luck in inauspicious years. For women, that means the

33rd year of life (for men, it is the 42nd). As you ascend the temple's stairwell, note how it divides, with 33 steps on the women's side and 42 on the men's. For good luck, leave a coin on every step.

RECOMMENDED READING

The Japanese Pilgrimage by Oliver Statler

RESOURCES

A Brief Shikoku Pilgrimage English Guide (www.mandala.co.jp/echoes/ jhguide.html)

67 *New Zealand*
The Maori

ACCORDING TO LEGEND, THE MAORI SET SAIL FROM THEIR Polynesian paradise on *waka,* or canoes, a thousand years ago and discovered a luscious new island inhabited primarily by birds. They stayed there in complete isolation for centuries, until the arrival of the Europeans. Though they battled bravely, they stood scant chance against the muskets and diseases. Soon after Queen Victoria annexed New Zealand in 1840, the Maori slipped into decline, and by the end of that century, many predicted they would eventually die out altogether. But then came the 1960s, which saw massive cultural revivals in indigenous communities around the globe. The Maori rejuvenated, and the novel *The Bone People* and film *Whale Rider* have since inspired an entire generation of travelers to learn more about them.

"The heart of my fascination is their idea of reciprocity between the land and the people," says Claire Alpern, an American who moved to New Zealand in 2005 after falling in love with Maori culture on an earlier trip. "Your actions on this earth are reflections not only of yourself, but of your immediate family, and most importantly of the *mana*—the respect, authority, prestige, and power—of all the ancestors who came before you."

WWW. www.nzmaori.co.nz · www.maoriculture.co.nz

These locales are ideal for exploring Maori culture:

* On the East Coast of North Island, Claire recommends the beachside town of Te Araroa, home to the nation's largest and oldest pohutukawa tree, called Te Waha-O-Rerekohu. According to Maori mythology, its red flowers represent the blood of Tawhaki, a spirit ancestor who died while showing his people the path to heaven. Traditional Maori bury the placenta of their newborns at the roots of pohutukawa trees, thus creating over the generations literal family trees. This particular one is thought to be around six hundred years old, and has twenty-two trunks. In the nearby town of Te Kaha, Maori Paul O'Brien and his family own and operate a home-stay called the Te Kaha Lodge. Evenings here include a welcome song and ceremony, a sunset soak in an outdoor hot tub overlooking White Island, dinner, and songs that last late into the night. By the end, everyone has become a *chay*, or friend, and many travelers extend their stay to work on Paul's kiwi farm. While in the area, also visit the Millennium Waka, the war canoe New Zealand contributed to the international celebration in 2000. Built by the finest Maori craftsmen, it was never finished and sits on a beach, exposed to the elements. "It is absolutely breathtaking," Claire says.

* The New Zealand Maori Arts and Crafts Institute in Te Puia, Rotorua welcomes visitors to their premises, where students from tribes across the country study traditional carving and weaving techniques. Maori concerts are held midday and a Mai Ora (song and dance feast) is thrown in the evening. You can also take a guided tour of the grounds, which include a habitat for New Zealand's national endangered

bird—the kiwi—and the neighboring Whakarewarewa Geothermal Valley.

* If traveling with easily awed children, consider the Tamaki Maori Village in Rotorua. Before you may enter, the village chief sends out a warrior to give your group a "challenge" to determine whether or not you've come in peace. Tribally painted and costumed performers then hold a grand *powhiri*, or welcome dance, and lead you to a meeting house for welcoming speeches. Afterward, you are free to walk the grounds to catch demonstrations of poi twirling, hand games, and chants. Join the other visitors in a sit-down traditional *hangi* feast, where baskets of meat, vegetables, and dessert are smoked and steamed atop hot stones beneath the earth. The evening concludes with a *poroporoaki*, or closing ceremony, of songs and speeches.

* A famous Maori legend tells of Pania, a lovely maiden who lived in the sea on the eastern coast of North Island. Because her stream had the sweetest water, a strapping young Maori named Karitoki sipped from it every evening. After weeks of gazing at him from afar, she finally stepped out of the water. Falling fast in love, they married on the spot and he whisked her off to his *whare*, or house. At sunrise, however, Pania's siren friends called her back. After a heated fight, Karitoki reluctantly allowed his bride to spend her days with her friends and her nights with him. Later, however, a village elder remarked that if Pania ate cooked food, she'd be forever banished from the sea. That night, Karitoki slipped a piece into her mouth but she promptly spat it out and bolted for the sea. He chased her to the water's edge, but she

slipped from his fingers and he never saw her again. In 1954, the Art Deco port city of Napier unveiled a 140-pound bronze statue of *Pania on the Reef* in commemoration of the sad tale. She's since become a prized symbol of New Zealand, though she went missing for a few days in 2005. The police found her, however, and plopped her back on her pedestal.

RECOMMENDED READING

The Bone People by Keri Hulme

68
Istanbul, Turkey
Whirling Dervishes

THEIR NAME MEANS "THOSE WHO HAVE CHOSEN THE ROAD OF suffering" and their ecstatic dance was born the afternoon a Sufi philosopher named Rumi strolled through the coppersmiths' bazaar in Konya, Turkey in the thirteenth century. Mesmerized by the rhythmic sound of their hammers on the metal, he began to twirl—right in the street—and one by one, the coppersmiths joined him. The Mevlevi Order was founded thereafter, better known today as the Whirling Dervishes.

When performing, Mevlevis usually enter the stage wearing black robes (which symbolize their coffins) and cone-shaped hats (their tombstones). After taking their places, they fling off the cloaks to reveal bright white tunics and bell-shaped skirts (their shroud). Then the music begins: a slow drum beat followed by a reed flute, a zither, and other ethereal instruments. The Mevlevis circle the stage several times, bowing deeply, before they begin to spin counter-clockwise with their right hands raised to receive the blessings of heaven and their left hands funneling the gifts down to earth. This ceremony, called *sema*, represents the Sufi's journey toward a closer union with God, and their attempt to see Him in every direction of the compass. "Dancing," as Rumi aptly described it, "is not rising to your feet painlessly like a speck of dust blown around the wind. Dancing is when you rise above both worlds, tearing your heart to pieces and giving up your soul."

Istanbul hosts a number of *sema,* the best of which is held at the Galata Mevlevi Monastery on Tunel Galip Dede Cadesi 15. Sufis twirl in reverence of Allah to live music here at least one Sunday a month (usually the last) around 3 P.M. Another highly recommended option is contacting Les Arts Turcs at Incili Çavus Sok 37 Kat 3 near the Aya Sophia. On Monday evenings they give lectures about Sufism in their gallery and then take groups to a small monastery in Istanbul-Fatih for a performance. Travelers and Turks alike enjoy Café Mesale, a tea garden and restaurant at Arasta Carsisi 45 near the Blue Mosque. In addition to savory foods, hot teas, and games like backgammon, Mesale holds live music nightly that often includes Dervishes. More performance than ceremony, this will suffice if no other shows are available. For a more unusual spectacle, go to the nineteenth-century Sirkeci Train Station, the old terminus for the *Orient Express.* Dervishes twirl here several nights a week (usually Sunday, Wednesday, and Friday) at Platform I in the exhibition hall.

Turks say that you can't appreciate the Mevlevis without understanding Rumi, and you can't get Rumi until you've visited his burial city of Konya. About three hundred miles southeast of Istanbul, this Anatolian city is a major pilgrimage site for Muslims. During its mid-December Mevlana Festival, Mevlevis whirl at the Mevlana Tekke Monastery. Dozens of dervishes lived here from Rumi's day until 1925, when the government shut it down because of its immense popularity with foreign tourists. (They feared the Dervishes symbolized the backwardness of the Turkish empire.) Mevlevis were suppressed for about twenty-five years, until the government recognized their cultural importance.

Fortunately, enough old dervishes remained to pass the techniques on to the next generation.

Some say that Rumi taught women to whirl as well (including his daughter-in-law Fatima), but they got nudged out of *sema*
in later generations. During the celebrations surrounding the
700-year anniversary of Rumi's passing, some women picked it
up again, and you can occasionally spot them twirling at *sema*
(albeit in red or blue tunics instead of white).

Keep in mind that however cosmopolitan Turkey seems, it is
conservative. Harassment can be intense if you don't dress mod-
estly, and it's best to travel here in a group or with a male.

RECOMMENDED READING

Women Called to the Path of Rumi by Shakina Reinhertz

Hawai'i
Island Goddesses

GODDESSES REIGN SUPREME IN THE TROPICAL ISLAND OF HAWAI'I. There's Laka, goddess of the hula, Hina of the moon, Namakaokahai of the waves, and Poliahu of the snow, but the grand diva is Pele, who presides over the volcanoes. Legend has it that she secretly envies her beautiful sister Poliahu, and the two often get into catfights over gods and mortals. Poliahu usu ally wins, causing Pele to erupt in fury, and Poliahu gets stuck cleaning the mess with her snow and ice afterward. (Geology lends credence to this story: traces of lava have been found seeping through glacial ice caps at various epochs in history.) Even when Pele triumphs, she soon tires of her lovers and sends them racing down the mountain, trailed by her hot, molten lava. Those who don't make it can be seen in the form of strange rock pillars that speckle the volcanic fields. Despite her flaws, Hawaiians revere Pele, calling her She Who Shapes The Sacred Land in their ancient chants. Indeed, her lava has been creating new land on the southeastern shore since 1983—more than seventy acres, at last count. (Though, truth be told, she has also destroyed more than one hundred structures.) To see Pele in action, head to the Big Island.

Within a few hours' drive on the Big Island, you'll pass every possible landscape, from black lava deserts to tropical forests to subarctic mountain peaks. Allow ample time to lounge upon the white-sand beaches at Kona Coast and the black-sand beaches at Puna district. Soak in a 90-degree thermal pool set in lava rock at Ahalanui Beach Park. Then continue on to Hawai'i Volcanoes National Park, home of the most active volcano on the planet: Kilauea. Rather than spew like a geyser, Kilauea oozes along the ground. At night, the mountain sometimes glows red with lava. The park also offers 140 miles of hiking trails over hills covered with pumice and cinder cones. Wear good hiking shoes and long pants, and be extremely wary of volcanic fumes, coastline collapses, and methane gas explosions. Pele is said to dwell in the Halema'uma'u Crater Overlook, where trails lead down to the 1982 lava-flow site. Devotees leave her offerings of flowers, gin, and ohelo berries. In 1824, a chieftess named Kapiolani defiantly ate the berries instead and then hiked up Pele's volcano and descended into her crater, saying "I fear not Pele." This was largely a ploy to encourage Hawaiians to convert to Christianity, but it was hardly successful: even non-Hawaiians make pilgrimages here today.

"I slipped a shell that had been with me for a long time into her crevice and said a prayer," says artist Rachel DayStar Payne of Corpus Christi, Texas. "I think women can relate to volcanoes because they are like hot juicy vulvas, and people bow down before them and honor the power within them. They are a direct cord to the center of the earth and spew forth for the world to see."

On your way out of the park, stop by the Volcano Art Center, a nonprofit arts organization that sells paintings, wood carvings, jewelry, quilts, and pottery by more than three hundred artists. It also offers special programs like Hawaiian music and dance concerts, language classes, and hula workshops. Then

www.nps.gov/havo/visitor/lava.htm

pay homage to Poliahu, whose frost and snow almost always crests the highest mountain peak on earth (if you count from the ocean floor to the top): Mauna Kea. This volcano is widely considered an ancestral burial ground, so protests were fierce when astronomers built the world's largest observatory here. Leave Poliahu or the goddess of your choice an offering at the altar and then find a good place to watch the sunset. You'll fast see why Hawaiians consider their homeland to be Earth's connecting point to the universe.

RECOMMENDED READING

Hawaiian Goddesses, 'Alua—Second Generation by Linda Ching

VIII
Just-Go-There Places

70 *Esfahān, Iran*

AN OLD PERSIAN PROVERB SAYS IT BEST: *ESFAHĀN NESF-E JAHĀN AST,*
or "Esfahān is half of the world." Full of gardens and tea houses,
palaces and covered bridges, this blue-tiled city is a paragon. A
few weeks here and you just might compose a song in its honor,
as did Duke Ellington.

Esfahān's architectural wonders date back to the eleventh
century. Of particular note is the exquisite Sioseh Pol bridge
spanning the Zayandeh river. Locals gather here to sing (the
thirty-three vaulted archways have great acoustics), picnic, and
sip tea in the tiny shop inside a pillar. Then there's the Sheikh
Lotfollah Mosque, a seventeenth-century structure covered with
mosaics that change color with the sunlight, from moccasin to
rose. It was once known as the Women's Mosque, as its underground tunnel to Ali Qapu Palace allowed women to attend
prayers incognito. Another not-to-be-missed site is the Grand
Bazaar, located on the northern side of Naghsh-I Jahan, or Imam
Square. One of the oldest and largest bazaars in the Middle East,
it is an explosion of color, spices, and music. Souvenir choices
range from antique silver jewelry to camel bone paintings, but
most travelers come here for the carpets: Turkomans, Gabbehs,
Qashqai bedrolls, and, of course, the luxurious Esfahans.

A fun goal in Esfahān is to sample every *ghahveh khaneh,* or
coffee house, in town. Most Iranians prefer tea to joe, and the

color and aroma of the leaves are equally as important as the taste. Shakes are another favorite, with flavors like banana, orange, and melon. And don't forget the sweets: *gaz,* a nougat chock-full of pistachios; *pashmak,* divinely spun sugar; and anything with saffron, including ice cream, *halva* (brownies), and rice pudding with almonds.

As a woman, you'll need to cover up in Iran—including your hair—but consider it your ticket into a world entirely unknown to men. Shirin Shokouhi, an Iranian-American psychotherapist in New York City, particularly enjoys the tradition of *rozeh* on her visits home. Whenever a woman feels in need of spiritual assistance, she invites over her inner-circle of female relatives, neighbors, and friends as well as a holy woman. Wearing their chadors, the women sit together upon cushions to pray and wail as the holy woman sings hymns. After a good hour of collective catharsis, the hostess brings out the food, which usually includes a hearty pot of soup called *ash-e reshteh* (whose noodles represent the different paths of life).

"And that's when the fun begins," says Shirin. "The women sit atop rugs and chat about their marriages, children, neighbors, one another. Then the hostess ladles out stew for each woman to take with her, so the spirit of the event will follow them home."

RECOMMENDED READING

Persepolis I and *Embroideries* by Marjane Satrapi

71 Places to Pet Fuzzy Animals

ADMIT IT. SMALL, FUZZY ANIMALS MAKE YOU SQUEAL. FOSTER THOSE feelings in the following spaces:

* The giant panda is one of the world's most endangered animals, with only 1,600 prowling in the wild and fewer than two hundred in captivity. Poaching is a problem—though it was punishable by death in China until a decade ago—but so is the difficulty inherent in reproduction. Baby pandas weigh about 1/900th of their mother's weight and are so helpless, mothers can only care for one at a time. Additional cubs are usually abandoned and die a few days after birth. Pandas also tend to refrain from mating in captivity, so have to be artificially inseminated. "Mr. Panda no like making love," is the explanation usually given to visitors of zoos and research institutes in Asia, but some scientists believe that captive pandas simply don't know how to procreate. A few keepers in China and Thailand have successfully remedied this problem by showing "panda porn" videos to their males (who are believed to be more stimulated from the

soundtrack than the images). Perhaps the best place to visit pandas is China's Sichuan province, home of the Giant Panda Breeding Research Base located six miles north of Chengdu. Between thirty to fifty pandas live here at any given time. Go in autumn to see the newborns sleeping in their nursery, and at 9:30 A.M. to watch the pandas feed. For a fee, you can cuddle with a young panda, feed it an apple, and snap a commemorative photo. The Research Base also has an assortment of red pandas, which resemble raccoons.

❋ Koalas can be spotted chewing eucalyptus leaves in the forks of trees throughout the eastern coast of Australia—from Adelaide to Cape York Peninsula—and into the hinterland. Like sloths, they have an extremely low metabolic rate and usually spend twenty hours of their day either sleeping or being utterly motionless. Their joeys are born the size of a jelly bean and have no hair, ears, or eyesight. They spend their first six months attached to their mother's nipples inside her pouch and another six clamped on to her back. The daughters then venture off on their own, while the sons—like all good mama's boys—stick around another year or two. Billabong Koala Park at 61 Billabong Drive in Port Macquarie, New South Wales, has three koala pattings a day, at 10:30 A.M., 1:30 P.M., and 3:30 P.M. The nearby Koala Hospital on Lord Street treats between 150 to 200 sick or injured koalas a year and accepts volunteers (or donations). Janet Jackson and Pope John Paul II are among the celebrities who've "cuddled" the 130-plus koalas at Lone Pine Koala Sanctuary. Located eight miles west of Brisbane, the sanctuary also has an assortment of

www.midcoast.com/users/koalabos

WWW.

wombats, dingoes, kangaroos, and Tasmanian devils. It is worth noting, however, that most regions of Australia have banned cuddling (as opposed to patting), claiming it stresses out the animals.

* In the mid-'90s, horrific forest fires and logging in the virgin forests of Central Borneo sent wild orangutans into villages looking for food. Many mothers were captured and eaten by equally hungry villagers, who then caged their infants for resale. The Forest Police managed to rescue hundreds of these infants, but hundreds more are believed to now be house pets (or worse) in other parts of the country (if not the world). Those that get confiscated during raids (or are voluntarily given up by their owners) are sent to the Nyaru Menteng Orangutan Reintroduction Project eighteen miles outside Palangka Raya, the capital of Central Kalimantan in Indonesia. Founded by a Danish woman, the Project returns the orangutans to protected forests after a carefully monitored transitional period that includes a health check and microchip insertion for future identification. They welcome volunteers and donations, but one of the best ways to help orangutans is to simply refrain from buying tropical hardwood furniture, picture frames, and other knickknacks, as it is often illegally logged.

www.orangutan.com/theprojects/
NyaruMenteng/nyarumenteng.htm

72 *Luang Prabang, Laos*

DURING THE VIETNAM WAR, JOURNALISTS RENAMED IT THE LAND of a Million Irrelevants from its former The Land of a Million Elephants. Soon after, it won the distinction of being history's most bombed nation—and land mines still lurk beneath its earth. Amazingly, its people are so laid back and peaceful, Asians say they don't grow rice, but rather, they sit back and *listen* to it grow.

"Laos is really beautiful like Thailand, but with little of its development," says Lisa Bosler, a Chicagoan who spent a year in Southeast Asia. "Traveling here is like walking into another time—another way of living through time."

About a hundred and twenty miles from the capital, hidden in the jungle, is a holy city that has been a backpacker favorite for years: Luang Prabang. Rise early in the morning to watch young monks in saffron robes flood into the streets, rattling their alms bowls. You can tell the phase of the moon by their heads: they shave when it's full. All of Luang Prabang's sixty-six temples are worth a visit, but if time only allows for one, it should be the Wat Xieng Thong. Built in 1560, it features a three-tiered roof that dips down to the earth before soaring toward the sky, and is crowned with delicately carved stupas that somehow escaped shelling by the Chinese Black Flag Haw Army in the 1880s. (Word has it, one of the invaders studied at the wat during his own monk days.) The walls are covered with mosaics that tell the stories of gods and kings. Explore the grounds, where monks-in-training play chess and tell jokes beneath shade trees.

For lunch, head to the cafes along the river front, where the Mekong meets the Nam Khan. Laotian cuisine is liberally spiced with fresh basil, lemongrass, mint, coriander, and lime juice, plus salty-sweet flavors like fish sauce, shrimp paste, and the occasional heap of dried river moss. Their tangy green papaya salad is especially good. Wash it all down with Beerlao, the national beverage, or some fermented rice wine sucked out of a clay jar with a reed straw. French colonists left behind their dessert tray: savor freshly baked croissants, pastries, and strong coffee along Sisavangvong Road. (Try Joma Bakery Café.)

You can do a fair amount of shopping damage in Luang Prabang. Pathana Boupha Antique House at 29/4 Ban Visoun sells jewelry, silver, and textiles. For naturally dyed Lao silk and cotton, try Ock Pop Tok at 73/5 Ban Wat Nong, which is both a gallery and workshop. (They make custom-tailored garments, too.) Nearly every night at dusk, hundreds of Hmong, Mien, and Thais descend from their mountain villages to set up shop along Sisavangvong Road. Haggle over woven-silk shawls, hand-stitched leather, and handmade paper in the lantern light, then enjoy a bowl of rice noodles and tofu, meat, or vegetables at one of the many food stalls.

Luang Prabang throws vibrant festivals. The three-day Songkan Water Festival kicks off the Lao New Year in April. While not as anarchic as it is in Thailand or Burma, you'll still get soaked by children armed with high-powered water guns. Watch the parade on the second day of festivities, and climb Phu Si on the fourth. Near the end of October, Laotians celebrate the end of wet season during Bun Awk Phansa. Watch locals set thousands of candles afloat in the river, then pick up a drum or firestick and head into the street to celebrate.

73 *Bountiful Gardens*

WHAT IS TRAVELING ALL ABOUT, IF NOT STOPPING TO SMELL THE roses? The following gardens feature the most fragrant ones:

* For many a Briton, gardening is second only to the weather when it comes to making small talk. They simply adore it, and thus boast some of the world's loveliest gardens. Not a petal is out of place at the Kew, 300 acres of botanical delights on the south bank of the Thames River in southwest London. Officially established by Princess Augusta in 1759, its grounds include Kew Palace, where King George III was quarantined during his fit of madness in the early 1800s; the Waterlily House, full of tropical ornamental aquatic plants and climbers; the Princess of Wales Conservatory, a greenhouse with ten climatic zones; the Rose Garden, with fifty-four rose beds; and 250-year-old ginkgo biloba trees reportedly undergoing sex changes.

   www.rbgkew.org.uk

   "All of the plants were brought back to Kew not just to satisfy curiosity or to increase the royal menagerie but to attempt to recreate the garden of Eden by uniting all of the plants of the world," says Nicole Fraser, an American who took up gardening soon after moving to Great Britain. "I love to take tea in the Orangerie on an inevitably wet day, looking out over the gardens. It is necessary for survival while living in London."

* The English are also quite proud of Sissinghurst Garden in Kent, designed by poet Vita Sackville-West. A bisexual who counted Virginia Woolf among her many lovers, Sackville-West wrote about gardening for years in her column in *The Observer.* Her (gay) husband did much of the architectural planning for this sumptuous garden, while she did all the planting. It is laid out as a series of rooms, each with a different theme or color, and the high hedges serve as walls.

* Kyoto, Japan showcases four types of traditional gardens: *funa asobi* (created for water "pleasures" like boat outings), *shuybe* (for strolling), *kansho* (for contemplation), and *kaiyu* (for all of the above). Daisen-In in Kita-ku, Murasakino, Daitokuji-cho (near Kitaoji station) is considered a masterpiece in Zen gardening and is far less crowded than the more famous Ryoan-ji. Its carefully-placed stones in white sand represent natural wonders like waterfalls and mountain lakes. Also visit the nearby Koto-In, a moss garden filled with bamboo and maple trees. Then take Bus 33 from Kyoto station to Nishikyo-ku, a seventcenth-century villa with tea houses set around a large pond and gardens (the forty-minute tour gives a detailed historial background). If you're lucky enough to be in Japan during plum or cherry blossom seasons in

March and April, visit the fabulous (and free) Kyoto Imperial Palace Park.

❋ Known as the Kyoto of China, Suzhou features rock and water gardens with great names like Pavilion of the Surging Waves and Garden to Linger In. Popular consensus is that the Garden of the Master of the Nets off Shiquan Jie on Wangshi Yuan is the best garden in Suzhou. Laid out in the twelfth century, it was abandoned for centuries before being restored in the 1900s. In the evenings, hop from pavilion to pavilion, watching traditional performing artists. Then check out the Couple's Garden on Ou Yuan near the Museum of Opera and Theater and stroll hand-in-hand with a lover or friend along the ponds, bridges, and canals.

❋ Every Russian, it seems, is born with an emerald thumb. Most families keep gardens in their *dacha*—or countryside cottage—that at minimum include tomatoes, cucumbers, potatoes, peppers, and mounds of dill. Urban dwellers, meanwhile, grow seedlings on their balconies and line their floors with jars of homemade pickles and jellies. Spend a significant amount of time in Russia and you're almost assured to land an invitation to a *dacha;* otherwise, hop a train to the countryside, where you can view the bountiful gardens, and the kerchiefed *babushki* tending them, from the window.

❋ To experience gardening in a pagan light, visit Manhattan's Lower East Side during a solstice or equinox for an Earth Celebration. Held by members of the fifty-plus community gardens, these pageants feature belly dancers, fire dancers, opera singers, and giant puppets who parade throughout the neighborhood beseeching passersby to "save our gardens" from developers. All events evolve into giant street parties, complete with drum circles and bonfires.

RECOMMENDED READING

Great Gardens of the World by Penelope Hobhouse

TOURS

Coopersmiths is one of the oldest garden tour companies, with ten to twelve tours to choose from each year (www.coopersmiths.com).

74 *Kraków, Poland*

ACCORDING TO HINDU LEGEND, LORD SHIVA ONCE CAST SEVEN stones into the world, and the sites where they landed became thriving centers of spiritual energy. The medieval city of Kraków was purportedly built upon one of them in the seventh century, and is today a magical destination. Situated on the banks of the Vistula River, it is studded with castles, stained-glass churches, palaces, and a 700-year-old university, all ornately adorned with Renaissance, Gothic, Romanesque, or Baroque finishes. You could spend weeks traversing the cobblestoned alleyways of Stare Miasto (Old Town) and Rynek Glowny (Grand Square), savoring wine in dark cellars and composing letters in dimly-lit cafes. (The Art Nouveau-styled Café Jama Michalika at Ulica Florianska 45 has particularly good ambiance.) Be sure to sample some Zubrowka, bison-grass vodka that was once forbidden in America because of its supposedly psychotropic properties.

Kraków has endured its share of anguish, particularly in World War II, when invading Nazis banished most of its Jewish community to nearby concentration camps (including Auschwitz). The old Jewish quarter of Kazimierz memorializes this genocide in the Remu'h Synagogue on Ulica Szeroka. The district has been revitalized in recent years—thanks in part to the movie *Schindler's List,* which was filmed here—and now has a vibrant café, bar, and club scene with live klezmer music and poetry slams. For traditional Jewish food, try Café Ariel at Ulica Szeroka 18; to soak in some communist kitsch, check out Propaganda on Ulica Miodowa.

Of its 2.5 million works of art, Kraków is proudest of Leonardo da Vinci's *Lady with an Ermine*. One of only three female portraits da Vinci painted, she has suffered a little damage in the past 500 years, but remains a knock-out. Her subject is said to be Cecilia Gallerani, the poetry-writing, music-composing, seventeen-year-old mistress of the Duke of Milan. The painting was stolen by the Nazis in 1939 but returned to Poland a year later and now resides in the Czartoryski Museum at Ulica Sw Jana 19. Another painting revered by Poles is the *Black Madonna* in the Jasna Góra Monastery in Częstochowa, seventy miles northwest of Kraków. Painted in the fourteenth century, she traveled to Poland all the way from Jerusalem, only to be captured in 1430 by a gang of Hussites who cut her face. When she started bleeding, the thieves dropped her and fled. As monks nursed her wounds, water sprung from the ground and continues to flow here to this day. A few centuries later, the *Black Madonna* saved her monastery from Swedish invaders (which some claim changed the course of the war) and she was crowned Queen and Protector of Poland. She still attracts crowds by the thousands, particularly on holidays, when pilgrims walk here from various parts of the country bearing gifts of cigarettes and kielbasa.

75 *Famed Opera Houses*

TRUTH BE TOLD, WOMEN FARE RATHER MISERABLY IN OPERA. Madame Butterfly commits suicide samurai-style when the father of her child marries another woman. Carmen is murdered by an old lover-turned-lunatic. Tosca may stab her would-be rapist with a triumphant "And this is Tosca's kiss!" in Act II, but by the end of Act III, she is leaping from the ramparts of a castle to her death. But, misogynistic plots aside, it's quite pleasant being a female observer of these spectacles. What better way to spend a starry night than slipping into a ball gown and sipping champagne while being royally entertained in some of the grandest buildings ever constructed?

* Start your opera house tour in Italy. Milan's Teatro alla Scala is one of the world's most celebrated houses. Inaugurated in 1778 with Salieri's opera-ballet *L'Europa Riconosciuta* (Europe Revealed), it featured a gallery called the *loggione* for less wealthy patrons, who gave performers real-time reviews via adoring cheers or contemptuous whistles (thus La Scala's reputation for being a "baptism by fire" establishment for performers). In the old days, the house was lit by more than a thousand oil lamps, which the managers kept in check with hundreds of nearby buckets of water. La Scala recently reopened after tens of millions in renovations, including the

installation of tiny, simultaneous-translation screens on each of the 1,800 seats so that audience members can follow the libretto in English, German, Italian, or French.

* Then head to Venice for an opera house aptly named La Fenice, or the Phoenix, as it helps operas "rise from the ashes" during their world premieres here. This house has actually risen a few times itself, having burned to the ground in 1774, 1836, and 1996. The first opera played after its grand reopening in 2003 was *La Traviata* (whose courtesan heroine sacrifices everything for love, only to die of consumption in the final act).

* Go next to Paris, home of the Palais Garnier on the northern end of avenue de l'Opéra. Palais Garnier was built upon ground so swampy, it had to be pumped for months before the foundation could be laid and later required a reservoir to be built beneath it (a situation that later inspired the *Phantom of the Opera*). Palais Garnier was inaugurated in 1875 with Fromental Halévy's *La Juive*, or *The Jewess* (whose heroine plunges into a bubbling cauldron of oil at the end of Act V). An ornate neo-Baroque building, it boasts a six-ton chandelier, marble friezes and columns, and ceilings painted by Marc Chagall.

* Perhaps the most distinctive opera house is situated on Bennelong Point in Sydney Harbour, Australia. Formally opened by Queen Elizabeth II in 1973, the Sydney Opera House consists of spherical-sectioned shells plastered with

www.teatrolafenice.it
www.operadeparis.fr
www.sydneyoperahouse.com

more than a million glazed white granite tiles. Inside are more than one thousand rooms, including five theaters, two main halls, five rehearsal studios, and a flurry of bars, shops, and restaurants. The Concert Hall contains the world's largest mechanical tracker action organ, with 10,000 pipes. All told, the Sydney Opera House uses the same amount of energy as a town of 25,000 people.

❂ The first house of the Metropolitan Opera of New York City caught ablaze; the second turned out to be too small. It reopened in its current Lincoln Center location in 1966 with *Antony and Cleopatra* (whose heroine kills herself with the poison of an asp after her lover dies in her arms). Today, 4,000 opera buffs can catch seven performances of four to five different productions a week. The Met features two Chagall murals, the world's largest tab curtain (custom-woven with gold damask), and berry tarts that are downright scrumptious at the bar.

www.metoperafamily.org
www.bolshoi.ru
W W W

❂ Although it is perpetually under *remont* (construction), Moscow's Bolshoi Theater is thrilling to behold. It, too, bursts into flames on occasion, but the latest building is a masterpiece of nineteenth-century Russian neoclassicism, with an eight-columned portico crested by Apollo, god of the arts. Renowned for its ballet, it premiered Tchaikovsky's *Swan Lake* in 1877 and remains the home of the Bolshoi Ballet. It has also been the site of major political events, including the first All Union Congress of Soviets, which officially announced the creation of the Soviet Union in 1922. It remains one of the cheapest places in the world to see first-rate opera, including Russian classics like *Yevgeny Onegin* (whose heroine actually stands up for herself and rejects Onegin in the final act, escaping with both her life and dignity intact). Celebrate this milestone victory with a glass of Soviet champagne in the parlor.

76 Senegal

SENEGAL'S CONFLUENCE OF FRENCH, MUSLIM, AND AFRICAN cultures means dining on croissants in the morning, lamb kebabs grilled over hot coals on the sidewalk in the afternoon, thick stews eaten with your fingertips in the evening, and fresh seafood drenched in lime juice and sprinkled with peanuts at any time of the day or night. Sprawled along the tip of the rocky Cap-Vert peninsula, capital city Dakar offers nearly year-round sunshine and is a good (albeit chaotic) base for exploring the rest of the vibrant nation. Just beware of price gouging: you must haggle for everything here.

❀ Thanks to pop star Youssou N'Dour, Senegalese music has gained international fame for its kinetic combination of West African drums and electric guitar riffs. Catching a live show is a must, if possible, at the legendary Thiossane in Dakar, which N'Dour owns and where he often makes special appearances when in town. Saint Louis hosts a jazz festival each May that lures tens of thousands of spectators, as does Goree Island. Drum and dance classes also abound, and Marie Basse Wiles—a famous dancer who emigrated to New York—leads annual tours of students here to study with the masters.

WWW · www.saintlouisjazz.com

● If Dakar proves overwhelming, take refuge in Toubab Diallo, a fishing village overlooking the Atlantic Ocean. Spend a few days in the Sobo-Bade, a hotel built of local stone and decorated with shells from the beach below. After an afternoon of drumming and batik classes, wash down curry with bottomless cups of *bissap,* or hibiscus flower tea, in its café.

● Twenty miles east of Dakar is an aptly named lake: the plankton in Lac Rose (Pink Lake) literally makes it shimmer pink. It is also so heavily salinized, you practically float to its surface. In January, Lac Rose is the ending point of the world's most dangerous off-road motorsport event, the Dakar Rally, in which five hundred or so motor vehicles race to get here from Portugal (via the Sahara Desert) in just sixteen days. Join in the festivities afterward.

● No woman should leave Senegal without a belly bracelet or two. Made of shells, beads, or leather, they are a traditional Senegalese accessory that, according to artisan Krista Claudene-Retto, were sometimes worn as blessings against evil. Men wore them above their biceps and around their waist; babies, on their ankle; and women, around their lower belly. Today, the larger, thicker beads that click are worn during community celebrations, while the more delicate ones are worn by women beneath their clothing as a quiet homage to the feminine. "Beware of men who try to break your bracelet," Krista warns. "They say in Senegal that he's the one you'll marry!"

www.kclaudene.com

77
Ubud, Bali

IT SEEMS THAT EVERY BALINESE IS A PAINTER, A DANCER, A MUSICIAN, or a singer, and after a few days soaking in their artwork, you'll start to believe that you are one, too. The city of Ubud is the perfect entrée into this colorful culture.

Museums are ubiquitous here, but start your tour at the Agung Rai Museum on Jalan Pengosekan. Housed in a Balinese-style building surrounded by four hectares of tropical gardens, ponds, and fountains, this cultural center showcases the wide range of arts on the island. The museum has a permanent exhibit of paintings, textiles, photography, and sculpture by famous Balinese artists as well as expats who've made their homes here, and dance performances are held every Saturday and Sunday night. The Agung Rai also offers more than a dozen workshops: everything from "offering making" and Hindu astrology to woodcarving, cooking, and batik-making. Browse through their bookstore and relax with a mango smoothie in their café.

Next stop should be the marvelous Seniwati Gallery of Art by Women at Jalan Sriwedari 2B. Founded by a British expat in 1991, the gallery features the artwork of more than one hundred Balinese, Indonesian, and expat women—the first of its kind in Asia. The difference from the artwork in the Agung

WWW.
www.armamuseum.com
www.seniwatigallery.com

Rai is immediately apparent: female subjects are never portrayed as sex objects, and the art is more straightforward and inviting. The Sewanti holds workshops and mentoring programs for young girls, whose paintings hang in the foyer and are sold in the store. Proceeds go to a scholarship fund that helps finance the college education of the most promising students.

Catching a traditional dance performance is a must. If possible, forgo the shows held in hotels and venture into the countryside. (The tourist office can give you a schedule for neighboring villages.) Twelve young women in floral crowns and twelve young men with painted mustaches artfully meld dance, music, and chorus in the Janger dance, a folk number dating back to the 1930s. Children will love the more touristy Kecak dance. Taken from the Hindu epic *Ramayana,* it tells the story of Princess Sita's kidnapping by the treacherous King of Lanka and subsequent rescue by Prince Rama. One hundred topless men serve as the chorus, swaying their bodies and pounding their chests as they cry out, *"Chack-achack-achack."* It is often performed at night around a bonfire.

Religion is an intrinsic part of Balinese life. Fresh fruits, flowers, candles, and incense are reverently laid out each morning as gifts to the gods; nearly every day of the year is marked with an ancient rite or ritual. Saraswati, goddess of knowledge and the literary arts, is held in especially high regard. Balinese honor her by intentionally *not* reading or writing on her holiday, opting instead to make offerings before stacks of books.

In Bali, even the dinkiest tourist-traps sell gems like Javanese puppets, Kalimantan-style textiles, and Sumbawan sarongs. A great place to purchase souvenirs is the Bali Cares Shop at Jalan Hanoman 44B, next to the Tegun Gallery. A not-for-profit cooperative that sells locally-made crafts like bone and coconut carving, rattan work, and weaving, Bali Cares sends its proceeds to community-based groups like Bali Jani (a foundation that provides legal aid and microcredit loans to women) and Yayasan Bumi Sehat (a health center where patients exchange handicrafts for free birthing and health care). Bali Cares also served as an information center after the December 2004 tsunami, mobilizing relief efforts and sending aid to families.

RESOURCES

Bali Blog: One Stop Travel Guide to Bali at www.baliblog.com.

78
Classic Castles

WHY DO WE LOVE CASTLES SO? THE UNABASHED POWER AND WEALTH, the tales of courtly intrigue, the knockout views of the inevitable seaside cliff? Or those long-harbored dreams of someday being whisked away to one by a dashing prince on a white stallion? Whatever the reason, here are some classics:

* High atop the volcanic crag of Castle Rock stands the mighty Edinburgh Castle of Scotland, visible from nearly every point in the city and—at 1 P.M.—audible, when its cannons roar. (In the days before timepieces, the cannon allowed sailors to reset their chronometers.) The site of innumerable battles and sieges, the castle kept a prison that brutalized so many captives, ghosts are ubiquitous, including a marching line  of headless drummers. Riches are also stored within the castle, including St. Margaret's Chapel (a stone structure built by David I in memory of his mother) and the Stone of Destiny upon which Scottish Kings were crowned. The optimal time to visit is during the Winter Festival of Hogmanay, when fireworks explode above the castle's towers and turrets as 100,000

revelers spill into the streets to herald the new year. If conscious the morning after, tie on your tennies and return to the castle for the mile-long "One O'Clock Run" down to Royal Park.

❉ Scotland's Stirling Castle has existed in some form or fashion since prehistoric times, and has seen its share of drama, though none as infamous as that endured by Mary, Queen of Scots. Crowned queen at just nine months of age, she endured three lousy marriages and a toxic relationship with her cousin, Queen Elizabeth I, before getting beheaded in three increments. (Her head finally rolled on to the floor when the executioner grabbed it by the wig.) One of Queen Mary's attendants, known as the Green Lady, is occasionally seen floating about the hallways. Stirling's sprawling esplanade is used for open-air concerts for acts like REM, Bob Dylan, and the Celtic band Runrig, as well as the city's Hogmanay celebrations.

www.edinburghcastle.biz
www.consy.com
W W W.

❉ Built in five years flat by King Edward I, the Conwy Castle is the most outstanding fortress in all North Wales, if not Europe. Dark-stoned and gritty, it features eight massive drum towers individually floodlit after nightfall, and panoramic views of the Snowdonia peaks and River Conwy. Enter via one of three jostling bridges and walk along its defensive walls, which stretch three quarters of a mile and are flanked by twenty-four towers and gateways. If visiting in May, drive seven miles south to the Bodnant Garden for the blossoming of its yellow laburnums (a.k.a. golden chain trees). Just don't eat any: laburnum poisoning causes incessant frothing at the mouth and convulsions, which would be highly unpleasant while actualizing fairy princess fantasies.

* Fans of horror flicks will get a kick out of Frankenstein's Castle in central Germany, a fifteen-minute drive outside Darmstadt. Built in 1252 by Conrad von Frankenstein, it is the quintessential haunted castle, desolate and spooky (thus Universal Pictures' decision to film its 1931 classic here). Some historians say that Mary Wollstonecraft Shelley (daughter of feminist Mary Wollstonecraft and anarchist William Godwin) based her classic novel on the castle after a trip to Germany in the early 1800s. The "real" Frankenstein is said to have been Johann Konrad Dippel, an alchemist who boiled hair and bones by candlelight in the seventeenth century, inventing new types of acid poison. If traveling with children, visit during the nine-day Frankenstein Halloween Fest, which includes monster shows with cameos by Dracula and Mr. Hyde.

79 *Morocco*

Travel books invariably describe Morocco as a "full-throttle assault on the senses," and there really is no better way to put it. Women traveling here should proceed with caution, however. Sexual harassment can be extreme, and it is best not to wander about alone unless you speak the language and are appropriately covered.

As the Moroccans say, "All roads lead to The Place." In Marrakesh, this Place is the Jemaa El-Fna: bus station by day, thriving souk by night. In its labyrinth, you'll spy men walking barefoot through fire while artists blow glass, dentists yank teeth, herbalists scribble prescriptive potions, and acrobats turn flips. Dance with transvestites to the sounds of reed flutes and wooden drums before haggling with vendors over their piles of bangles, silverware, pottery, and Persian rugs. Then hit the food stalls, where old men stir fragrant delights in bubbling cauldrons as waiters beckon from low-to-the-ground tables. Moroccan cuisine dips into Berber, Arab, and Mediterranean traditions, with hearty *tagine* (meat and vegetable stew) served in clay bowls with couscous, and kebabs roasted on spits. The adventurous can sample snails and sheep heads, while vegetarians can choose dried fruits, nuts, dates, or freshly-crushed pomegranate juice. Then light up some apple-scented tobacco in a waterpipe and watch the marvelous bedlam around you.

"Jemaa El-Fna is best enjoyed with lots of women friends so you can pool your resources for that great chicken-olive dish, or get an opinion on that shawl or pair of earrings you'd never find elsewhere," says Monica Flores, who spent two years criss-crossing the globe as a correspondent for The Odyssey: World Trek. "Plus, you can prevent each other from being hypnotized by those snake charmers!"

If Marrakesh proves overwhelming, never fear: Kasbah du Toubkal is only forty miles away. Situated near the foot of North Africa's highest mountain, this retreat overlooks three major valleys and the rocky High Atlas range. Local guides offer day-long outings to nearby villages and week-long treks through the mountain ranges with pack mules. Upon your return, slip on some leather *babouches* (slippers) and a wool djellaba (robe) and relax with a mint tea on the rooftop terrace before a hot soak in the *hammam* (steam bath). Run by local Berbers, Kasbah du Toubkal recently won a Green Globe for sustainable tourism, and uses part of its profits for purchases like four-wheel-drive ambulances that serve remote communities.

Two hours from Marrakesh is a coastal town beloved by locals and tourists alike: Essaouira. Explore its bustling souks tucked within the whitewashed medina, where surprises await behind every azure door. Boats unload their cargo and fishermen auction their catches along the harbor, and you can have a fish prepared any way you like on a sizzling grill in the nearby street stalls. Then visit the artisan market beneath the Skala fortress, where musicians serenade passersby and poets recite their work beneath the thuya trees. If possible, come during the Gnaoua and World Music Festival in June. Deeply rooted in sub-Saharan

www.kasbahdutoubkal.com

Africa, Gnaoua music is deeply hypnotic, with call-and-response singing, cymbals, hand-clapping, and lute-playing. Its musicians are considered healers who can treat anything from scorpion stings to psychic disorders.

Another can't-be-missed festival is the Bride's Fair, held each September in a remote valley in the Atlas Mountains near the town of Imilchil. According to legend, it began when the families of two young lovers forbade them to marry, as they were from opposing tribes. The two were so heartbroken, they cried themselves to death, creating two neighboring lakes. Their families were so aghast, they organized an intertribal meeting on the anniversary of the deaths where couples were permitted to marry. Today, hundreds of Ait Hadiddou Berbers carry on the tradition. Prospective brides paint rouge on their cheeks and kohl on their eyelids, slip on their best silver and amber jewelry, and crown themselves with a rounded headdress if they've never been married and a pointed one if they're widowed or divorced. Eager groomsmen, meanwhile, wear white turbans. They then mill about, making suggestive glances and small talk, before introducing potential mates to friends and family. If a suitor is deemed unworthy, his offering of a handshake will either be broken or refused altogether. At the end of the fair, a mass wedding ceremony is performed, where dozens of couples marry and dance to traditional songs played by hand drums and flutes. Then they hop on their donkeys and return to their villages, confident that if it doesn't work out, there's always next year.

80 *Dubrovnik, Croatia*

LORD BYRON CALLED IT THE "PEARL OF THE ADRIATIC"; GEORGE Bernard Shaw preferred "Heaven on Earth." David DeVoss compared it to Camelot. Whatever the moniker, Dubrovnik has been enchanting travelers for ages. Come see why before another Mediterranean cruise ship beats you to it.

Enter Stari Grad—the well-preserved Old Town—through Pile Gate, a high wall built eons ago to ward off attacks from the sea. The marble promenade spilling before you is called the Stradun, or Placa. Adjacent to the St. Savior Church on the left is a fourteenth-century Franciscan Monastery that contains a prized library of ancient manuscripts and liturgical objects as well as Europe's third oldest functioning pharmacy (now a museum). Behold the Pietà hanging over its doorway. Next, follow the Placa toward the center, peeking into the old churches and synagogues, forts and palaces, galleries and boutiques. A great pit stop is the Museum of Modern Art at Frana Supilla 23, which spotlights works by contemporary Croatian artists. Then savor a platter of just-caught mussels with a glass of white wine in an outdoor café while taking in the scenery. The rooftops of Dubrovnik read like a history book. The rarer red, green, and white tiles symbolize the once-united Yugoslavia—the era before rockets and mortar shells pelted the city as Croats and Serbs engaged in a bloody civil war for five frightening months in the early '90s. You can still see bullet holes on the sides of some buildings, and those terra cotta tiles—which got blown to smithereens—were replaced by flowerpot-red shingles, courtesy of UNESCO. For a moving depiction of not only this but other wars, drop by War Photo Limited at Antuninska 6, dedicated exclusively to war photography.

Now follow any alleyway until laundry lines appear, weighed down with the day's wash. Here, you'll find children skipping rope alongside mothers selling baskets of homegrown pears, figs, and olives. Sample one of their cheeses and soak in the quiet. Then return to the waterfront and catch a water taxi to one of the hundreds of islands dotting the Adriatic coast. Lokrum is one of the closest. Join the peacocks roaming wild through its national park before exploring the botanical garden and scenic ruins of a medieval Benedictine monastery. For a longer day-trip, try the Elafiti Islands, which consist of a dozen sparsely populated islands. Kolocep is known for its fragrant orange trees; Sipan, for its churches. Fresh fish are grilled right aboard the boat at lunchtime.

Though the city will be mobbed, mid-July is a fun time to visit Dubrovnik for its Summer Festival. The celebration commences with fireworks and a band on Luža Square, and over the next few weeks, hundreds of singers, dancers, actors, and musicians perform around Old Town in indoor venues as well as beneath the stars. Early February is also great (and far less crowded) for watching the pageants and parades of the Feast of St. Blaise.

www.dubrovnik-festival.br

81 Best Places to Spot a Mermaid

NEARLY EVERY SEA CULTURE HAS TALES OF LOVELY MAIDENS WHO propel through the ocean with fish-like tails. The first known legend dates back to Assyria in about 1,000 B.C. When the goddess Atargatis accidentally killed her mortal lover, she threw herself into a lake in despair, prompting the gods to turn her feet into fins so that she could not drown. As recently as the 2004 tsunami, islanders have claimed that dead mermaids have washed upon their shores. (For some reason, the photos released are inevitably of a monkey hacked in half with a sewed-on tail.) A few cultures believe mermaids help steer ships from harm's way, but most claim they are seductresses who, like the Sirens of myth, lure sailors into the water with their songs and then sink their ships. European legends hold that mermaids can grant wishes, while the Japanese say that eating their flesh can make you immortal. (Would they be served sashimi-style, or as a deep-fried tempura?)

One place where mermaids are thought to be alive and well is the island of Eleuthera in the Bahamas. Locals say that if you rise early enough, you can sometimes catch them washing their golden locks on the rocks of Whale Point, an old swimming hole. Bahamian children believe that their parents have seen this, and they will too someday. But if your own sunrise outing is in vain, worry not: mermaid art abounds. You can buy mermaid jewelry, pottery, t-shirts, doorstops, and figurines made of everything from shells to banana leaves. (Interestingly enough, these representations almost always resemble Daryl Hannah in *Splash*, with long, curly blonde hair, blue eyes, and cleavage. They are never black, like the majority of Bahamians.)

Or, you could opt to become a mermaid yourself.

"There is little to do here but be in the water, and you can swim and walk around naked all day because there is absolutely no one to see you, so it's a little like being a mermaid," says Karla Cosgriff, an American who grew up on the island and flies back regularly on business. "There are no signs here either, so finding a good beach is all about self-discovery."

It is certainly worth the effort: Eleuthera's beaches (in particular, Harbour Island) have crystalline waters filled with colorful reefs, eagle rays, octopus, and dolphins. Whales migrate through here annually. After a long day of playing in the ocean, you can pass the night at Elbina's in Gregory Town, where locals gather every Tuesday and Friday night to sing along to live Southern Caribbean music. Ask the old-timers about their own mermaid encounters; you'll hear some great stories.

If you still haven't gotten your mermaid fix, head out to Coney Island in New York around the summer solstice for their annual Mermaid Parade. Participants prance about dressed as mermaids, Neptune, sea creatures, and walking lighthouses, while vintage cars with fins roll past. At some point, the Queen Mermaid and King Neptune, usually celebrities like Queen Latifah and Moby, will cut the ribbon separating the boardwalk from the sea and toss offerings of fruit to the goddesses and gods of the Atlantic, thus signaling the start of the summer swimming season. Everyone then rushes home to primp for the evening Mermaid Parade Ball.

www.coneyisland.com/mermaid.shtml

82 Samarkand, Uzbekistan

MIDDLE EASTERN LEGEND TELLS OF A KING WHO WAS SO DISTRAUGHT by his wife's love affairs, he had her killed. The same fate befell a succession of new brides, each executed the dawn after the King took their virginity, until the clever daughter of a vizier intervened. Named Scheherazade, this maiden married the King, then kept him up all night telling a fantastical tale about a wish-granting genie who lived inside a lamp. When the sun rose the next morning, she left the story at such a cliff-hanger, the King spared her life to hear the ending the following night—only to be told another story. On this went until the two fell in love and the King revoked his brutish decree. Scheherazade's stories, now collectively known as *The Book of One Thousand and One Nights,* made literary history, and you can visit her supposed motherland in Samarkand, Uzbekistan.

One of the world's oldest cities, Samarkand was razed several times by warlords like Alexander the Great and Genghis Khan until Tamerlane turned it into a key post on the Great Silk Road. It retains this sense of antiquity, with public squares surrounded by terra cotta minarets, arches, and *madrassas,* or Islamic colleges. Azure tile mosaics coat many of its mosques. Of particular interest is the Shah-I-Zinda, where many of the women in Tamerlane's life are buried. (They say if you count the same number of stairs both on the way up and back, you have no sins.)

Also visit the Bibi Khanum Mosque, built in 1399 and named after Tamerlane's favorite wife. As the story goes, the mosque's architect fell so in love with her, he threatened to stop working on construction until she let him kiss her. She did, and his lips left a mark that Tamerlane noticed upon his return. Enraged, he beheaded the architect and ordered all women to wear veils so that only their husbands could enjoy what was beneath. Modern Uzbek women, however, usually do not take the veil. Mini-skirts and stiletto heels are *de rigeur* in the capital Tashkent, and in the countryside, women mainly wear scarves to block out the sun.

The bazaars of Samarkand are treasure troves of silver jewelry, embroidered robes, celestially-patterned wall hangings, and *dupalars,* or colorful skull caps. In the markets, old women sell bottles of homemade yogurt alongside bins of eggplants, cherry tomatoes, and honey dew. Nomadic nibbles abound, from sun-dried raisins and apricots, to almonds and pistachios. The culinary-inclined will want to buy some of the tiny gourds and fill them with fresh spices like saffron, cloves, and cumin.

Above all, meet Scheherazade's hospitable descendants. The high wooden doors of family compounds lead to inner court-yards that serve as dining nooks, with low-to-the-ground tables set atop Persian-style rugs, and brocade pillows sufficing as seats. Spend enough time strolling through the residential districts and someone will eventually invite you inside for a bowl of tea and some fresh *lepeshka,* or unleavened bread. *Lepeshka* is considered sacred, so don't set it face-down anywhere, or leave leftovers to be thrown away.

83 *Famed Teahouses*

WHILING AWAY THE AFTERNOON WITH A HOT POT OF TEA AND A friend is an activity that has been celebrated for millennia. In some nations, like Japan, the very act of preparing a cup is worthy of an hour-long ceremony (as is serving and drinking it). Renowned for its medicinal and healing properties, tea also possesses a social lubricant, enhancing any conversation. Two countries with heralded tea traditions are China and England.

* China claims to be the birthplace of tea, and records show that they have been drinking its infusion for at least three thousand years. Their love of the drink is so deep, they consider it to be one of the seven necessities of life (along with fuel, oil, rice, vinegar, soy sauce, and salt). Many teahouses were torn down during the Cultural Revolution but new ones have been mushrooming in recent years. Their menus are often impressive—from the standards (green, black, and oolong) to mixtures like Ba Bao Cha, or Eight Treasure Tea (which contains dried chrysanthemum, rock sugar, wolfberries, golden raisins, pinenuts, dates, and dried longan fruit, in addition to green tea leaves). In Beijing, try the Sanwei Bookstore at 60 Fuxingmennei Dajie opposite the Minzu Hotel. Their second-floor teahouse has a nice selection and features live traditional Chinese music on Saturday nights

that attracts old-timers and expats alike. Shanghai's famed teahouse is the lovely (albeit touristy) Huxinting, accessible by the zigzag bridge to Lotus Flower Pond in the heart of the Old City. Quail eggs are served alongside the tea in the upstairs rooms, and women in long silk *qipao* dresses perform the tea ceremony most evenings. If you'd rather hang out with Shanghai (and international) hipsters, check out the Taiwanese-style Harn Sheh, which serves bubble tea and other fun concoctions until about three in the morning in locales throughout the city.

* The British trace their tea rituals back 150 years, to a duchess named Anna who grew so hungry by late afternoon, she sometimes fainted. Her doctor's prescription of a light meal  before dinner spread throughout the land, and modern-day Britons now enjoy two types of tea: Afternoon and High. In addition to the bottomless pot of fine tea, the former traditionally consists of crustless sandwiches; warm scones with heaps of butter, fresh jam, and clotted Devonshire cream; and a cake or pastry (or two); the latter always includes a hot entrée, like Welsh rarebit (toast with melted cheese) or sausages. London's most renowned tea establishment—as well as its most expensive, touristy, and exclusive—is the Ritz at 150 Piccadilly Street. Guests book a solid month in advance to sip $45 tea out of fine bone china and nibble on dainty goodies served on triple-tier silver stands. If your companion is male, dress him in a jacket and tie (or he'll be loaned a ghastly one). Tea time is at 3:30 and 5:30 P.M. If your budget (or conscience) doesn't allow for

such extravagance, there are excellent alternatives, starting with the Ritz's neighbor, The Wolseley, at 160 Piccadilly. Set in the former showroom of the Wolseley car manufacturer, this café offers two tea services: Cream Tea with scones, clotted cream, and tea; and Afternoon Tea that throws in some jam and sandwiches. Service here is excellent (for London) and business is always bustling. For tea with a Middle Eastern kick, try Mo, the little sister of the Moroccan restaurant, Momo. Along with hot pots of orange blossom tea, Mo's serves treats like *harira*, *zaalouk*, Berber pancakes, and sweet pastries—all of which can be enjoyed while reclining on their low-level sofas and floor cushions. Visit them at 25 Heddon Street.

RECOMMENDED READING

The London Ritz Book of Afternoon Tea by Helen Simpson
The Way of Tea: The Sublime Art of Oriental Tea Drinking by Kim Chuen Lam and Kai Sin Lam

84 *Sites Worth the Hype*

WE'VE ALL BEEN DISAPPOINTED BY BLOCKBUSTER LOCALES. THE Statue of Liberty isn't nearly as tall as she seems in the movies; the poor Sphinx lost its feline features long ago. But the following sites are truly worth their hype, even for the most jaded traveler:

- The Taj Mahal might be architecture's greatest love story. Nineteen-year-old Arjumand Bann Begum was such a beautiful maiden, the moon was said to hide in shame. Future Mughal Emperor Shah Jahan fell fast in love with her, and took her as his second (and favorite) wife. They traveled throughout the land together, where she rallied on behalf of the destitute. Tragically, she died giving birth to their fourteenth child, but not before making the Shah promise to build a symbol of their love. After a year of deep mourning, the Shah brought in the world's greatest architects; precious stones and lapis lazuli from central Asia, Russia, and China; and glistening white marble from throughout India. For the next twenty years, some twenty thousand people worked around the clock, creating a "tear [that] would hang on the cheek of time," in the words of Bengali poet Rabindranath Tagore. Soon after the completion of the Taj Mahal, Shah Jahan was overthrown by one of his sons and imprisoned in a fort a mile away. He spent the rest of his days gazing through

a window at his tribute to love, until his body was interred next to his wife's in 1666.

Located near the bank of the Yamuna River in Agra, Uttar Pradesh, the Taj Mahal is open from sunrise to sunset. Visit early in the week to avoid the thickest crowds, and don't rush: no matter how many times you've glimpsed images of this sensuous building in world geography classes and Indian restaurants, it will move you. Drop in the Taj Museum to see a portrait of the "beloved ornament of the palace," Arjumand Bann Begum.

* Commenced in the third century, the Great Wall of China is said to be "so tall, because it is stuffed with the bones of soldiers" and "so deep, because it is watered with the soldier's blood." Twenty-three feet high and wide enough for ten soldiers to march abreast, it spans the same distance as New York to Los Angeles. While it utterly failed at keeping out the barbarians (Genghis Khan simply bribed the sentries so he could cross it) the Wall is a positively thrilling site. It is imperative, however, to avoid the reconstructed sections (namely Badaling and Mutianyu near Beijing), as they've been overrun with tourists, aggressive vendors, and Western fast food chains. Rather, pack a lunch (and, if time allows, a tent) and head into the countryside for a long hike and picnic on a desolate stretch of the ancient rubble. From Beijing, try the eight-mile hike between Jinshanling and Simitai, reachable by catching a bus from the Dongzhimen bus station to Miyun, transferring to another bus to Gubeikou, and

hopping off at Bakeshiying. Or join one of Explore Worldwide's eleven-day "Walk the Great Wall" expeditions along some fairly remote sections. Runners can tackle the Great Wall Marathon in Huangyaguan, Tianjin, which includes ascending and descending 37,000 steps.

* Chilean poet Pablo Neruda once wrote, "Machu Picchu is a trip to the serenity of the soul, to eternal fusion with the cosmos, there we feel our own fragility." Located forty-four miles northwest of Cusco in Peru, this "Lost City of the Incas" is thought to have been built as a country retreat for nobility in about 1440 and was inhabited until the Spanish invaded in 1532. An American historian "re-discovered" it in 1911 (taking so many thousands of artifacts back with him to Yale that Peru is now threatening to sue), and tourists have been flocking here ever since. Its 140 structures include temples, sanctuaries, and residences, all built with stones so perfectly cut, no mortar was needed to bind them (and, in many places, not even a butter knife can fit between them). Many travelers visit Machu Picchu as a day-trip from Cusco, but if your time and fitness allow, it is far more rewarding to hike here along the Inca Trail. Depending on the starting point, this trip can take either two or four days, and includes rugged passages through several different biomes, from cloud forest to mountain tops. Pack warm clothing, good boots, and a flashlight; chew on coca leaves for energy; and prepare for some hallucinatory views, including entire sides of mountains blooming with wild orchids.

* A Portuguese monk who visited Angkor Wat in 1586 claimed, "it is of such extraordinary construction that it is not possi-

ble to describe it with a pen." Five centuries later, words still defy. Located just a few miles north of Siem Reap in Cambodia, this site was built in the twelfth century as a state temple and capital city to King Suryavarman II. The epitome of the highly classical Khmer-style architecture, it features redented towers shaped like lotus buds, balustered windows, and high walls covered with ornate bas-reliefs. Especially delightful are the two thousand or so *devatas*—celestial dancing girls—flirting from every angle (except for the ones south of the entrance, who bare their teeth). Archeologists are still uncovering new sections of Angkor buried in the jungle. Visit with a tour or hire a private guide on the premises.

TOURS

Explore: Leading the World in Adventure Travel offers small group holidays to 120 countries and historical sites around the world (www.explore.co.uk).

IX

Best All 'Round Places

85 San Cristobal de las Casas, Mexico

A COLONIAL CITY TUCKED IN THE HIGHLANDS OF CHIAPAS IN southern Mexico, San Cristobal de las Casas leaped into the international spotlight on New Year's Day in 1994, when an army of Mayan Indians called the Zapatistas marched in with machetes and AK-47 rifles, announcing it was payback time for 500 years of exploitation. The Mexican Army quickly overcame the uprising, but not before their ski-masked spokesperson, Subcomandante Marcos, became a poster child of the anti-globalization movement. Today, San Cristobal is a pilgrimage site for activists, artists, and travelers who enjoy its organic cafes, *mercados,* fair-trade crafts shops, and political consciousness. Be sure to hit the following:

* Every Mayan is said to have "an ancient library in their heart." Even those who cannot read can recite stories that predate the Spanish conquest. In 1975, American Ambar Past founded Taller Leñateros, a cooperative artist workshop dedicated to the preservation of traditional Mayan bookmaking. Stop by Flavio Paniagua 54 to watch the artists (nearly all of whom are indigenous women) create paper out of everything from old cardboard and palm fronds to coffee, corn silk, and pansy petals.

www.tallerlenateros.com

Journals, cards, and silk-screen calendars are for sale in the connecting gift shop. Ask for a copy of *Incantations,* the wondrous collection of translated Mayan prayers, spells, poems, and stories that the cooperative published in 2005. The three-dimensional front cover features a haunting bas-relief mask of Kaxail, the Mayan goddess of the wilderness. Proceeds go directly back into the cooperative, which supports 150 members of thirty local families.

- For the past forty-five years, Sergio Castro (a.k.a. Mexico's Mother Teresa) has worked with Indians in almost every capacity—sanitation engineer, farmer, teacher, construction worker—always for free and often at great risk to his personal safety. Along the way, he gathered hundreds of traditional costumes, art work, tools, and instruments. Every week night at six, he gives tours of his collection in Spanish, English, French, and Italian at the Museo Trajes Regionales de Sergio Castro at Calle Guadalupe Victoria 6. This hour-long presentation and slideshow is free, but donations go toward his work as a burn healer in the rural countryside. (Indigenous Chiapanecos always keep their cooking fires burning in their cramped huts, and young children, drunken men, and people with epileptic seizures tend to fall in.) Visitors can also donate medical supplies, such as bandages and ointments.

- Madre Tierra at Avenida Insurgentes 19 has it all: a nightclub featuring live Mexican ska and reggae music until the early hours of the morning, an excellent vegetarian restaurant, a bakery specializing in whole-grain pastries and bread, a travel agency, and a theater with nightly screenings of Zapatista-oriented documentaries and the latest in Mexican cinema.

Another great center is La Casa de Luna Creciente, a restaurant and bookstore run by a collective of Mexican female artists, whose artwork adorns the walls. Their food is organic, delicious, and cheap ($3.50 for a soup, main course, freshly-squeezed fruit drink, and dessert). Find them in the courtyard at Chiapa de Corzo 19.

- Before leaving Chiapas, explore the primeval Mayan city of Palenque, magnificently set in a jungle inhabited by howler monkeys. Travel agencies in San Cristobal offer day-trips to the ruins that include pit stops at the waterfalls of Misol-Ha and Agua Azul as well. Check in with Zapata Tours in Madre Tierra for details.

86 *Kerala, India*

IN THE TREASURE CHEST OF INDIA, KERALA IS THE JEWEL THAT gleams brightest. It is the nation's most progressive state, boasting higher literacy and life-expectancy rates than the United States. An old matriarchal society, its women are fully emancipated, thanks in part to feisty community leaders like Mary Roy, who successfully fought archaic laws denying women the right to their parents' property, and Roy's famous activist daughter Arundhati (author of *The God of Small Things*). In 1975, Kerala became the world's first state to democratically elect Marxist leaders, and it remains the only place on the planet where Communists worship Krishna, Christ, Allah, and assorted Boddhisatvas side by side in harmony.

Kerala is also gorgeous. Coconuts, jackfruit, mangos, and bananas grow wild here, as do spices like cinnamon, nutmeg, and cloves. Its coast is lined with beaches, but only Westerners spend much time there, eating salads and drinking beer. Indians and travelers-in-the-know head instead to the backwaters, a network of channels linking three major rivers, forty-four smaller rivers, and countless tributaries and lagoons. Here you can rent an old *kettuvallam,* or houseboat, constructed entirely of planks of jackwood tied with coconut rope. Once used to transport rice and spices, *kettuvallam* now feature bedrooms, modern bathrooms, living rooms, and well-stocked kitchens that churn

out fresh seafood and coconut curries. Spend a day or two gliding along the soothing waters dotted with African reeds. Vanilla,
betelnut, and cocoa groves, rice paddies, tea plantations, and
rural villages will slowly pass by as flocks of herons, egrets, king-
fishers, and brahminy kites fly overhead.

For a transcendent experience, ask your *kettuvallam* captain to
dock at the Matha Amritanandamayi Mission in Amritapuri.
Built in a fishing village, this ashram considers itself the center of
a "silent spiritual revolution." At its helm sits Amma, a guru
known as the Hugging Mother, as she is said to have physically
embraced more than 24 million people in the last thirty years. "I
was skeptical the first time, as it looked a little cultish with everyone in white robes and barefoot, and my number for a hug was in
the thousands," says Sonya Tsuchigane, an actress in New York
City. "But Amma's was the closest to unconditional love I've ever
experienced. Her energy comes down to that hole we all
have inside of us, and fills it up with love and light."

Amma spends much of the year traveling over-
seas, so check her schedule to ensure she'll be here
(although her ashram is worth a visit regardless).

Kerala is also the birthplace of *ayurveda,* the
study of prolonging life through homeopathic
medicine and massage. A particularly rejuvenating treatment entails stripping naked and
lying on a wooden bench as not one but two
therapists pour hot oil over your entire body and
then rub it in with long, sweeping strokes to break
down bodily toxins and eliminate any imbalances.
Clinics can be found on practically every street corner in
Kerala; for deluxe treatment, try the Coconut Lagoon Resort in
the backwaters.

WWW.
www.amritapuri.org
www.asiatravel.com/india/hotels/
kerala/cocolagoon/index.html

87 Sweden

So where in the world is the best place to be a woman? Sweden, according to studies by the United Nations and World Economic Forum. This Nordic land ranks at or near the top in the number of women who graduate from college, hold down a job, win a public office, and serve as a cabinet member. Swedish mothers (and fathers) can take up to eighteen months of paid parental leave, day care centers are heavily subsidized, and Swedish men are said to clean up after themselves more than any other member of their gender. The nation also abides by a philosophy called "Allemansratten," which allows citizens to pitch tents just about anywhere they please, free from worry of trespassing (an unknown concept here).

"This has contributed significantly to nurturing the special relationship that Swedes have with nature, a romanticism and love for the homeland," says Anna-Karin Jatfors, a Swede currently living in Indonesia. "That is why we get all starry-eyed and patriotic talking about it!"

Some Swedes say they only have two cities—Stockholm and Goteborg—and that everything else is just a village of varying size. The following are some highlights:

* Every November since 1990, international artists and engineers have gathered in Jukkasjarvi, Norrland to build a

swanky hotel entirely out of snow and ice—4,000 tons of it. In the four months before it melts, some fifteen thousand guests will pay between $400 and $800 to sleep in this marvel of human ingenuity. In addition to the nearly one hundred rooms and suites—some decked out with sculpted ice castles, flocks of penguins, piles of mammoth bones, or life-sized statues of the Beatles—there are art galleries, a cinema, a chapel, and the 400-seat Ice Globe Theatre that stages magic shows, concerts, and plays. (Attendees are given insulated capes to keep warm.) Daylight hours are spent snow-mobiling, dog-sledding, ice fishing, cross-country skiing, and designing your own ice creations in ice-sculpting classes. Reindeer safaris can also be arranged, as can visits to communities of nomadic reindeer herders known as the Sami. Retire late at night to an ice-block bed draped with reindeer hides and a high-tech sleeping bag. (Don't drink too much beforehand: getting up to pee will be painful!) The Ice Hotel is located about 125 miles north of the Arctic Circle. If you have $700 to spare, request a dogsled pick-up from the airport. Store anything that might freeze (like cameras or Ipods) in the lockers at the front desk. Warm accommodations are offered in nearby hotels and cabins if the cold is unbearable or the wallet is waning.

www.icehotel.com

* If sub-zero temperatures are a turn-off, come in late June, when Swedes head into the countryside en masse to celebrate Midsummer. Friends and family decorate enormous maypoles with flowers and greenery and pass the evening (and early morn) singing, dancing, and carousing around it,

stopping intermittently for games. There are boot tosses, egg tosses, and relay races where teams compete to create the longest line of clothing by ripping off their own, piece by piece. Traditional foods include pickled herring and the first potatoes and strawberries of the season, all washed down with considerable aquavit (a potent beverage distilled from potato or grain, like vodka). Midsummer also has mystical connotations. Wild flowers are said to absorb special powers at midnight, and girls slip seven different kinds beneath their pillows to dream of their future mates.

The best way to spend Midsummers is with Swedish friends, but if you're new to the country, travel to Leksand about 150 miles northwest of Stockholm. Located in the region of Dalarna—the nation's folksy heartland—Leksand throws some of the liveliest celebrations, with maypole-raising ceremonies held throughout the weekend. Friday night draws the largest crowds, when people in native dress float down the river in church boats, waving their garlands. Then everyone marches to the amphitheater, where they fiddle and dance into the night.

88 *Austin, Texas*

NO MATTER WHERE YOU'RE FROM, IT'S GOING TO SEEM A LOT LESS fun after a romp in this big city/college town. Austin is the kind of place where only two forms of footwear are needed: flip flops and cowboy boots. Just don't forget that everything is bigger (not to mention better) in Texas: the margarita you order at Baby Acapulco's will be the size of your head; the chicken enchilada platter at Chuy's, the width of your torso.

They don't call it the Live Music Capital of the World for nothing. Some one hundred and fifty live music venues—from the airport to Sixth Street to the legendary Austin City Limits—crank out the Austin sound (a special blend of country, rock, blues, and jazz with a Latin beat and a Western swing) every night of the week. Bask in the muses floating above the old filling-station-turned-restaurant where Janis Joplin once jammed at Threadgills, located at 6416 North Lamar Boulevard (and have chicken-fried steak smothered with gravy while you're at it). Then head to the Continental Club at 1315 South Congress Avenue any Tuesday at 7 P.M. for a Hippie Hour performance by Toni Price that NPR once described as "something like a holiness revival and a Harley rally and a Phish concert and an Appalachian wedding party." Other must-catch local songstresses include Christina

WWW.www.sxsw.com

Marrs, Patrice Pike, and Tish Hinojosa. In March, the city hosts the South by Southwest Music Conference, which features nearly 1,500 shows by stars like Lucinda Williams and the Dixie Chicks.

Indeed, artists flock to Austin like flies to cow chips. One of the earlier expats was the flamboyant European sculptor Elisabet Ney, who shocked locals by wearing a smock that barely graced her knees in the late nineteenth century. She also made such public statements as "Women are fools...to be bothered with housework. Look at me. I sleep in a hammock, which requires no making up; I break an egg for my brekkie and sip it raw from a shell; I make lemonade in a glass and then rinse the glass—and my housework is done for the day!" Visit her studio at 304 East 44th Street, then head to Women & Their Work on 1710 Lavaca Street. This gallery throws fifty events a year in the film, music, dance, and visual arts, and has recently showcased artists like Tina Medina, Liliana Wilson, and Angela Fraleigh.

As you wander around this funky town, you'll notice the "Keep Austin Weird" bumperstickers plastered to cars. This isn't just a nostalgic cry for a return to Austin's (better) pre-dot-com days, but a tribute to the city's infinite quirks, like Eeyore's Birthday Party. Held every April in Pease Park, this celebration draws in costumed thousands who strut about in the Hippie Queen Pageant, dance barefoot in the community drum circles, and eat birthday cake in honor of Winnie the Pooh's melancholic friend. In December, head to 37th Street for a display of Yuletide fever that can only be described as anarchic, with reams of Christmas lights wound around every inanimate object available, from trash cans and lounge chairs to junked-out cars. A giant volcano of green lights erupts with red-light lava; Mermaid Barbie casts Sailor Ken into the open jaws of sea creatures; and highly unflattering effigies of political figures are twisted into compromising positions. And then there are the bats—1.5 million, at last count—that live beneath the Ann W. Richards Congress Avenue Bridge. Huge crowds gather to watch them swarm out at night, an electrifying process that can take up to forty-five minutes. The best time to visit is in August, when mothers take out their tiny pups, or September, when locals throw a Batfest of arts and crafts, live music, and bat viewing. (If you sit up close, bring an umbrella!) Call the Bat Hotline at 512-416-5700 ext. 3636 for details.

89 *Berlin, Germany*

WHAT COULD TOP BERLIN? IT IS DEEPLY COSMOPOLITAN. (ONE IN every 7.5 citizens is an immigrant.) The populace cares about the environment. (Recycling centers anchor every neighborhood; shoppers bring cloth bags from home for their purchases; bicycling is such an accepted mode of transportation, cyclists have their own lanes and traffic lights.) It throws great parties. (Once a year, tens of thousands spill into the streets for the world's largest techno celebration—the Love Parade—as well as its anti-globalization counter-parade, the Fuck Parade). And it pays homage to its women, at the following locales:

* Berlin bleeds art. Not only have the remnants of the Berlin Wall become a painted canvas, but many abandoned factories have been transformed into thriving art spaces. In the early 1990s, squatters created Kunsthaus Tacheles, a multifloor complex of studios, galleries, a café, a theater, a cinema, and a rather chichi restaurant called Milagro. Visit it at Oranienburger Strasse 54-56 (via the U-Bahn Oranienburger Tor). Kunst-Werke Berlin at Auguststrasse 69 (S-Bahn Oranienburger Strasse) is an old butter-factory-turned-non-profit-art-space for international artists. Another favorite is Begine at Potsdamer Strasse 139 in

www.tacheles.de

Schoneberg (U-Bahn Bulowstrasse), which hosts concerts, readings, and films by and for women.

* Das Verborgene Museum: Dokumentation der Kunst von Frauen, otherwise known as the Hidden Museum, was founded by feminist artists and historians in 1986 to honor forgotten art works by early twentieth century Berlin women artists who were retired, exiled, or murdered by the Nazis. Now a nonprofit with a gallery, the museum regularly organizes exhibitions of contemporary and historical women's art. Visit it on Schüterstrasse 70 (S-Bahn Savigny Platz).

* While at the Hidden Museum, you'll undoubtedly fall for artist Käthe Kollwitz, who has a museum of her own at Fasanenstrasse 24 (U-Bahn Uhlandstrasse). Drawing inspiration from the work of her husband (a physician who made house-calls in the slums) and the deaths of her son in WWI and grandson in WWII, Kollwitz imbued much of her work with socialist realism. She is best known for an antihunger lithography series called "Bread" and a woodcut series called "War," but excelled in other forms as well, including sculptures, graphics, and drawings.

* Marlene Dietrich—a.k.a. The Blue Angel—also hails from Berlin. The blond bombshell received an Oscar nomination for her role in *Morocco* and perfected her *femme fatale* personae in such classics as *Scarlet Empress* and *Shanghai Express*. An American citizen by 1937, she raised war bonds, entertained U.S. and Allied troops, and recorded anti-Nazi songs (in German). Despite this "disloyalty," Hitler remained an avid fan, and purportedly offered Marlene a queenly sum to come

back home. She replied that she'd only do so if her Jewish friends could, too. When she did return in 1960, protesters pelted her with tomatoes and eggs, to which she quipped: "I guess they have a love-hate feeling for me." Marlene is buried at Stubenrauchstrasse 43-45, in Friedenau Cemetery (U-Bahn Friedrich-Wilhelm-Platz). Her tomb is a simple one, noting: "Here I stand on the marker of my days." To check out her extravagant costumes, photos, and personal effects, visit the Filmmuseum Berlin at Potsdamer Strasser 2 (U/S-Bahn Potsdamer Strasse).

90 *Vietnam*

A WILD CONFLUENCE OF FRENCH COLONIAL VILLAS, BUDDHIST temples, communist kitsch, and rice paddies, Vietnam intoxicates and replenishes. Rise with the sun to enjoy the first sights of the day, such as the elderly practicing *tai chi* beneath tamarind trees; the entrepreneurs setting out foot-high stools on the pavement for impromptu sidewalk cafes; the women in white silk *ao dai,* elbow-length gloves, and sunglasses tearing through traffic on motorcycles; the bands of school children calling out "Hello!"

Then hit the streets for the following:

* In Saigon/Ho Chi Minh City, first stop at the Nam Bo Women's Museum, where three floors showcase the heroics of Vietnamese women during the many wars this nation fought in the twentieth century (against France, Japan, the United States, China, and Cambodia). There is also a fashion gallery of costumes from different regions and eras with accompanying accoutrement at 202 Vo Thi Sau Street, District 3. Then brace yourself for the War Remnants Museum on Vo Van Tan Street. Built in 1975, the museum meticulously documents the atrocities committed by U.S. troops during the Vietnam War. Amidst the tanks, helicopters, grenade launchers, and torture chambers are mannequins of tall blond soldiers

smoking Marlboros as they shoot off their MI6s. One display case, however, contains seven medals—including a Purple Heart—along with the inscription: "To the people of a United Viet Nam: I was wrong. I am sorry." It is a chilling but imperative experience.

- Vietnam's national mythology revolves around a remarkable young woman named Thúy Kiều, or "water wanderer." The poster child of filial piety, she saves her father and brother from a prison sentence by becoming a prostitute. But there is redemption: she later marries a famous rebel and conquers much of the nation. If you arrive during Tet, the lunar new year, take part in the Vietnamese tradition of predicting the future by asking a question, closing your eyes, and opening the story book of her life. Whatever verse your finger finds is said to be a telling indicator of what's to come.

- Don't be surprised if you extend your trip for the cuisine. Some favorites include *pho,* beef or chicken noodle soup with fistfuls of cilantro; *banh mi thit,* paté smeared on a French baugette with pork, pickle, daikon, carrot, and cucumber; and *bánh chung,* sticky rice stuffed with mung beans, pork, and black sesame seeds and steamed in a banana leaf. For a memorable meal in Hanoi, try Koto at 61 Va Mieu Street in the Dong Da District. Owned by an Australian nonprofit organization called Street Voices, Koto is staffed almost entirely by former street kids who can whip up anything from Vietnamese stir-fry and clay pots to European-style sandwiches, pastas, and salads. Top off any meal with *ca phe sua nong,* French-style drip coffee served hot in a glass with a hefty dollop of sweetened condensed milk. Just one serving will keep you wired half the day: order it iced, or *ca phe sua da,* to dilute the potency.

* Every inch of Vietnam's countryside yields another wonder: jungles, mountain peaks, winding rivers, rice paddies full of water buffalo. From Hanoi, head out to Ninh Binh province, where the ancient royal capital of Hoa Lu offers decadent shrines and temples, as well as the ruins of the Dinh Dynasty palace. Villagers will gladly row you past rice paddies and limestone formations to see the Tam Coc, or Three Caves. Inquire about the local legends; they are vivid storytellers.

RECOMMENDED READING

Hitchhiking Vietnam by Karin Muller

91 *Iceland*

WHY ICELAND? BECAUSE YOU CAN TAKE A SHUTTLE STRAIGHT FROM the airport to a geothermal pool. Because its landscapes are so barren, NASA astronauts trained here to walk on the moon. Because its people speak the language of the Vikings, believe in elves, and include Björk. Still not convinced? Let's start with Reykjavik.

Like most great cities, Iceland's capital never sleeps—especially in the summer, when the sun shines almost continuously. Sixty-two percent of the population lives here in wooden houses with colorful tin roofs, and the city's center swells with cafes, bookstores, museums, and galleries. Consider investing in a one-, two-, or three-day Reykjavik tourist card, which includes admission to most of the attractions, plus unlimited rides on the city buses and dips in the thermal pools. Not to be missed is the *Volcano Show* at the Red Rock Cinema at Hellusund 6A, which includes shocking images of lava swallowing houses whole. Stop by the Harbor House at Tryggvagata 17 to see paintings by the famed Icelandic contemporary artist, Erro, then hit the boutiques for one of those fabulous wool sweaters. On weekends, check out the bargains at Kolaportid Flea Market by the harbor on Geirsgata. Björk fans should drop by Japis at Laugavegur 13 for a retrospective of her entire career, neatly filed into CD bins. For a glimpse of the pickled penises of every mammal in the land, visit the Icelandic Phallological Museum at Laugavegur 24. At some point in the day, hop in a watery hole. There are no less than sixteen in the Reykjavik area alone, including the famous Blue Lagoon, a 1.2-acre geothermally-warmed pool, a forty-minute bus ride away. The waters here are said to both exfoliate and invigorate, and are surrounded by scenic views of hardened lava.

Foodies will delight in the dinner options: anything from halibut and sea bream with bacon, capers, and shiso leaves, to salted cod with artichokes and tomato lobster jus. If you've over-gorged on seafood, try horsemeat, reindeer, or a hot dog with all the trimmings. For a dairy treat, try *skyr*—a yogurt-like curd with a creamy texture brought to Iceland by the Vikings more than a thousand years ago. Traditionally eaten with milk or cream and a little sugar, it is sold in grocery stores in every conceivable flavor.

By now it should be nightfall, if not another day entirely. If it is showing, catch "The Saga of Guðríður," a one-woman show about an obscure Viking tale that has been playing at the Skemmtihúsið Theatre at Laufásvegur 22 for years. Otherwise, venture forth on a *runtur,* or pub crawl. The bars start hopping around 11 P.M. on Friday and Saturday, and crowds don't thin out until at least 3 A.M. (if not dawn). Vodka-spiked beer is the brew of choice, and tabs accrue quickly.

Sleep off the hangover before exploring the countryside by taking Route 1 southeast of Reykjavik to Hveragerdi, or Hot Springs Garden. Behind it is a valley full of mud pots, steaming vents, fumaroles, and hot springs, but the primary attraction is Gryla, a forty-foot geyser that explodes several times a day. (She is named for the witch mother of the mischievous Jolasveinarn, or Christmas lads, who cause much trouble on Christmas Eve.) You can also go out on horseback excursions that last anywhere from a couple of hours to eight or nine days.

www.eldhestar.is

As you wander about the Land of Fire and Ice, beware that beyond a certain point, maps become inaccurate and compasses falter, due to magnetic anomalies. Rent a four-wheel drive and bring a friend with an excellent sense of direction.

92 *California*

CALIFORNIA IS NOT FOR THE INDECISIVE. YOU'LL AWAKE EACH morning too overwhelmed by the choices: *huevos rancheros* or *dim sum*? The vineyards, the mountains, the desert, or the beach? Should you spend the day surfing, hiking, and cycling? Or shopping, club-hopping, and celebrity-watching? No matter how bad your wanderlust, you are sure to quench it here, in what might be the greatest of the United States.

* Let's start with the national parks. There's Yosemite. Sequoia. Kings Canyon. Channel Islands. Death Valley. If time allows for only one, pick Joshua Tree, if for no reason than it has the best soundtrack (U2's 1987 album, of course). Here, the Colorado Desert collides with the Mojave Desert, exploding in creosote bush, ocotillo, cholla cactus, and fan palm oases, as well as the park's quirky namesake. No two Joshua trees look alike: in clumps, they resemble dysfunctional family portraits. To get here from Los Angeles, pack hiking boots and plenty of water and drive east 140 miles.

  www.nps.gov/jotr

* For another arboreal excursion, venture to the coastal hills of Northern California, where thousand-year-old redwood

trees reach into the clouds. Here in the Headwaters Forest, a twenty-three-year-old woman named Julia Butterfly Hill climbed up one named "Luna" in 1997 to protest logging and clear-cutting by Pacific Lumber Company. She didn't come down for 738 days, during which she became a powerful voice in the environmental movement. Luna got attacked by a chain-saw soon after the sit-in ended, but Julia managed to save a 2.9-acre buffer zone around her. Catch a glimpse of her from Highway 101 near the Stafford exit.

* To fully appreciate California's phenomenal landscapes, cruise down State Route 1 (a.k.a. Highway 1) with the sunroof open and the music blasting. This 549-mile road follows the rugged coastline from San Juan Capistrano to Leggett, passing Orange County, Los Angeles, Santa Cruz, and San Francisco. Big Sur is the most popular stretch, with knock-out Pacific vistas at every turn.

"My girlfriends and I drive the coast when we need to sort out our lives, careers, boy drama, etc. You can pull over and pop down to a beach or to a cute cafe in Half Moon Bay, or you can just drive," says Neda Farzan, who once logged in 40,000 cross-country miles as a documentary historian for The Odyssey: U.S. Trek. "For a Californian, it is also a rite of passage. I took my cousin on a Highway 1 drive for her seventeenth birthday so she would know that the freedom of the open road is there for the taking."

* There are infinitely many ways to pass the day in San Francisco: gorging sourdough bread at Boudin's, strolling

across Golden Gate Bridge, hopping cable cars at random. But don't miss the Mission District, home to a thriving arts scene and Latino community (check out the murals on Balmy and Clarion Alleys). Load up on some locally-grown, organic goodies at Bi-Rite on 18th Street between Dolores and Guerrero—or a burrito anywhere on Mission Street—and then hit the funky shops.

Looking to reignite your sex life or improve upon your self-love techniques? Stop by Good Vibrations on 603 Valencia Street at 17th Street. Opened by pioneering sex therapist Joani Blank in 1977, this worker-owned cooperative sells novelty gifts like "Our First Bondage Kit" as well as high-end products like Yva, a $1,500 splash-proof, ergonomically designed, 18-karat gold-plate vibrator/*objet d'art* that can last up to seven hours. Then walk a few blocks to 826 Valencia Street to stock up on spy glasses, eye patches, or a message-in-a-bottle. That's right: author Dave Eggers (of *A Heartbreaking Work of Staggering Genius* fame) opened a writing center for students age eight to eighteen here that moonlights as a pirate supply store. Go ahead and buy that $100 limited edition glass eye book set; all proceeds go back to the kids.

www.oaklandnet.com/parks/parks/lakemerritt.asp

Surely you're now in the mood for a new tattoo—and what luck: Black & Blue Tattoo is right on 381 Guerrero Street at 14th Street. Owned and operated by women, it won the *Guardian*'s "Best of the Bay" Readers Poll in 2005. If needles frighten you, head instead to the women-only *osento* on 955 Valencia Street. Housed in a white Victorian, it features a 104-degree hot tub, a cold plunge pool, wet and dry sauna, and wooden deck. Then take the BART across the bay to Oakland to watch the sun set over Lake Merritt, a saltwater lagoon/wildlife refuge with a gritty, urban skyline. Sit on a bench and take in the vibrant peoplescape: African-American youth, Ukrainian grandmothers, Cambodian lovers, Guatemalan families.

❋ Top off your Golden State adventures with a tour of its wineries. The Benziger Winery in Sonoma practices a holistic farming technique called biodynamics that integrates their vineyards with the surrounding ecology. Take a forty-five-minute tour of their estate—which includes gardens and wildlife sanctuaries—on a tram pulled by a tractor, then try a glass of their famous Fumé Blanc. Benziger Family Winery is located at 1883 London Ranch Road in Glen Ellen.

While Sonoma and Napa Valley are the best known wine regions, they are by no means the only ones. Kathy Joseph opened Fiddlehead Cellars in Santa Barbara County to "capture the pure essence" of her two favorite grape varietals: Sauvignon Blanc and Pinot Noir. She and her "FiddleChix" now produce 5,000 cases a year in their "Lompoc Wine Ghetto" at 1597 East Chestnut Avenue in Lompoc. Call ahead to arrange a tasting. Twelve miles north of Fort Bragg along the Mendocino Coast, Sally Ottoson runs a winery called Pacific Star. Enjoy a complimentary tasting inside her barrel cellar, then relax on the outdoor picnic tables with a bottle of Petite Sirah. (If the season is right, a gray whale brigade might pass by.) Other women-owned vineyards in California

www.benziger.com

www.2.ibgcheckout.com/pacstar/index.jsp

www.fiddleheadcellars.com

include: Kathryn Kennedy Winery, La Sirena Wine, Tres Sabores, Selene, and Lane Tanner.

Another woman who has contributed to the state of California grapes is Dolores Huerta. Along with Cesar Chavez, she led the massive grape boycotts of the 1960s in an attempt to educate the public about the abhorrent treatment of migrant workers as well as the rampant use of pesticides. (A cofounder of United Farm Workers, she also raised 11 children, mostly as a single mom!) The Dolores Huerta Foundation still rallies on behalf of farmworkers from its headquarters in Bakersfield. Get a feel for her legacy (and that of other Chicano leaders) by strolling through San Diego's Chicano Park, where brilliant outdoor murals adorn the pylons holding up the Coronado Bridge. The Latino community gathers here every April 22 (or the weekend closest to it) to celebrate the many battles endured in keeping bulldozers out of the park.

www.doloreshuerta.org
www.chicano-park.org

RECOMMENDED READING

Legacy of Luna by Julia Butterfly Hill

93 *Mongolia*

MONGOLIA. THE VERY WORD CONJURES A LANDSCAPE THAT IS BLEAK and forbidding—the epitome of desolation. Yet, this "last frontier" is steeped in ritual and tradition and surrounded by stark, natural beauty. Come to race a pony (or yak or camel) across a grassland speckled with wildflowers, to meditate in hidden Tibetan Lamaist temples, to flirt with 300-pound wrestlers clad only in boots, briefs, and sleeves. Come to bask in the legacy of Genghis Khan, who created history's largest empire by inspiring his warriors to "live by the sword instead of the plow" in the twelfth century, and of Mandhai-Setsen, the Wise Queen who re-unified her turbulent nation by leading her troops into battle in the fifteenth century. Whatever the reason, come.

Roughly one-third of Mongolians live in capital Ulan Bator—or UB, as expats call it—which is fast becoming a cosmopolitan city. Amidst the oppressive, Soviet-style apartment blocks are raucous nightclubs, coffee houses, Indian restaurants, and hipsters who sell calls from their cell phones for a few *tugrik* apiece. Ulan Bator's is arts scene is also growing. Visit the Union of Mongolian Artists Art Gallery on the second floor of the Arts Center at 1 Chinggis Avenue, and have tea with the artists afterward in the café of the Art Club next door. Then drop by the Choijin Lama Museum on the first floor of the Marco Polo Plaza, the Red Ger Gallery on Barilagchdiinn Talbai, and the

Bartsch Gallery in Misheel Center in the Khan Uul district. However much you might love Ulan Bator, though, limit your stay, as the heart of this nation beats in the countryside. Find a good guide at a travel agency (or better yet, through an expat); stock up on food, supplies, and gifts for host families; and pray for a safe journey in Mongolia's holy center, the Gandantegchinlen Monastery (the sole Lamaist Buddhist temple to survive the Communist purges). Then venture off into the steppe.

There are few roads in Mongolia and most vehicles are Soviet, so wear a good sports bra (or two). Occasionally, you'll pass by an *ovoo,* or collection of stones piled high in deference to gods worshipped eons before Tibetan Buddhism. Join your driver in solemnly circling the stones three times in a clock-wise direction and toss a new pebble in for good luck. Then drive on...and on...and on. At last you'll come upon a small community, where your host family awaits. Most Mongolians live in *gers,* round, wooden-framed felt tents covered in heavy white canvas that can be disassembled in half an hour and transported on an ox cart: perfect for the nomad-on-the-go. *Ger* etiquette should be carefully heeded: make a bit of noise before entering; step over the threshold with your right foot; move throughout the space in a clockwise fashion if you're female (counterclockwise if you're not); and above all—cheerfully ingest whatever the host offers, usually a small bowl of vodka (if you're lucky) or a potent brew of fermented mare's milk called *airag* (if you're not). Drink every drop and then hold the bowl upside down over your head to prove it. In the summertime, you might be offered fresh yogurt instead. Lick it clean with your tongue.

And then the fun begins! Mongolians are a horse-centric culture; many children learn to ride before they can walk. Your hosts, or guide, will take you out for a memorable ride through

Sherwood-like forests, Ghobi desert, or tundra, depending on the area. If possible, plan a trip to Lake Hovsgal, one of the deepest freshwater lakes on Earth. While too frigid for swimming (unless you're Russian), the lake is surrounded by gorgeous peaks and tundra and home to bears, moose, and ibex.

The best month to visit Mongolia is July—not just for the sunny weather, but for Naadam, a three-day, Olympic-style festival celebrated in every corner of the nation. In archery, women fire twenty arrows made of willow branches and vulture feathers from a distance of sixty meters and men shoot forty arrows from seventy-five meters, while judges stand on either side of the target, singing old folk songs. In horseracing, 600 horses gallop across the steppe with jockeys as young as five years old. Winners are baptized in mare's milk and honored with songs. And then there is wrestling, which is said to date back thousands of years. Hulky men clutch each other for hours (and hours) until their strength wears out and they knock each other over. Winners go on to become major public figures, such as ambassadors to countries like France. Ulan Bator hosts the biggest Naadam, but to avoid the tourists, stay out in the steppe. You just might be pulled out of the crowd to help congratulate the winners.

94 *Lithuania*

THE FORTITUDE OF THE LITHUANIAN PEOPLE IS IMMEDIATELY palpable, and their history reveals why. Their empire once stretched from the Baltic Sea to the Black Sea, but the Russians invaded in the nineteenth century and started Russifying the place, closing down universities, abolishing legal codes, and banning the language. During the two world wars, they endured German, Soviet, and Nazi invasions, and much of their Jewish population was exterminated. (Survivors lead tear-jerking tours through the Museum of Genocide Victims at Aukų g. 2A in the capital, Vilnius.) Incredibly, throughout the four decades of Soviet occupation that followed, Lithuanians held on to their cultural heritage—even at risk of banishment to Siberia. And in March 1990, they shocked the world by declaring independence. Gorbachev dispatched troops to seize control of the main television tower in Vilnius, but thousands of unarmed civilians fended them off and then impaled their Soviet passports on wooden stakes and torched them in protest. Though barely the size of West Virginia, Lithuania won the battle against Mother Russia and became the first Soviet satellite to be free.

The nation's spirituality is equally omnipresent. A matriarchal culture, Lithuanians worshipped many female deities in

www.genocid.lt/muziejus/en

primeval times, including Saule (Goddess of the Sun), Laima (of Fate), and Gabija (of Fire). See their mosaics within the walls of Vilnius University. Then climb the Hill of Three Crosses, which commemorates the spot where a pagan tribe crucified Franciscan friars centuries ago. Soviets mowed down the crosses in the 1950s, but locals risked their lives sneaking up the hill to prop them back up. A hundred miles north of Vilnius, another hill has been a shrine of thousands of crosses in varying shapes, sizes, designs, and metals since the fourteenth century. Soviets razed this site at least three times as well, but the crosses always mysteriously sprung up soon after. St. Peter and Paul's Church in Vilnius is also a marvel to behold, with 2,000 creamy-white friezes of angels, beasts, and maidens climbing its walls and dripping from its high-vaulted ceilings, each symbolizing a different biblical passage, battle, or allegory.

Despite their historical drama, Lithuanians are a laid-back people with a good sense of humor. (They are, after all, the only country in the world with a statue to Frank Zappa. Sculpted by a man who used to make Lenins, it stands in the courtyard of Kalinausko Gatve.) Huge crowds gather for the Skamba Skamba Kankles folk festival during the last weekend of May, and cafes and restaurants spill onto the sidewalks throughout the summer. Užupio Kaviné on Užupio 2 has a great deck overlooking the river, which is inhabited by a silver mermaid.

For centuries, Lithuanians have traveled to Druskininkai, eighty miles south of Vilnius, to relax in its sanitorium. Rent a bicycle and ride to the banks of the Nemunas river, where people swarm around a water fountain believed to have healing powers. Some actually drink the water, despite its high salt content. Then hit the spas. The recently renovated Druskininkų Gydykla offers hour-long mud baths, while Afroditė has a sauna, Turkish bath, and two different massages, one involving honey. Top off the treatment with a swim at the Vilnius Spa, reputed to have the best mineral water around.

Now explore Lithuania's landscape. Aukstaitija National Park, for starters, is 250 square miles of pine forests, 100-plus lakes, and 80 historic villages, some of which retain their traditional wooden architecture (including an eighteenth century octagonal church). For a panoramic view, climb up Ladakalnis, where ancient pagans made sacrifices to the goddess Lada. (And with good reason: she supposedly gave birth to the entire planet!)

95 *Jordan*

FROM ITS UNDULATING DESERTS TO ITS GODDESS TEMPLES, JORDAN is full of surprises. Where else can you trek in the tracks of Lawrence of Arabia in the morning and indulge in the beauty regimen of Cleopatra in the evening? The most accessible nation in the Middle East, Jordan warmly welcomes travelers, and women can wander about with relatively little hassle.

* Start your journey in capital Amman's artsy districts, which are lined with cafes, bars, and galleries. Not to be missed is the Darat al-Funun on Nimer bin Adwan Street. Housed in three buildings alongside the ruins of a sixth-century Byzantine church, this cultural center includes a contemporary art gallery and library and holds workshops, films, musical and theatrical performances, and lectures by Arab artists and critics. Ask about their monthly literary events, where poets recite verses beneath illuminated Roman columns. Then stroll about, ducking into teahouses for puffs on water pipes and cups of hot *yansoon*, an aniseed-based drink. To experience a traditional *hammam*, stop in Al-Pasha on Al-Mahmoud Taha Street between ten A.M. and midnight for some rigorous body scrubbing followed by a steam bath and forty-minute massage. Wind down at the upscale Blue

WWW www.daratalfunun.org

Fig on Abdoun (a gallery, café, bar, and restaurant with world fusion music), Books@Café on Jabal Amman, First Circle—a hotspot popular with expats and young Jordanians. On Fridays, hit the Souk JARA, an open-air flea market of pottery, crafts, and antiques by the Jordan River Foundation showroom near the First Circle.

* Next, head to the Dead Sea for a 2,000-year-old beauty and health treatment. Located 1,300 feet below sea level, these sacred waters are loaded with bromine, magnesium, iodine, and calcium, and are considered so healing for asthma, arthritis, skin diseases, and hypertension, some European Union countries—namely Austria and Germany—cover extended stays in their health insurance plans. Before you go, pack a kit of soap, shampoo, a washcloth, and a towel, and ensure you have no open wounds (which will sting like hornets in the heavily salinized water). Within a few dozen steps out to sea, your feet will magically levitate to the surface, leaving you floating like a cork. Have a blast turning somersaults, but try not to swallow—just one drop will induce gagging if not retching. Scrub off the salty slime as soon as you emerge and proceed to a mud hut, where you'll pay a small fee to slap mud all over your body and bake in the sun. The Dead Sea is an easy day trip from Amman; most budget hotels and travel agencies offer outings.

* Though it's been called "the rose red city half as old as time," Petra actually contains stones of many colors. The Nabataeans carved this magical city right out of the cliffs in the third century B.C.: temples, palaces, tombs, banquet halls, even a theater. For eons, its locale was ideal, smack

where camel caravans from the Silk Road crossed paths with spice routes. But Petra began to decline during Roman rule and was severely damaged in an earthquake in A.D. 363. For centuries, it was known as the Lost City until a Swiss explorer rediscovered it in the 1800s and Harrison Ford sauntered about it in the 1900s (indeed, that is Petra you see in *Indiana Jones and the Last Crusade*). Enter it through a canyon so narrow, you can almost touch both sides, and visit the many temples built in honor of Allat, the pre-Islamic Arabian goddess. (The Nabataeans equated her with Athena.)

- Best known for the exploits of Lawrence of Arabia—who was based here during the Arab Revolt of 1917—the Wadi Rum is a dramatic valley cut into sandstone and granite rock. It has housed many a people who left behind grand temples and rock paintings—some of them prehistoric. Bedouin tribes live here today and offer camel-trekking and rock-climbing expeditions.

96 *Canada*

WHAT'S NOT TO LOVE ABOUT CANADA? FOR ITS CITIZENS, THERE'S universal health care, a terrific public education system, progressive social welfare programs, and a remarkably low crime rate. For travelers, there's rich landscapes of mountains, tundra, glaciers, forests, and shimmering lakes, plus activities like polar bear tracking, seal spotting, and whale watching. Best of all, Canadians are a welcoming and unpretentious people who go out of their way to distinguish themselves from their cocky southern neighbors. Visit the following locales:

- The world's second largest French-speaking city, Montreal knows a thing or two about *joie de vivre.* Its summer Festival International de Jazz de Montréal draws in 2 million spectators for 500 mostly free concerts by 2,000 musicians, including sensations like Diana Krall, Norah Jones, and Dee Dee Bridgewater. Some 700 comedians—such as Margaret Cho and the Canadian comedy troupe Women Fully Clothed—keep 2 million more in stitches at the Just For Laughs Humor Festival in July; and yet another 2 million gather around the Jacques Cartier Bridge to watch fireworks carefully synchronized to musical scores at the L'International

www.montrealjazzfest.com
www.hahaha.com

des Feux Loto-Québec. When Montreal gets blanketed with snow in the wintertime, the party simply slips underground, where walkways link up the city's malls, cinemas, and hotels.

* Peter Ustinov summed it best when he said Toronto is "New York run by the Swiss." Nearly half of its population was born elsewhere, and their cultures are honored and respected here. Toronto is also the site of some major museums and galleries. Shoe fiends should check out the Bata Shoe Museum which contains more than ten thousand pairs—from ancient Egyptian sandals to chestnut crushing clogs, plus stilettos worn by great dames like Princess Diane and Elizabeth Taylor. And don't forget the Toronto Women's Bookstore at 73 Harbord Street. A community center for three decades and counting, this nonprofit organization hosts writing workshops, book launches, and lunar eclipse evenings of poetry, spoken word, and art.

www.batashoemuseum.ca
www.womensbookstore.com

* Where else but Vancouver can you be transported from a major urban city to the top of a snowy ski slope in fifteen minutes flat? Grouse Mountain offers snowboarding, ice skating, snowshoeing, and a bevy of shops, bars, and restaurants. For something extravagant, sign up for their "Fly, Dine, and Drive Package," where a Helijet whisks you from downtown to the top of the peak for a candlelit dinner at the Observatory, followed by a limousine ride back downtown. Summers in Vancouver see the International Dragon Boat Festival, the Bard on the Beach Shakespeare Festival, assorted classical, jazz, and world music festivals, and one of the funnest gay-pride parades in North America.

* No Canadian adventure is complete without an exploration of the countryside. Fans of the 2002 film *Atanarjuat: The Fast Runner* will enjoy Inuit areas such as the Northwest Territories, Nunavut, Nunavik, and Labrador. These indigenous people lived communally off Arctic animals until the arrival of traders, missionaries, and government agencies in the late nineteenth and early twentieth centuries. Modernization disrupted their traditional ways of life, and many now rely on tourism and arts-and-crafts to care for their families. The Inuit Art Foundation sells soapstone carvings, printmaking, and textiles made by such families at 2081 Merivale Road in Ottawa.

www.inuitart.org

97 *Chengdu, China*

A WISE CHINESE PROVERB ADVISES: "DO NOT VISIT SICHUAN WHEN you are young." Once you've glimpsed its mountainous landscape and Taoist temples, its spicy cuisine and noontime operas, you'll never want to leave. Deemed China's "Party City" by the *Los Angeles Times*, Chengdu has more tea houses and bars per capita than Shanghai (which has twice the population). Yet it is somewhat off the typical tourist circuit, meaning fewer crowds at the following places:

* The Sichuanese boast that their food burns three times: on the way in, in the middle, and on the way out. They aren't kidding: simply standing at the intersection of Huaxing Street and Chunxi Road, where the Chuanchuanxiang, or strip of hotpot restaurants, begins, will cause your eyes to water and nose to run. Take a basket and fill it with skewers: raw mutton, fish, chicken, mushrooms, Chinese broccoli. Then sit at one of the hotpot tables built around a bubbling cauldron of peppercorns that, in earlier times, were used as anesthetic. (This is where the burning comes in.) Dunk your skewers and let them cook for a long time (especially the chicken) before fishing them out with chopsticks. If you can't handle much spice, request that your cauldron be *baiwei*, for wimps. Otherwise, order plenty of cold *pijiu*, or beer. You'll

likely find hotpot to be numbingly delicious. Another Sichuan culinary treat is *mapo doufu,* tofu and pork blended in a spicy bean sauce and laced with water chestnuts, cloud ear fungus, and, of course, chili. According to legend, Ma Po was a leperous old widow quarantined in the boondocks who took in a farmer and son caught in a heavy rainstorm one night and cooked them her favorite dish. Although they feared her skin condition, they couldn't refuse her cooking, and stayed with her every time they passed through town. Her reputation grew, and her recipe remains a Sichuan favorite.

* One of Sichuan's most historic figures is Wu Zetian, a female emperor who ruled the Zhou Dynasty from 690 to 705. Machiavellian and beautiful, she plotted, schemed, and slept her way to the Dragon Throne. While there, she reinforced Sichuan's tribute system to ensure such a steady supply of teas, her descendants claim their region as the birthplace of China's beverage of choice. Teahouses proliferate throughout Chengdu, with old men in Mao jackets nibbling sunflower seeds in some, businessmen in power suits signing contracts in others. A few (like the Jinjiang Theater on Huaxingzheng Jie) stage operas, plays, and stand-up comedy for entertainment. Play a mean game of mahjongg or get your ears cleaned while downing bottomless cups of jasmine tea at the Renmin Teashop in Renmin Gongyuan, or People's Park.

* *The way which can be uttered, is not the eternal Way. / The name which can be named, is not the eternal Name.* Thus goes a tenet of Taoism, an ancient religion and philosophy that once flourished in Sichuan. Sadly, many of its sacred sites were eradicated during

the Cultural Revolution of 1966-1976 and its monks sent into exile, but a few lovely ones remain. In northwest Chengdu, worshipers light long sticks of incense and kowtow to the spirits at Qingyang Gong, or Green Ram Temple. Another important site is Qingcheng Mountain, considered by some scholars to be the very birthplace of Taoism. It offers a tranquil setting for reflection and meditation.

RECOMMENDED READING

Iron and Silk by Mark Salzman

Becoming Madame Mao and *Red Azaleas* by Anchee Min

98 *Mozambique*

THEY DON'T CALL THIS THE "LISBON OF AFRICA" FOR NOTHING. Mozambique may have endured everything from drought-induced famine to brutal warfare to severe economic oppression in recent decades, but it is making a tantalizing comeback. You'll fast see why this former Portuguese colony is reeling in everyone from backpackers to luxury-seekers:

* Start your journey in the capital of Maputo, where must-see stops include the palatial train station (designed by the same Eiffel who did the famed tower) and the National Art Museum on Avenida Ho Chi Minh 1233, which showcases the nation's contemporary artists. At Mercado Municipal on Avenida 25 de Setembro, vendors peddle everything from spices to fresh fish to cashews to baskets. For a fascinating glimpse of traditional medicine, check out the Mercado Xipamanine, where claws and tails are sold out of gunny sacks. Arts and crafts hounds should drop by Praça 25 de Junho on Saturday mornings for batiks, masks, and sandalwood. History buffs and Che Guevara fans, meanwhile, should check out the National Museum of the Revolution, which chronicles—through four floors of grainy photographs and crumpled uniforms—the revolt against the Portuguese and the Civil War. (Note the assault rifle emblazoned on the

national flag.) Round it out with the mural depicting Mozambique's struggle for independence en route to the airport, on Avenida Acordos de Lusaka. (Only don't walk on the grass here: it's against the law and you'll get slapped with a fine.)

- By now, you should be hungry. Stroll down the Feira Popular on Avenida 25 de Setembro to sample Mozambique's myriad culinary influences—from the traditional Portuguese restaurant Escorpião (famous for its steaks cooked and served on a hot rock) to the Zambézia-inspired Coqueiros, which serves up tasty *galinha zambeziana,* or chicken cooked with coconut. Mozambican specialties include curried crab (lightly stir-fried and smothered in red curry) and *matapa* (prawns cooked in coconut and served with peanuts, greens, and fruit). On the weekends, you can't beat Costa do Sol on the Marginal just outside town. Order a platter of foot-long prawns grilled with *piri-piri,* a razor-blade chili sauce, and wash them down with cold Dois M or Manica beer.

- Nightlife in Maputo rages from dusk to dawn. Along Feira Popular, locals and tourists pack into ramshackle bars to enjoy loud music and cheap beer. Nearby Rua do Bagamoio is another hotspot, where dancers crowd into discos to do the *passada,* a cross between the merengue and the lambada. (To actually hear what your companions are saying, try the laid-back Gypsy Bar instead.) Be forewarned that prostitutes and pickpockets frequent these places as well. Under no circumstance should you walk from Feira Popular to Rua do Bagamoio—however close they seem.

* Now for the back roads. Hiking is especially good in the Penha Longa mountains along the Zimbabwe border, but most travelers head straight for the Indian Ocean. Go swimming around the coral reefs of Ponta d'Ouro, and you'll likely spy hammerheads, manta rays, potato bass, and even whale sharks passing by. But nothing outshines Pemba, a coastal town in the far north of the country, where emerald mangroves surround white-sand islands. Unknown for years to all but the most intrepid travelers, it is now home to a five-star resort that is attracting crowds from every continent. Yet you can still find thatch-roofed cafes serving fresh lobster by candlelight, and dhows leading sunset safaris to view six-foot manta rays and the occasional dugong. The Makua women here are famously feisty, and paint their black faces with a thick white root paste called *muciro* to moisturize their skin. Buy one of their batiks or ebony sculptures at the market.

* The Bazaruto Archipelago is a diving paradise full of florescent fish, moray eels, and clams the size of linebackers. The islands of this archipelago, including Benguerra and Santa Carolina, are accessible via Vilankulos, a quiet fishing village in Inhambane province. Luxury resorts abound, but the budget-conscious can land a good deal at a lodge called Baobab's, which will amicably arrange a boat outing for you.

99 New York City, New York

IF YOU CAN'T MAKE IT TO ANY OTHER DESTINATION IN THIS guidebook, visit New York City to experience them all. Want to roast in a banya with a room full of sweaty Russian women and pop open a bottle of Soviet Champagne? Go to Brighton Beach in Brooklyn. How about tattooing your palms with henna and slipping on a sari sewn for a princess? Head to Jackson Heights in Queens. Want to slam down some *caipirinhas* and samba with boys from Rio? Black Betty on 366 Metropolitan Avenue, Williamsburg. And we're just getting started.

- For inspired works of art, begin with the obvious (the Metropolitan on 1000 Fifth Avenue at 82nd Street; the Museum of Modern Art on 11 West 53rd Street; the Guggenheim on 1071 Fifth Avenue at 89th Street; the Whitney on 945 Madison Avenue at 75th Street) and then head to Chelsea. Between 20th and 26th Streets and Tenth and Eleventh Avenues, you'll find a wide array of independent galleries. Women own and operate the Bellwether Gallery on 134 Tenth Avenue, the Denise Bibro Fine Art Gallery on 529 West 20th Street, and the Barbara Gladstone Gallery on 515 West 24th Street. Next, hop on the 7 train to Long Island City and visit P.S. 1 on 22-25 Jackson Avenue. Founded under a 1970s project to transform New York City's abandoned buildings into public spaces, this contemporary art center is located inside an old school-house and features cutting-edge art exhibitions, films, and concerts. Round off the day (or week) with another train (or two) to survey El Museo del Barrio's collection at 1230 Fifth Avenue at 104th Street. Founded by Puerto Rican artists and activists in 1969, this is the city's premier Latino museum and a major gathering point for the Spanish Harlem community.

* Summertime in New York City means festivals. In just about every borough, you'll find live music, readings, dance performances, film screenings, and street fairs—most held outdoors and many free. Grab a copy of the *Village Voice* and start planning. Manhattanites gravitate to Central Park for its SummerStage festival. The 2006 line-up included Canadian songstress Feist, U.K. hip-hop artist Lady Sovereign, blues rocker Bonnie Raitt, indie music star Ani DiFranco, and Pulitzer Prize finalist Joan Didion. The New York Philharmonic and the Metropolitan Opera also hold free nighttime performances in the park; sit in the back to chat. Bryant Park on 40th Street and Sixth Avenue holds free screenings of classic movies all summer long; New Yorkers pack elaborate picnics and start trickling in at 5 P.M. for 8 P.M. shows. Brooklynites, meanwhile, head to Prospect Park to Celebrate Brooklyn, which has in recent years head-lined La India, Leela James, and Angelique Kidjo.

www.villagevoice.com
www.summerstage.org
www.bryantpark.org
www.celebratebrooklyn.org

* But what you really want to do is shop, you say? As a New York cabbie once said, "Anything you can't find anywhere else in

the world, this city has two of 'em. And if you can find it
somewhere else, we've got five of 'em." Looking for a bamboo bird cage, a silk kimono, a sushi-and-sake set, or a hot
cup of oolong tea? Try Pearl River Market on 477 Broadway.
Want those strappy kittens Carrie Bradshaw swoons over in
Sex and the City? Go to Jimmy Choo's on 645 Fifth Avenue at
51st Street (and if you need to justify that $1,200 price tag,
repeat Bette Midler's credo: "Give a girl the correct footwear
and she can conquer the world"). Need a touch-up on your
makeup before hitting the town? Europe's leading beauty
chain, Sephora, is your answer (with ten locations in
Manhattan alone). Bargain hunting? It doesn't get better
than Century 21 on 22 Cortlandt Street between Church and
Broadway. (Just be forewarned that on weekends, shopping
here is a full-contact sport.) And then there's that holy grail
of consignment shopping—INA—where celebrities and fashion magazine editors dump their gently-worn Marni jackets,
Prada shirts, Manolo Blahnik stilettos, and handbags by
Chanel, Mui Mui, Marc Jacobs, and Gucci. (It was also the
site of the famous *Sex and the City* Wardrobe Sale, when
hundreds of fans waited in lines that wrapped around
the block to buy "a piece of fashion history" after the
show's end.) Much of INA's clothing only runs to
size 10, but shoes generally come in all sizes. Of the
four locations, Soho is the best, at 101 Thompson
Street (nearest subway: C or E to Spring Street).
Watch out for their seasonal sales, when prices can be
slashed up to 70 percent (which, when you're talking
about a hand-me-down from Barney's, will still set you
back several hundred bucks, but for a fashionista, that deal is
a steal).

www.inanyc.com

❋ A "rest stop for rare individuals," the Hotel Chelsea on 222 West 23rd Street opened as a housing cooperative in 1884 before shifting toward transient occupancy, and has long attracted writers, artists, musicians, and other larger-than-lifes. Somewhere within its eleven canvas-lined floors, Sir Arthur C. Clarke wrote *2001: A Space Odyssey*, poet Dylan Thomas "sailed out to die," Janis Joplin had an affair with Leonard Cohen, Arthur Miller wrote *After the Fall*, and Sid Vicious of the Sex Pistols killed his girlfriend, Nancy. Famous women residents include song-writer Patti Smith, filmmaker Shirley Clarke, and communist Elizabeth Gurley Flynn. "This is a feeling hotel, unlike any other," says Stanely Bard, the hotel's long-time managing director. "Lovely, sensitive, and beautiful people stay here."

www.hotelchelsea.com

❋ Don't leave the Big Apple without paying homage to its most famous female resident. A gift from the French in the late nineteenth century, Lady Liberty holds a torch in her right hand, a tablet in her left, and stands on a chain that symbolizes her acquired freedom. The seven spikes in her crown represent the seven seas (or continents), and her plaque is inscribed with a sonnet by Emma Lazarus that begins: *"Give me your tired, your poor/Your huddled masses yearning to breathe free."* From her perch at the mouth of the Hudson River, she welcomes (in theory, at least) all immigrants, visitors, and returning Americans to the United States. Pay her a proper visit by catching a ferry from Battery Park in New York or Liberty State Park in New Jersey

www.nps.gov/stli

and taking either the Statue of Liberty Observatory Tour or the Promenade Tour, both of which include admission to her museum.

TOURS

Gutsy Women Travel offers a women-only Discover New York Tour (www.gutsywomentravel.com).

100 *Motherlands*

Of all the destinations spotlighted in this book, none are as meaningful as our own motherlands. At some point in life, return to your ancestral home, be it a specific neighborhood or an entire continent, to learn from the roots within you.

Start by conducting a little research. Heritage Quest—one of the largest genealogical data providers in the United States—offers an online tutorial called "Genealogy 101" with tips on everything from drawing a family tree to obtaining vital information (such as old birth, death, and marriage records). They also sell CD-ROMs with titles like "Your Family Name in 1870 America." Another excellent resource is the Family History Library, which has more than thirty-four hundred branches in sixty-four countries. Founded to assist members of the Church of Jesus Christ of Latter-day Saints (a.k.a. the Mormons) in tracing their lineages, these libraries allow non-members to peruse their extensive microfilm collections as well. There are also thousands of organizations dedicated to genealogy, many of which host web sites and annual conferences where root-seekers can swap branches. Simply type in your racial or ethnic group and "Genealogical Society" on Google and see what pops up.

If your family's origins remain a mystery, simply go with what you do know. Soul Planet Travel, for instance, offers "Black

History Tours" to Nigeria and Salvador Bahia in Brazil which have become popular with African-Americans who are curious about their heritage but don't know their exact tribe.

Even those of us who were adopted can find some way to explore our roots. Take artist Rachel DayStar Payne of Corpus Christi, Texas. She knows only that her biological parents attended the University of Texas at Austin in 1969, but that one fact has given her a sense of connection.

"Whenever I find people who were in Austin at that time, I try to meet my parents through them," she says. "Those are my family stories—as close as I'll ever get to them. And I love just wandering around Austin, knowing I'm from that hippie haven, that place of art and Bohemian ideals."

If your genealogical inquiries lead you to an actual ancestral village, spend as much time there as possible. You just might stumble upon long-lost kin, as writer Barbara Belejack did on her recent trip to Slovakia. Thanks to an uncle who had visited thirty years prior, she had a general idea of her village's location. Clutching an old photograph of her grandfather, she knocked on a door at random. The woman inside thought he looked like a man in the neighboring village, and advised her to meet him. Barbara did, and sure enough—met her father's first cousin.

"I always used to think that I must have been switched at birth, because I never really understood my Slovak culture. I tried studying Russian in college but it never took, and I spent most of my adult life exploring Latin America," she says. "But there was a connection with him. We spent the afternoon together, and it almost felt like I was back in my grandparent's kitchen."

www.heritagequest.com
www.familysearch.org
www.soulplanettravel.com

If you can't locate a living family member, ask around for the local historian (or oldest living resident) to see if they know anything about your family name. Request relevant birth, marriage, or death certificates at the equivalent of the county clerk's office; make rubbings of tombstones engraved with your family name at the local cemetery; fill a jar with earth. Above all, talk with the old-timers, for your own version of "family stories."

If nothing else, you'll leave with the satisfaction that you witnessed the same sunset as your ancestors, and that your boots collected the same dust.

Women's Tours

A Broad Adventure
www.abroadadventure.com

Adventure Associates
www.adventureassociates.net

Adventure Cycling Tours & Vacations
for Women
www.femtoursguide.com

Adventures in Good Company
www.adventuresingoodcompany.
com

Adventures in New Zealand
for Women
www.driftwooddreamers.com

Adventures in Perspective
www.livingadventure.com

AdventurePlanet
www.adventureplanet.com

AdventureWomen
www.adventurewomen.com

Adventurous Wench
www.adventurouswench.com

American Woman Road & Travel
www.roadandtravel.com

Annapurna Journeys
www.goldenhilltravel.co.uk/
nepal/annapurna-journeys.html

Arctic Ladies
www.arcticladies.com

Armstrong & Hedges
http://teagardentravel.com

Artista
www.artistacreative.com

The Association of Women Travel
Executives, London
www.awte-london.co.uk

Astra
www.astragreece.com

Azores Walks
www.azoreswalks.com

Bev Gruber's Everyday Gourmet
Traveler
www.gourmetravel.com

Blue Moon Explorations
http://home.cio.net/bluemoon

Broad Horizons
www.broadhorizonsnetwork.com

Bushwise Women
www.bushwise.co.nz

Call of the Wild
www.callwild.com

Canadian Woman Traveller
www.cwtraveller.ca

Canyon Calling Tours
www.canyoncalling.com

Caribbean Bike & Adventure Tours
www.caribbeanbiketours.com

Chimo Club Toronto
www.chimoclubtoronto.org

Cloud Canyon Expeditions
www.cloudcanyon.com

Costa Rican Luxury Vacation
www.vacationscostarica.com

Country Walkers
www.countrywalkers.com

Destinations Europe
www.womens-tours.com

Direct Approach Golf School
www.golfschoolpi.com

Diva Expeditions
www.divaexpeditions.com

EarthWise Journeys
http://home.teleport.com/
~earthwyz

Ela Brasil Tours
www.elabrasil.com

Eliotropica Travelling
www.eliotropica.com

Elderhostel
www.elderhostel.org

Equinox Wilderness Expeditions
www.equinoxexpeditions.com

*Eurynome Journeys of Leisure
Markets: Travel Adventures for
Women*
www.wanderwoman.com

Explorations in Travel
www.exploretravel.com

Fresh Tracks
www.freshtracks.ca

GATE
www.gate-travel.org

Genuine Romance Adventures
www.GenuineRomance
Adventures.com

Global Fitness Adventures
www.globalfitnessadventures.com

Going Places!
www.goingplacestours.com

Go-Outdoors
www.go-outdoors.ca

GORP Travel
www.gorptravel.com

Grape Adventures
www.grapeadventures.com

Gutsy Gals Travel
www.gutsygalstravel.com

Gutsy Women Travel
www.gutsywomentravel.com

High Wild & Lonesome
www.hwl.net

The Historic Pines Ranch
www.historicpines.com

Holiday Expeditions
www.bikeraft.com

Il Chiostro
www.ilchiostro.com

Journey Weavers Educational Travel
www.journeyweavers.com

Journeys International
www.journeys-intl.com

Journeys of the Spirit
www.journeysofthespirit.com

Inspiring Ireland
www.inspiringireland.com/
CromCastleRetreat.htm

Las Olas
www.surflasolas.com

Las Verdes
www.golflasverdes.com

Loners on Wheels
www.lonersonwheels.com

Mama Tembo Tours
www.mamatembotours.com

Mariah Wilderness Expeditions
www.mariahwomen.com

Menopausal Tours
www.menopausaltours.com

Mind Over Mountains
www.mindovermountains.com

Mountain Spirit Adventures
www.mountainspiritadventures.
com

Newage Travel
www.newage-travel.com

Olivia Cruises & Resorts
www.olivia.com

Ontdek Kenya
www.ontdekkenya.com

Outdoor Beyond
www.outdoorbeyond.com

Painting Tours in Italy
www.portray.it

PanTours of Australasia
www.pantoursindia.com

Paris du Jour
www.parisdujour.com

Peaceful Choices
http://internet.cybermesa.com/
~innerpeace

Phyllis Trips
www.phyllistrips.com

RVing Women
www.rvingwomen.org

Sacred Earth Journeys
www.sacredearthjourneys.ca

Sacred Journeys for Women
www.sacredjourneys.com

Sacred Sites Tours
www.sacredsitestours.com

Sanddrifters
www.sanddrifters.com

Seagypsy
www.seagypsysailing.com

Senior Women's Travel
www.poshnosh.com

Shesailing
www.shesailing.nl

Shop Around Tours
www.shoparoundtours.com

Sights and Soul Travels
www.sightsandsoul.com

Sila Sojourns
www.silasojourns.com

Soul Purpose Adventures
www.soulpurpose.bc.ca

Soul Trekking
www.soultrekking.com

Sounds & Furies Productions
www.soundsandfuries.com

South Sea Mermaid Tours
www.southseamermaids.co.nz

Surf Goddess Retreats
www.surfgoddessretreats.com

Tanguera Tours
www.tangueratours.com

Tea Garden Traveler
www.teagardentravel.com

Tiger Travel
www.tigertravel.co.uk

Tours Explore
www.toursexplore.com

Towanda Women
www.towanda.org

Transcend Travel Switzerland
www.transcendtravel.com

Transition Counseling Services
www.transitioncounselingser-
vices.com

Travel with Women
www.travelwithwomen.com

Trips for Women
www.tripsforwomen.com

A Twisty Road
www.twistyroad.com

Unleashed Adventures
www.unleashedadventures.com

Valentine Travel
www.valentinetravel.com

Walking Women Holidays
www.walkingwomen.com

Well Arranged Travel
www.wellarrangedtravel.com

West Coast Women Adventures
www.westcoastwomen.ca

Wild Women Expeditions
www.wildwomenexp.com

Woman Tours
www.womantours.com

Womanship
www.womanship.com

WomanWalkers Travel Service
www.womenwalkers.com

Woman's World Travel
www.womansworldtravel.com

Woman Xplore
www.womenxplore.com

Women in Florence
www.womeninflorence.com

Women's Only Mountain Biking
www.womensonly.com

Women Summit
www.womensummit.com

Women's Quest
www.womensquest.com

Women's Travel Network
www.womenstravelnetwork.ca

Women Travel New Zealand
www.womentravel.co.nz

Women Traveling Together
www.women-traveling.com

Women Travelling
www.womentravelling.com

Women's Travel Club
www.womenstravelclub.com

Women Welcome Women
www.womenwelcomewomen.org.
uk

The World Outdoors
www.theworldoutdoors.com

Index

Acknowledgments

I am deeply indebted to the following women who shared their favorite places with me: Stacy Aab, the Alaska Women's Network, Claire Alpern, Sarah M. Anderson, Aliana Apodaca, Natasha Lycia Ora Bannan, Barbara Belejack, Donna Bernhardt, Joan Bertin, Lisa Bosler, Shelley Buckingham, Bianca Calabresi, Irma Cantu, Irene Carranza, Trina Chattoraj and family, Krista Claudene-Retto, Karla Cosgriff, Carolina Varga-Dinicu, Larisa Dinsmoor, Marie Doezema, Stephanie Emory, Lauren Erdreich, Neda Farzan, Monica Flores, Susan Frances, Nicole Fraser, Mercedes Gallego, Wang Huaiyu, Anna-Karin Jatfors, Lila Rose Kaplan, Claire Karpen, Debby Katz, Suzanne Kratzig, Rebecca Kroll, Victoria Langland, Ana Lara, Jen Leo, Cheng Lijie, Irene Lin, Amaya Moro-Martin, Sylvia Martinez, Svetlana Mintcheva, Aya Nakashima, Carolena Nericcio, Sheryl Oring, Stacey Panousopoulos, Catharine Patha, Rachel DayStar Payne, Dena Qaddumi, Kavitha Rao, Amy Robben, Lori Robinson, Maria Sacchetti, Amy Schapiro, Michele Serros, Betty Shamieh, Elena Shishkina, Sherry Shokouhi, Jessie Sholl, Jo Slater, Sylvia Smullin, Daphne Sorensen, Laima Sruoginis, Danya Steele, Sonya Tsuchigane, Annie Wald, Beth Weinstein, Betsy White, and Jackie Yang.

Thanks also to these women-loving men for their insight: Leo Arriola, Stanley Bard, Michael Coren, Robert Edgerly, David Farley, Harley Feldbaum, Harry Finley, Jeff Golden, Brendon Levitt, Fred Magerrison, Eddy Malesky, Tom Miller, Paul Muldoon, Mansir Petrie, Rolf Potts, Michael Robertson, Greg Rubio, Eli Shalom, and Peter Silys.

I am also profoundly grateful for the wonderful resources out there which we travelers rely upon in our journeys and which I consulted for basic logistical and descriptive information, especially Lonely Planet's guidebooks, Time Out Guidebooks, and Moon Travel Guides. Thanks also to the travel sections of *The New York Times, New Yorker, New York Magazine, Washington Post, San Francisco Chronicle, Seattle Post-Intelligencer, Village Voice, San Francisco Bay Guardian, Globe and Mail, The Observer,* and other journals archived on Lexis/Nexis; Wikipedia and Alternet; and the following books: Patricia Schultz's *1,000 Places to See Before You Die* (Workman Publishing, New York 2003); R. W. Apple Jr.'s *Apple's America: The Discriminating Traveler's Guide to 40 Great Cities in the US and Canada* (North Point Press, New York 2005); Lynn Sherr and Jurate Kazickas's *Susan B. Anthony Slept Here: A Guide to American Women's Landmarks* (Time Books Random House, New York 1984); and Dave Freeman and Neil Teplica's *100 Things to Do Before You Die: Travel Events You Just Can't Miss* (Taylor Publishing Company, Dallas Texas 1999).

Heart-felt thanks goes to James and Sean O'Reilly and Larry Habegger at *Travelers' Tales* for inviting me to join this project, and to Susan Brady and Emilia Thiuri, who served as its wise midwives. My agent Sarah Jane Freymann remains my literary angel and friend. Words defy my gratitude to the Council of Humanities and Department of Creative Writing at Princeton University for the Hodder Fellowship that allowed me the time to research and write this book. My Princeton posse—Tori, Amaya, Jo, Sylvia, Lauren, Maayani, Karla, and Elliot—kept me sane this crazy year: *mil gracias* for the memories. Without my family, I'd be lost and lonely: Irene and Dick Griest, and Barbara, Alex, Jordan, and Analina Devora.

The final thanks goes to Mother Road, who makes all journeys possible.

About the Author

Stephanie Elizondo Griest has mingled with the Russian Mafiya, polished Chinese propaganda, and belly danced with Cuban rumba queens. These adventures are the subject of her award-winning first book: *Around the Bloc: My Life in Moscow, Beijing, and Havana.* Atria/Simon & Schuster will publish her memoirs from Mexico in 2008. She has also written for the *New York Times, Washington Post, Latina Magazine,* and numerous Travelers' Tales anthologies. An avid traveler, she has explored 25 countries and once spent a year driving 45,000 miles across the United States, documenting its history for a web site for kids. She is currently a Hodder Fellow at Princeton University and a Senior Fellow at the World Policy Institute. Visit her web site at www.aroundthebloc.com.